FIGHT FOR FREEDOM:

BLACK RESISTANCE AND IDENTITY

First published in Ghana 2017
by **Sub-Saharan Publishers**
P.O.Box 358
Legon-Accra
Ghana
Email: saharanp@africaonline.com.gh

© Mousa Traore & Tony Talburt 2017

ISBN: 978-9988-647-67-4

Typesetting and cover design: Kwabena Agyepong

Contents

Acknowledgements

The writing of this book has been a truly collaborative effort. We received tremendous professional encouragement and support from a number of individuals. First, we must say a special word of thanks to all the contributors for their patience and understanding as we continually kept asking them for additional information or clarity on sections of their chapters. There a few individuals who helped us much more than they probably realised. Professor Kwarteng in the History Department at the University of Cape Coast was able to read small sections of the study and we only wish he could have read more, but we appreciate the time taken to consider our publication. We would also like to express our thanks to Dr. Daive Dunkley, Assistant Professor in the Black Studies Department at the University of Missouri, who made a number of invaluable suggestions in chapter five. We would also like to express our thanks to the Geography Information Systems, Cartography and Remote Sensing Section, Department of Geography and Regional Planning, University of Cape Coast, for producing the map used in chapter two and for granting us permission to use it in this publication.

We would also like to express or thanks and heartfelt appreciation to Akoss Ofori-Mensah and the entire editorial staff at Sub-Saharan Publishers for their patience, diligence and professionalism in the publication of this book, from its draft manuscript stage through to its completion.

And finally, we would like to express our heartfelt appreciation to Dr. Awo Sarpong from the Depatment of Basic Education, UCC, for her sterling work in designing the cover of this book.

List of Contributors

Emmanuel Saboro (PhD) received his doctoral degree at the Wilberforce Institute for the Study of Slavery and Emancipation (WISE), University of Hull, England. His PhD was an interdisciplinary study predicated on how communities in northern Ghana continue to endure the legacies of enslavement through the rich culture of folklore. He is currently a lecturer of Literatures in English at the University of Cape Coast, Ghana. His research interests are centred generally on the interface between Oral Literature and History and specifically on the Literary Manifestations of the Slave Experience in Folklore, Postcolonial Literature, Cultural Memory, Verbal Texts and Literature of the African Diaspora. He is working on a monograph predicated on Memory and Representations of the Slave Experience in Ghanaian Folklore.

De-Valera N.Y.M. Botchway (PhD) Associate Professor in History in the Department of History at the University of Cape Coast, Ghana and also teaches courses in African Studies at the Centre for African and international studies at the same university. He has research interests in several fields of African and African Diaspora history and studies. These include West African history, black religious and cultural nationalism(s), sports (boxing) in Ghana, African indigenous knowledge systems, biography, and Africans in dispersion. He was in the University of Cambridge, England, as a Fellow of the Centre of African Studies from 2006 to 2007 and is also a member of the Historical Society of Ghana.

Wilson K. Yayoh (PhD) is a Senior Lecturer and Acting Director of the Centre for African and International Studies, University of Cape Coast, Ghana. He obtained his PhD in History from the School of Oriental and African Studies, SOAS, University of London. His research interests are in the areas of ethnic history, colonial policies in Africa, Africa in world affairs and historical perspectives on democratisation in Africa. Dr Yayoh is currently working on a British Academy sponsored research project which will culminate in the publication of a book: 'ABLODESAFUI': *Writing the Nation in a West Africa Borderland.* He is also working on another book entitled *Contested Territory: Governing Colonial and Post-Colonial Ewedome (British Trust Territory), 1870s to 1970s.*

Orville W. Beckford (PhD) is a lecturer in sociology in the Department of Sociology, Psychology and Social Work at the University of the West Indies (UWI), Mona. He teaches Introduction to Sociology, Caribbean Culture, and Industrial Sociology. Orville Beckford worked on the Mona Commons Township Project Social Report for the UWI and received The Excellence in Teaching Award from The Faculty of Social Sciences in 2012-2013. His research interests are institutional building, industrial sociology, and the culture of the inner city.

Christopher A.D. Charles (PhD) is a senior lecturer in political psychology in the Department of Government at the UWI, Mona and operates a psychology consultancy in Kingston and is a fellow of the Institute of Cultural Policy and Innovation. He did doctoral training in psychology and political science and holds a Ph.D. in psychology from the City University of New York. His main research interests are sport psychology, criminological psychology, political psychology, and Black identity, body modification, popular culture, and sexuality. Before going to the UWI, he taught at John Jay College of Criminal Justice of the City University of New York, and The King Graduate School at Monroe College in New York.

Moussa Traoré (PhD) is a Senior lecturer at the Department of English of the University of Cape Coast in Ghana where he teaches Literature and he is also a part-time lecturer at the French Department of the same university. Moussa holds a

PhD in Comparative Literature from Illinois State University (USA). His main research interests are Pan-Africanism, Diasporan Studies, Postcolonialism, Environmental Studies and Sustainable Development, English as a Foreign Language (EFL) and Bilingual Translation (French-English). His publication includes: the book *Intersecting Pan-Africanisms: Africa, North America and the Caribbean* (2012) He presented papers at several international conferences and Dr. Traoré is currently working on the translation of a French into English *La vie en rouge* (2008) by the Burkinabe writer Vincent Ouattara.

Tony Talburt (PhD) is a lecturer in the Centre for African and International Studies at the University of Cape Coast, Ghana. His main research interest is in the areas of international development and African and Caribbean politics and history. He is the author of a number of books including: *Food of the Plantation Slaves of Jamaica,* (2004) *Rum, Rivalry and Resistance: Fighting for the Caribbean* (2010) as well as the ground-breaking children's novel *History on the Page: Adventures in Black British History* (2012), and *Andrew Watson: the World's First Black Football Superstar* published by Hansib publishers in July of 2016. He was programme coordinator and on the part time degree course at the Univrsity of Birmingham in African and Caribbean studies.

FIGHT FOR FREEDOM:

BLACK RESISTANCE AND IDENTITY

Edited by

Moussa Traoré and Tony Talburt

SUB-SAHARAN PUBLISHERS

CHAPTER ONE

Black Resistance and Identity: Overview of A Global Struggle

Tony Talburt

Black campaigns of political and cultural resistance in Africa and throughout the African Diaspora, in response to European systems of control and dominance are neither recent nor infrequent occurrences. The historical experiences of Black people in Africa and displaced Black people across its diaspora is replete with examples of freedom fighters who fought or campaigned for some form of political change and independence in their encounters with European slavery, colonialism and racial discrimination. The very long list which reads like a Black Resisters' Hall of Fame could typically include such prominent individuals like: Toussaint L'Ouverture in Haiti in the 1790s, Paul Bogle in Jamaica in 1865, Marcus Garvey in Jamaica, Central America and the USA in the 1920s or Claudia Jones in Britain during the late 1950s and early 1960s. In Africa itself, during the late nineteenth and early twentieth centuries, powerful and influential political leaders such as Yaa Asantewaa, Queen of the Asante Empire in what is today part of modern Ghana, and Menelik 11 of Ethiopia both played significant roles in confronting European colonialism in their respective countries. In the post-war period within Africa, the stand-out names who tirelessly campaigned for African liberation and identity include Kwame Nkrumah of Ghana, Julius Nyerere of Tanzania and also Nelson Mandela of South Africa. Of course, there are so many other worthy names which could be added to this list. What these individuals have in common, was their determination to challenge systems of European oppressive domination and thereby assert, and also attempt to preserve their own Black identity.

The central unifying theme and purpose of this collection of original essays, is to examine how Black people in Africa, Britain and the Caribbean organised campaigns of resistance against European slavery, colonialism and racial discrimination in attempts to assert their own freedom and identity. Drawing upon original material from different academic disciplines such as African and Caribbean history, literature, politics and psychology, these essays serve to demonstrate how Black people engaged in organised campaigns of resistance using a whole range of strategies to confront European colonial systems of dominance. It covers the broad period from the fifteenth century when European slavery and colonial exploitation started in Africa through to the post war period. This book, therefore, continues the process of recapturing and reclaiming some of these encounters and experiences of Black people by bringing to bear, new case studies, insights and approaches to these debates. Whilst academic studies on the broad themes of Black resistance and identity are not new, what is particularly refreshing in this book, is the fact that most of the essays are based on very specific case studies or alternative approaches to generally accepted viewpoints on Black resistance and, therefore, helps to challenge some of the prevailing predominant positions on these subjects.

Black resistance took on a variety of forms and methods both in Africa and the Diaspora. Some of these forms of resistance and key themes which are examined in this study include: slave and oral narratives, nationalism and religion in Africa, local African resistance to colonial rule, an examination of Jamaica as a micro-study where a wide variety of Black resistance occurred, case studies of maronage in the French Caribbean, coping with Black identity and skin bleaching, and also realigning and reframing Pan Africanist ideology.

Given the obvious wide range of possible strategies and initiatives that could have been brought to bear on this subject, in this present volume, it has to be quickly pointed out that this work has a number of necessary limitations. Firstly, these essays in no way attempt to provide an exhaustive and chronological account or narrative of the story of Black resistance from the fifteenth century to the present. The significance of the various case studies and discussions in this volume rests principally with their emphasis upon the strategies used by Black people to firstly organise their resistance campaigns and secondly to challenge aspects of the very political, economic and social foundations of European systems of control and dominance which adversely affected their lives and identity. More specifically, our attempt is to focus on particular studies and debates drawn from Africa, Britain and the Caribbean which demonstrate a universal theme of Black people fighting and organising their own campaigns of resistance using a variety of methods.

The second point worth noting regarding the limitations of this book, is that its main focus is on organised campaigns of resistance based around strong and distinct individual personalities and, or, clear ideologies of strategies of resistance against European colonialism. For this reason, spontaneous and short-lived acts of slave rebellions whether collectively or by individuals, important though these were, receive very little attention. The third issue which needs to be pointed out is that, whilst not attempting to be exhaustive in its coverage, the study never-the-less draws upon material both in Africa as well as in sections of the Black Diaspora. More precisely, the first part of the book focuses primarily upon studies drawn primarily from historical accounts in Ghana. The second section concentrates on studies pertaining to Black resistance and identity in Britain and the Caribbean. Therefore, this study attempts to look at different case studies and discussions of Black resistance in three different parts of world on both sides of the Atlantic. This is important because many studies on Black resistance (discussed below) have tended to focus primarily on one geographical area or region.

The term resistance is extremely broad and is used in this book to refer to organised and sustained campaigns by Black people against European domination in the form of slavery, colonialism and also aspects of psychological and socio-cultural forms of control. In a similar manner, the term 'African' or 'Black' needs some clarification. Although there are a number of different meanings and usages which can be applied to the terms 'Black' and 'African', throughout this book, these terms are used interchangeably within two contexts. Especially in the first part of the book, the term Black is used to refer to people born and living in Africa who were not part of the forced exodus of people during the trans-Atlantic slavery systems which saw millions of Africans transported to the Americas. Secondly, the term Black is also used to refer to those people of African descent who, precisely because they became victims of the trans-Atlantic slavery experiences, ended up living in the Americas or Europe which have variously been described as the African Diaspora or the Black Atlantic (Gilroy, 1998; Rice 2003) or New World Africans (Martin, 2012).

The initial impetus behind the writing of this book stemmed from discussions among academic colleagues at the University of Cape Coast, Ghana across different departments and centres, all of whom teach courses which address various aspects of African Studies. Dialogues with other academic colleagues at the University of the West Indies (Mona Campus) also resulted in contributions from Orville Beckford and Christopher Charles. The central motivation was to examine some of the different ways through which Black people have engaged in resistance campaigns both in Africa as well as within the African Diaspora. What quickly became apparent was the extent to which so many of us were examining similar themes through our independent studies and academic courses. From these initial discussions, therefore, we decided to collaboratively work together on this study. This also accounts for the eclectic and multidisciplinary nature of the book. In addition to the wide academic background of the contributors, the other over-riding reason for this publication was the desire and need to add to the existing literature on this broad subject of Black resistance and identity.

Of course, there have been numerous studies on different aspects of Black resistance, but very few of these have focused on specific case studies of the different ways in which Black people engaged in organised and sustained campaigns of resistance in their fight for freedom in Africa, the Caribbean and Britain. Therefore, whilst there have been numerous studies pertaining to different aspects of Black resistance across numerous academic disciplines (Campbell, 1992; Marable and Mullings, 2000; Sivanandan, 1982; Thompson, 2006), very few of these have focused on the variety of methods actually employed by organised Black resistance campaigners and activists in Africa as well as parts of the diaspora within a single volume.

A brief summary of a few of these studies demonstrate this point. Manning Marable's book on *race, resistance and radicalism* (1996) provides an overview of the different ways in which Black people have been either affected by White domination in America, or the different ways in which they have had to confront this. Whilst part one of the book deals with the Black experience in America, the second section provides more of a global perspective and examines such issues as socialism, and the Cold War and their impact on the Black community in America. There is also a chapter on Pan Africanism which focuses on the need for African Americans to adopt, or recognise the significance of this concept in terms of liberating Americans and the world's poor Blacks from poverty in capitalist societies throughout the Third World. In this sense, therefore, Marable's primary concern is with the plight of the Black community in America using a wide range of examples in his presentations. In his later work with Mullings (2000), these essays and discussions once again focused primarily on the

African American experiences during and after slavery. In this sense, therefore, his work is typical of a study on Black resistance which centres upon a particular community or region.

In a similar vein, Alvin Thompson's work on the Maroons was, because of the nature of the subject, necessarily focused on the Americas. Maroon communities were located throughout the Americas, from Brazil in South America, Ecuador in Central America and numerous communities across the Caribbean. This longevity of maronage constituted a significant part of the struggle of Black people for their freedom (Thompson, 2006, p. 2). This also helps to explain why, as Thompson points out, that writers from almost every discipline have studied Maroon societies.

Vincent Thompson (1987) and Ronald Segal (1995) both provide excellent discussions on the history and significance of the Black presence in world history. Segal's powerful and insightful work focused on the wide experiences of Black people primarily outside of Africa. In this regard, he focuses on the slaves' defiance within the Spanish Americas from very early in the sixteenth century. After also discussing the significance of the Maroons in the Caribbean, he then examines the Haitian Revolution. Understandably, Segal's work focuses on the African Diaspora so Black resistance in Africa is not a significant priority. Thompson's work traces the general forms of Black resistance from Africa through to their efforts in the Americas. Whilst Thompson provides a good comprehensive discussion on the Black experience and resistance in general, our work differs in one important respect. This present study intends to present case studies and discussions on particular resistance strategies used by Black people rather than a comprehensive and coherent discussion on the nature of Black resistance.

The main emphasis of many of these works on resistance is their focus largely on African resistance to the slave trade. However, Robbie Shilliam's work on the Black Pacific (2015) demonstrates the global reach and extent to which Black organised resistance campaigns were influential in stimulating anti-colonial struggles outside of the traditional Black Atlantic geographical arena. In this regard, it shows that the nature of European colonialism and racial discrimination had adverse effects on local peoples regardless of whether they were located within the traditional arena of what has come to be called the 'Black Atlantic'. Despite the fact that these studies have not tended to have a global emphasis, they demonstrate that wherever the Black communities found themselves, they were often confronted with aspects of European colonial domination and control which they sought to challenge at every level and through a variety of strategies.

Furthermore, a number of other important studies on the wider experiences of Black people have often overlooked this issue of how they confronted the political systems which had sought to disempower them. The works by Edwards and Dabydeen (1991) on the writings of Black people in Britain during the slavery period is a good example of studies on Black people who were clearly engaged in resisting the slavery and colonial systems around them, but receive very little emphasis by the authors. Their work centred upon what the people wrote, rather than the nature of the resistance struggles which often formed the context for much of what the Black people in Britain wrote about. The powerful collection of essays by Rice on Black narratives (2003) provides a platform from which we can see how Black people articulated their experiences about a number of issues which they encountered. Although many of these experiences were set within the context of European domination, the emphasis of that particular study was not on the extent to which Black people sought to confront and engage in organised resistance, but rather, their actual stories.

The key point that is being made is that Black resistance against European slavery and colonialism was universal and was clearly visible in Africa and the Americas and, as will be discussed in this book, also in Britain. Although Sivanandan referred to the presence of the 'Black intellectual' in Britain, he also suggested that 'Black people exist on the margins of European culture and...

he is a creature of two worlds and of none… marginal man par excellence' (Sivanandan, 1982, p. 82), this concept of the 'marginal man' whether in Africa or the African Diaspora, has been the central reason why Black people have engaged in fights and campaigns to de-marginalise and assert their own identity. These, of course, are only historical struggles, but can still be observed today within the context of the global economy and society where many Black people have had to find ways to exist within a European or Western dominated global political, economic and social world, over which they have little or no control. As long as this situation persists, Black people will continue to fight for freedom through whatever means appropriate. It is to these varieties of resistance strategies that the next section of this chapter briefly examines.

Overview of Black Resistance Strategies and Campaigns

Wherever Europeans sought to impose their political, economic and social control over Africa or its Diaspora, Black people used every opportunity to plan campaigns of resistance. Black people resisted at every possible opportunity, whether they were on the coasts of Africa, across the Middle Passage or in the Americas and Europe. In Africa these forms of resistance were not only universal across the entire continent, but also diverse in their manifestations and methods of operation. In this regard, Ali Mazrui is absolutely correct. From the moment Europeans engaged with Africa and sought to control or dominate them, by attempting to control and exploit them or their countries' resources, African resistance campaigns, specifically against European domination and control, were established (Mazrui, 1986). Had there been no European slavery, colonisation and exploitation, there would have been no Black resistance and Pan African Movement. From the very beginning of the European colonisation process into Africa, its leaders sought to resist these advances and insist on retaining their own political sovereignty and identity.

Ranger (1985) makes it very clear that African leaders were prepared to resist the European take over and control of their kingdoms (Ranger, 1985, pp. 48, 49). Thompson further asserts that once the partition of Africa was officially sanctioned by European powers in 1885, resistance took place everywhere from the north to the south of the African continent, from the Battle of Adowa in 1896 and as well as the Zulu wars in the 1870s (Thompson, 1962, p. 9). In this respect, however, Thompson is only partially correct. Black resistance in Africa started almost four hundred years earlier as soon as it became clear to the Africans that some aspects of European interests were closely associated with economic exploitation. This point was powerfully made by Mazrui when he spoke about 'primary resistance' meaning forms of African resistance which occurred on the African continent from the very moment when the Europeans arrived to conquer it (Mazrui, 1986, p. 283).

In this sense, Black resistance against European colonialism could be seen through the numerous wars which were fought against European regimes. These included: the Ashanti wars in Ghana, the Bunyoro wars in Uganda and the Zulu wars in South Africa in the late nineteenth and early twentieth centuries. Mazrui also used primary resistance to mean African struggles against European symbolisms of control. For example the Mau-Mau in Kenya in the 1950s fought the British largely on the basis of Kikuyu values and related religious beliefs incorporating indigenous combat cultures, from oath ceremonies to the drinking of blood. The significance of African cultural symbolisms is a crucial point which Saboro makes in his chapter of this study on the use of oral history and songs as forms of resistance. Although the Mau-Mau fighters were militarily defeated by the British, they were victorious in breaking the 'white settler political will and destiny' and helped to change the nature of British colonial relations with not only that colony, but also other countries in Africa more generally (Mazrui, 1986, p. 283). In West Africa, one outstanding example of an African who resisted European colonialism was Samori who was a great military leader who fought the French in parts of Guinea, Mali and the Ivory Coast during the 1880s. In this sense he was prepared to stand up to the colonial authorities in order to fight for the freedom of the country.

European eventual domination of Africa came only after years of resistance struggles with Africans who were not prepared to simply allow European colonists free and easy access to their territories. Thomson (1987) points out that the English slave trader and sea captain, Sir John Hawkins, on his second and third visits to the West African coast to secure African labourers to sell in the Americas, was frustrated by the organised attacks which they experienced at the hands of local Black people (Thompson, 1987, pp. 107, 108). Thompson also describes how, at times, Black people were very often involved in open warfare and regular military campaigns against European slave traders on the African coast. He cited examples from John Hawkins in 1564 who claimed that he lost some of his best men who were killed by a band of Africans after some of his crew members had gone into the interior against his own advice (Thompson, 1987, pp. 107-112). Even the African slaves who were captured and forced to walk to the coasts of Africa, engaged in acts of resistance, from disobedience and running away to acts of violence and fights. Africans later staged a whole range of mutinies while on board ships sailing across the Middle Passage (Thompson, 1987, pp. 109-127).

There were also some forms of resistance in Africa which were influenced by religious beliefs and traditions among Africans. Some of the resistance campaigns had the advantage of 'spiritual leaders who enunciated the message of wider unity' (Ranger, 1985, p. 52). There were widespread Islamic influences in the resistance campaigns which occurred across the Sudanic belt of Africa from east to west as well as other protestant Christian ideas and influences which were embraced by Hendrik Wittboi in the Nama people against the Germans. The risings in southern

Rhodesia in 1896 were influenced by religious leaders (Ranger, 1985, p. 52). In similar manner Makana was able to use a blend of African religions and Protestant Christian ideas based on spiritual or religious views to form the basis of an ideological resistance perspective for the Xhosa nation which focused on the importance of sovereignty (Ranger, 1985, pp. 52, 53).

This theme of resistance through Black-led religious movements is a particular issue which is examined in chapter three by Botchway as well as part of Beckford and Charles' chapter on Jamaica, as well as Talburt's chapter. In particular, Botchway discusses the significance of the key African personality of William Joseph Egyanka Appiah, alias Prophet Jemisimiham Jehu Appiah. He was, as we will see in chapter three of this study, a critical figure in establishing African nationalist philosophies and liberation theologies which sought to challenge Euro-centric Christianity and propose a more Afro-centric one in order to salvage aspects of indigenous African cultural beliefs and practices. As a direct rejection of the Christian tradition, many Black people sought for messiahship from within their own communities rather than from a perceived European inspired source. Thus in Beckford and Charles' chapter on Jamaica, the significance of Bedward in the early twentieth century would serve a similar purpose of appealing to the spiritual needs of the Black people in Jamaica. This issue of Black people Africanising the Christian religion to make it more personal and also to use this as a form of cultural resistance is briefly examined in part of Talburt's chapter on the eighteenth and nineteenth century roots of Pan African struggle in the Black Diaspora. Though these three chapters are entirely independent of each other, they nonetheless demonstrate that some Black people used religion as a vehicle of resistance in the liberation struggle against European systems of domination.

Upon surviving the horrors of the Middle Passage and arriving in the Americas, Black resistance continued. Even though there might be considerations that many of these forms of Black resistance were unsuccessful, their significance rests with the effect they had of wearing down, or eroding the effectiveness and, thereby, some of the power of the White planter elites or the plantocracy. Ranger also points out that some people generally accepted the wrong idea that 'resistances had been dead ends, leading nowhere' (Ranger, 1985, p. 56). However, as he asserts, even if these violent resistance campaigns did not always result in immediate political freedom, they played a part in the long struggle or fight for freedom which continued and in some respects reached maturity many years later. In other words, whereas one unsuccessful revolt might not have had a significant impact in weakening or bringing the eventual system of slavery and colonialism to an end, several hundreds of revolts and other forms of resistance certainly played their part in the gradual erosion of these systems.

One of the ways through which Black people resisted European control and domination was through the use of either violent or non-violent forms of actions. In terms of examples of non-violent forms of resistance, one such strategy employed was through the use of songs and slave narratives. Patterson's work on slavery in Jamaica, showed how slaves often sang songs to give vent to their feelings (Patterson, 1973). These forms of resistance were carried out by men and women and there was certainly plenty of evidence of women taking active part in slave resistance through songs and satire. More generally however, women in slave resistance was highlighted by Hilary McD Beckles in his work on Slave women in Barbados (1989) and also the Bush's work on slave women the Caribbean more generally (1990).

More specifically with regard to oral evidence, this was, however, not only confined to the plantations of the Caribbean but also present in Africa. Chapter two of this study, by Saboro, clearly demonstrates the extent to which songs and oral accounts were used in Africa as tools of resistance both historically as well as in the contemporary period. In this way Black people were able to use the medium of music and oral evidence to articulate their feelings and thus use these as tools to speak out against social and political injustices which they encountered at the hands of the European colonists. Very importantly, they were able to use these cultural forms of resistance as ways of asserting their own independence and Black identity which was part of their strategy of maintaining the survival of these very important aspects of their very existence. Whereas European colonialism sought to remove many aspects of African culture, such non-violent forms of resistance were important in helping to keep such African stories and cultural values firmly entrenched in their collective consciousness.

One of the central themes of Black resistance which is examined in part two of this book especially by Moussa Traore, is that of the impact of Maroons. What makes the study of the history of Maroons or maronage important in this study, is the fact that it is an excellent example of organised resistance campaign where slaves or captive Africans in the Americas not only sought to escape from slavery but, as Alvin Thompson informs us, maintain their freedom and independence within the slavocracies throughout the Americas (Thompson, 2006). In fact, Segal quite correctly adds that the very act of running away involved a level of defiance that reached beyond any fear of the ferocious penalties such individuals could face if captured by the colonial authorities (Segal, 1995). Mavis Campbell also expresses similar sentiments on her case study of Maroons in Jamaica. According to her, 'if the key to human dignity lies in action' then the Maroons possessed this trait fully, for their lives bespoke resistance (Campbell, 1992, p. 89). For example, Campbell makes the very powerful point that after several unsuccessful attempts by the British colonial authorities to subdue the Maroons in Jamaica, the British officials finally signed a formal peace treaty with them in 1738-'39. Because this was a clear example of a group of black people fighting for their freedom, Campbell regarded this, and by extension, other examples of maronage, as remarkable achievements of resistance.

Throughout the Caribbean and the Central American region the Maroons were, against the seemingly difficult European military and economic odds stacked against them, able to fight for, and establish their own independent communities within, but yet outside these slavocracies. From as early as the 1540s, 1570s and early 1600s in Hispaniola, Panama and Mexico respectively the Spanish colonial authorities were forced to make peace treaties with these Black freedom fighters (Campbell, 1992, p. 89).

Furthermore, Maroon communities constituted the first independent polities from European colonial rule, even if the colonial authorities did not recognise them as such at that time (Thompson, 2006, p. 13). In this sense, therefore, maronage was probably the most extreme form of Black resistance because it involved opting out of the system of oppression altogether (Thompson, 2006, p. 9). This is why Alvin Thompson refers to the Maroons as self-liberated persons (Thompson, 2006, p. 11). Therefore, the act of running away or escaping from slavery was only the first phase in Maroon resistance. The more important aspect, that of remaining away or setting up alternative independent Black communities within a slavocracy, constituted the second important phase in Maroon resistance.

Nor were all the Maroon leaders necessarily outright fighters using violent means as their main weapon against the colonial regimes of Europe. The case of Montague James is most insightful in terms of demonstrating how powerful the Maroons were at the time in their struggle with the various colonial governments of Europe. Montague James of the Trelawney Maroons in Jamaica was very highly and favourably regarded by the colonial government of Jamaica, and by the late 1770s or early 1780s, had been made or appointed captain of the Maroons and was also paid a salary of £200 per annum. He seems to have been the only Maroon leader to have held such a commission which would normally be reserved for White colonists especially since Maroon leaders did not normally receive official salaries (Campbell, 1992, pp. 90, 91).

Following a disagreement between the colonial government and Montague initially over his requests for more lands for the maroons and the subsequent rejection of this, he, and about 600 other maroons were, in 1796, deported to Nova Scotia and then Sierra Leone where he continued to be actively involved in resistance campaigns against the colonial regimes. These organised resistance campaigns took the form of letters to British colonial officials requesting that at the very least, they be removed from such a cold environment to a warmer one or else they would not engaged in any agricultural work which had been deemed necessary for their general subsistence (Campbell, 1992). Throughout the Caribbean region, therefore, maroon resistance was an extremely powerful example of organised and sustained Black resistance struggle.

Within Britain during the eighteenth and nineteenth centuries, the emerging Black population was also engaged in organising campaigns of resistance which took similar forms to those we have briefly described in Africa and the Americas. Some of these forms of resistance included running away from their masters, the use of religious movements and also the formation of their own pressure groups specifically focused on particular issues of social injustice which they sought to address. Religion was also a very important tool used by many Black people as a form of resistance. Because many slaves and free Black people were prevented from joining the established churches attended by the colonial class, the Black communities responded in two main ways. Firstly, they established their own Christian churches where they could worship more freely and where they could also challenge the European imposed systems of entrapment. Secondly, some Black people developed more Afro-centric forms of religion which were based on a rejection of many aspects of the basic Christian theology in favour of a distinct Black theology. Walvin points us to the fact that the Christian religion was often used by some Europeans as a way for Black people to block out of their minds totally, the problems and discrimination they were facing in their daily lives by not concentrating on the here and now, but focusing instead, on the life to come. For example, a morning prayer, which Walvin says was written especially for the Black population in England in the eighteenth century said, 'O merciful God, grant that I may perform my duty this day faithfully and cheerfully; and that I may never murmur, be uneasy, or impatient under any of the troubles of this life' (Walvin, 1973, p. 69). In this way, therefore, there was a belief that Black people should be content with their lot in society and not offer any resistance but be cheerfully obedient. It seems, however, that many Black people in Britain were probably ignorant of this prayer or desirous of developing their own creed and philosophy in response to the social and economic injustices which they encountered in Britain.

Although they were speaking with specific reference to Jamaica during the nineteenth century, Moore and Johnson argued that the post emancipation period witnessed the wholesale importation of the cultural items and symbols from Victorian Britain into Jamaica (Moore and Johnson, 2002, p. 353). This was equally true for much of the Anglophone Caribbean. Whilst there is much truth in this statement, it should be equally borne in mind that some Black people chose to resist these wholesale importation and acceptance of European (or more specifically British Victorian cultural values). Far from believing that Christianity made Black people more obedient and passive towards European colonialism, Black religion and resistance challenged this assertion. One aspect of this European cultural value was that the practice of Christian religion was not readily accepted by many Black people and was in fact resisted. In Britain, therefore, during the nineteenth century, some Black people were becoming disillusioned with main-steam or orthodox Christianity.

Faced by constant animosity and dangers, the Black population in England turned to the reliable support of their 'own numbers and a sense of community' (Walvin, 1973, p. 61). In this way they could form natural points for the combined purposes of community protection and preservation, as well as the basis for community resistance against European oppression. Commenting on the British Government's attempt to enable or assist three hundred and fifty members of the Black community in Britain to go back to Africa, specifically Sierra Leone, in the late eighteenth century, or as he put it, 'to get rid of them', most of them were dead within five years (Fryer. 1984, p. 203). Fryer also asserted that from the late 1700s, Britain's Black slaves often engaged in individual acts of resistance. These were multiplied many times over which contributed to the eventual pressure being placed on the government to formally bring the system of slavery to an end (Fryer 1984, p. 203).

It was clear therefore, that the Black population in Britain would also seek to organise aspects of their own resistance and campaigns of Black identity through such organisations as the Sons of Africa Movement of the eighteenth century of which the former slaves and free Blacks, Equiano and Cugoano, were members. In addition, there were cases of Black radical activists who were prepared to engage in violent acts to challenge and undermine the British Government. One of the most notable examples was the Jamaican-born radical preacher named Robert Wedderburn, who lived in London in the 1820s. Wedderburn was born in 1762 in Jamaica to a White Scottish father and a Jamaican slave mother but was later sent to live in England. He was very much involved in organising a Black resistance campaign in the 1820s aimed broadly at improving the living conditions Black people were experiencing in Britain at the time, as well as a campaigner for violent actions against Whites if necessary. His Black resistance campaign receives more discussion in chapter nine of this study.

Organisation of the Book

This chapter has served to provide an overview of some of the main ways through which Black people have engaged in organised and sustained campaigns of resistance against European forms of domination and control. It has therefore helped to contextualise the main rationale and key ideological framework within which these discussions take place. The book is broadly organised into two main sections. Chapters one to four constitute the first part of the study and considers how Africans resisted European slavery, colonialism and cultural domination within Africa. This section focuses on particular issues such as the impact of slave songs and narratives, local resistance against colonial government administration, and the impact of religion and resistance. The second section of the study focuses on resistance struggles in the African Diaspora, with particular emphasis on Britain and the Caribbean. The focus in this part of the book is on Black resistance struggles in Jamaica, slave resistance in the Caribbean through maronage in the French Caribbean, skin bleaching and identity and finally the roots of Pan African campaigns of resistance in the eighteenth and nineteenth centuries. What these independent studies have in common, is their focus on how Black people have had to fight for their own freedom against European systems of control in order to assert their own independence of thought and cultural identity and ensure their very survival and existence.

Chapter two by Emmanuel Saboro examines a particular case study in Northern Ghana, West Africa and draws upon oral evidence based on his extensive field work within the Bulsa and Kasena communities through recordings of songs and oral narrative accounts of slavery and enslavement. The study pays particular attention to the ways in which indigenous perspectives of slavery and resistance are metaphorised within these cultures and have, to a large extent, been preserved through oral tradition and referred to by members of the community as cultural references of their past resistance struggles against European attacks. This is particularly important as it demonstrates how Africans, who might otherwise have been regarded as defeated peoples, used these songs to reflect upon, and celebrate their attempts to challenge African slave raiders who sought to supply the Europeans with captured Africans. In chapter three, Botchway examines the significance of William Joseph Egyanka Appiah, alias Prophet Jemisimiham Jehu Appiah in establishing African nationalist philosophies and liberation theologies which sought to reform Euro-centric Christianity into an Afro-centric religion. His primary objective was to fight against a Euro-centric form of religion which down-played the relevance of African cultural traditions and values. He therefore attempted to salvage aspects of indigenous African cultural beliefs and practices in order to create nationalist awareness in the Gold Coast and racial consciousness among colonial Africans.

Chapter four by Wilson Yayoh, focuses on an Ewe community in Ghana which sought to challenge the colonial authorities over the nature of land demarcation and boundaries as well as attempts at colonial coercion. These attempts by the Brtish Colonial regime, which were supported by Nkrumah's newly formed political party and his subsequent government, seemed destined to wipe out the very existence of this local ethnic community. It is their resistance strategies, which forms the basis of Yayoh's study. Even though the local political party led by Kwame Nkrumah was also complicit in these colonial arrangements, this chapter demonstrates how local community activists fought to maintain their traditional homeland and geographical territory in the face of overwhelming odds. These three chapters focus on particular case studies in Ghana and show different approaches being employed to resist European-initiated systems of domination.

The second part of this study begins with chapter five by Beckford and Charles which is effectively a powerful micro study of Black resistance campaigns in Jamaica, the largest English-speaking Caribbean island. Here the authors use a wide variety of examples to demonstrate how, from the beginning of its colonial encounters until the present period, Jamaica has been at the centre of Black resistance campaigns. In this sense, Jamaica is examined here as an island in which the Black radical tradition has also manifested itself in almost every generation since the second half of the seventeenth century. Some of the stand out Black resistance campaigns which are examined in the chapter include: the Morant Bay Rebellion, the ideas and activities of Alexander Bedward, the ideas and work of Marcus Garvey, Leonard Howell and Rastafari, Claudius Henry, the Coral Gardens incident, the anti-Chinese riot, the Walter Rodney riot, and the lyrics of some popular songs.

It should not be assumed that Black resistance was the exclusive preoccupation of men. Traore's work in chapters six and seven discuss the significance of Caribbean men and women through their experiences as Maroons in the French Caribbean. What is particularly important about these two chapters is the emphasis they place on the desire on the part of these women to reconnect with their African ancestral home. Traoré examines the role of women in the pan African Francophone Caribbean. Through the use of English literature, this chapter shows that several Caribbean women took up the challenge of fighting slavery by embarking on a search for their roots, which meant a journey to Africa. Chapter six examines the case of Veronica's quest for "wholeness" or a search for her roots in Guinea, West Africa. In Chapter seven Traoré explores the case of Siméon Louis Jerome's attempt to reconnect with his roots and literally to return to Africa which is often referred to as *pays d'avant* -- the country before-- ,or where we came from or *Pays Guinée* (Guinea in West Africa), after he has killed his white master. Throughout this chapter Traoré demonstrates that this novel presents the *marronnage* process as one of the battle strategies used by Black people to challenge and undermine the systems of slavery and colonialism.

One popular argument which is often cited as an effect of slavery and colonialism is that Black people have low self-esteem and as a consequence, engage in skin bleaching. Chapter eight by Christopher Charles discusses the debates pertaining to the popular explanation for skin bleaching among Black people as one done for reasons of self-hate, which is a legacy of slavery. Far from accepting that there is a crisis of Black identity and low self-esteem, this chapter rejects the self-hate or internalised oppression thesis as the reason for skin bleaching in Jamaica with empirical evidence and posits the alternative explanations of colourism and miseducation that are the legacies of White domination. The self-hate thesis is a one-size- fits- all explanation that ignores the variegated history and culture of Black people as an ethnic group and their resistance and resilience in the face of oppression. Some skin bleachers do suffer from self-hate, but the large majority do not hate themselves, so it is important to interrogate the culture and their engagement of oppression that influences them to alter their black physicality. This interrogation requires a study, which measures the self-esteem of Jamaicans who bleach their skin and those who do not and compare the mean self-esteem scores of the two groups that are interpreted and contextualized within the voices of the participants and the Jamaican culture in terms of how the study participants in particular and Black people in general diverge in their response to oppression.

Chapter nine by Talburt discusses the idea of reframing and realignment of the Pan African ideologies by critiquing the over reliance on the twentieth century Pan-African conferences, Black initiatives and ideologies as the central basis for discussing the Pan-Africanist Movement. Pan Africanism can be regarded as one of the most formal and sustained forms of organised campaigns against European colonial domination. This chapter demonstrates that many of the features and issues of Pan-Africanism, which are generally discussed within the context of the twentieth century, could be traced to earlier periods in Britain and America within the Black communities as they encountered and responded to various forms of European oppression. This discussion briefly examines such ideas as 'back to Africa,' calls for African independence, as well as African unity which were evident long before the year 1900. The primary focus, however, is on the attempts by Black people to organise campaigns to reconnect and resist White entrapment and domination in the African Diaspora primarily through religious campaigns and Black-based pressure groups in the nineteenth century. In this sense, therefore, Talburt argues that the roots of Pan-African ideology can be traced to Black resistance campaigns before the start of the twentieth century and that studies which rely so much on twentieth century examples of Pan-Africanism lose the real sense of the more general understanding of Pan-Africanist struggle.

Conclusion

What this introductory chapter has sought to do is demonstrate a universal theme which runs through all the chapters in different ways, and that is, the extent to which Black people had to fight for their own freedom in order to preserve their own identity and existence. Black resistance started in Africa at the points along the West African coasts where Europeans sought to exploit them. It continued as they journeyed from the interior to the coasts before being forcefully transported to the plantations of the Americas. Finally, Black people resisted in the Americas and Britain. The uniqueness of this book is not in the theme of Black resistance itself, but in the new case studies and discussions pertaining to this universal theme.

References

Bush, Barbara. (1990). Slave Women in Caribbean Society 1650-1838, Kingston, Jamaica, Heinemann Publishers, Indiana University Press, James Currey Publishers London.

Campbell, Mavis. (1992). 'Early Resistance to Colonialism: Montague James and the Maroons in Jamaica, Nova Scotia and Sierra Leone' in Ajayi, J.F. and Peel, J.D.Y eds. *People and Empires in African History: Essays in Memory of Michael Crowder*, London and New York, Longman Publishers.

Edwards, Paul and Dabydeen, David eds. (1991). *Black Writers in Britain 1760-1890 an Anthology*, Edinburgh University Press.

Fryer, Peter. (1984). *Staying Power: The History of Black People in Britain*, London, Pluto Press.

Gilroy, Paul. (1998). *There Ain't no Black in the Union Jack: The Cultural Politics of Race and Nation*, London, Routledge Pubishers.

Marable, Manning. (1996). *Speaking Truth to Power: Essays on Race, Resistance and Radicalism*, Colorado, Westview Press.

Marable, Manning and Mullings, Leith. (2000). *Let Nobody Turn Us Around: Voices of Resistance, Reform and Renewal*, Lanham, Boulder, New York and Oxford, Rowan and Littlefield Publishers.

Martin, Tony. (2012). *Caribbean History: From Pre-Colonial Origins to the Present*, Boston, London, Pearson Publishers.

Mazrui, Ali. (1986). *The Africans: A Triple Heritage*, London, BBC Publications.

Mcd Beckles, Hilary. (1989). *Natural Rebels: A Social History of Enslaved Black Women in Barbados*, London, Zed Books.

Moore, Brian. (1998). 'The Culture of the Colonial Elites of nineteenth-Century Guyana' in Johnson, Howards and Watson Karl eds. *The White Minority in the Caribbean*, Kingston, Jamaica Oxford and Princeton, Ian Randle, James Curry and Markus Wiener Publishers.

Moore, Brian and Johnson, Michelle. (2002). 'Challenging the Civilising Mission: Cricket as a Field of Socio-cultural Contestation in Jamaica 1865-1920' in Thompson, Alvin eds. *In the Shadow of the Plantation Caribbean History and Legacy*, Kingston, Ian Randle Publishers.

Patterson, Orlando. (1973). *The Sociology of Slavery: An Analysis of the Origins, Development and Structure of Negro Slave Society in Jamaica*, Jamaica, Sangsters's Book Stores Limited in Association with Granada Publishing Limited.

Ranger, T.O. (1985). 'African Initiatives and Resistance in the Face of Partition and Conquest' in Boahen, Adu eds. *General History of Africa Vol. V11, Africa Under Colonial Domination 1880-1935*, London, Heinemann Educational Books.

Rice, Alan. (2003). *Radical Narratives of the Black Atlantic*, London, Continuum Publishers.

Shilliam, Robbie. (2015). *The Black Pacific: Anti-Colonial Struggles and Oceanic Connections*, London, Bloomsbury Publishing.

Sivanandan, A. (1982). *A Different Hunger: Writings on Black Resistance*, London, Pluto Press.

Segal, Ronald. (1950). *The Black Diaspora*, London and Boston, Faber and Faber Limited.

Thompson, Alvin. (2006). *Flight to Freedom, African Runaways and Maroons in the Americas*, Kingston Jamaica, University of the West Indies Press.

Thompson, Vincent. (1962). *Africa and Unity: The Evolution of Pan Africanism*, London and Harlow, Longman Publishers.

Thompson, Vincent. (1987). *The Making of the African Diaspora in the Americas 1441-1900*, New York, Longman Publishers.

Walvin, James. (1973). *Black and White: The Negro and English Society 1555-1945*, London, Allen Lane the Penguin Press.

CHAPTER TWO

Our Fathers Shot Arrows: Songs of Resistance to the Slave Trade in Northern Ghana

Emmanuel Saboro

Introduction

This chapter examines the centrality of the experience of
enslavement and resistance to the slave trade within two
communities in northern Ghana: the Bulsa and Kasena, as it is
reflected in their contemporary oral traditions. The chapter
particularly focuses on examples of popular songs, oral traditions,
and various forms of public culture that reveal how the memory
of slavery and enslavement shapes public representations of
identity in these societies. Drawing from fieldwork within these
communities that involved the recording of songs and oral accounts
of the slave trade and enslavement, the chapter examines the ways
in which resistance to enslavement in the nineteenth century is
presented today as a dominant metaphor in public and private
representations of local identity. What emerges from this chapter
is the attempt by communities hitherto perceived as victims, to
actively reshape their role through identity politics that actively
transforms dominant ideas of victimhood, and replaces them
with narratives of resistance and common struggles to retain free
status.

Cressida, (2012) has provided some insights into the concept of identity politics and how it relates to vulnerable and marginalised groups within the body politic.

'Identity politics,' Cressida has argued, has come to signify a wide range of political activity and theorising founded in the shared experience of injustice of members of certain groups (Cressida, 2012). Although the concept may not fit exactly within the context of the Bulsa and Kasena's collective experience of the slave trade, we can borrow Cressida's formulations to inform certain aspects of their experience. For example, Cressida sees Identity politics as a mode of organising intimately connected to the idea that some social groups are oppressed and that one's identity as part of the oppressed group makes one 'peculiarly vulnerable' to certain influences such as cultural imperialism violence, exploitation, marginalisation, or powerlessness. Cressida goes further to argue that, rather than accepting the negative scripts offered by a dominant culture about one's own inferiority, one transforms one's own sense of self and community, often through consciousness-raising (Cressida, 2012). In this chapter, therefore, the main claim being made is that the Bulsa and Kasena have attempted this consciousness-raising, through their songs and thereby seek to subvert the narratives of passivity and docility often ascribed to enslaved people.

The songs which are discussed in this chapter showcase a narrative of communal redemption predicated on pain, struggle, and eventual triumph (Saboro, 2013). The songs suggest that while slave raiding and enslavement may have eroded solidarities that had bound communities together, contemporary discourse is transforming this past of defeat and division by producing a new narrative of a past that is not divisive, but potentially empowering.

Although the nature of memory and the oral tradition is often beset with a number of methodological constraints, the songs examined in this chapter still offer a significant window into how marginalised communities often understood and responded to their plight of enslavement. Whilst these songs do not tell us about numbers, what they reveal is a compelling story of a people's fears and hopes. The songs have also come to constitute a testament of individual and communal response of a strong and resilient people who survived in the midst of the tragedy of predation and European exploitation.

As part of a larger attempt at interrogating and documenting the oral expressions of the slave trade in Ghana, the process of conducting interviews and collecting songs from among the Bulsa ethnic group from 2005 and later the Kasena between 2012 and 2013, had to be undertaken. In the interviews which were conducted, the slave trade and enslavement always came up as one of the significant traumatic events within their collective history. Whenever they were asked about how these memories are preserved and conveyed, informants always alluded to songs. It was then decided to proceed to record these songs from popular singing groups. The songs were then transcribed and translated into English with the help of translation experts, and constituted them into texts for analysis. Although it is always difficult to capture certain cultural specifics into the English language, and the fact that the very nature of memory itself is fluid and can be subject to distortions, careful attempts were made to present the translated data as close to the original local texts as practicable.

The wealth and diversity of documentation of the slave experience, resistance and the notions of freedom to the slave trade within the general body of historical literature is enormous (Genovese 1979; Thompson 1987; Bah 2003; Cordell 2003; Klein, 2003; Richardson 2003; Beckles 2007; Opoku-Agyemang 2007, Saboro 2013; 2016). These scholars have particularly shown how the enslaved within most parts of Africa often negotiated and resisted their oppression through various forms and strategies. Within the African-American historiography for example, there is also a wealth of documentation on slave resistance reflected through the autobiographical writing of ex-slave such as Olaudah Equiano and Frederick Douglass.

Indeed, scholars have long acknowledged that 'struggle is the core of history and that the principal dialectic in that struggle is between oppression and exploitation, on the one hand and resistance on the other. As was already pointed out in chapter one, African resistance to the slave trade began in the interior even before captives were put on board slave ships for the Middle Passage (Thompson, 1987). Several accounts by European slave dealers and travellers on the coast for example, attest to resistance by some Africans either avoiding capture or trying to escape enslavement. Furthermore, upon arrival in the Americas, slaves continued their organised resistance campaigns as part of their quest and determination to re-establish their own physical and cultural freedom and identity.

Within the specific case of the communities under review, there are communal memories of how such societies often adapted and resisted the threats of enslavement within their collective imagination. This representation of resistance is conveyed through a variety of means: the exploitation of the landscape and the use of local architecture, flight from slave raiders and songs. One of the interviewees noted during one of my field trips undertaken while conducting some of this research, that 'the events of this history were not written down in formal documents, but we remember them through proverbs, narratives, stories and songs' (Wemegura, 2012).

The song is one of the most pervasive oral forms in Africa and is an important part of a people's literature. These songs which are discussed in this chapter are composed imaginatively, and have come to constitute a way in which these subaltern groups articulate their individual and collective experiences. People sing when they are happy and when they are sad. Songs are thus one of the cultural resources that are sometimes used to give expression to what would not ordinarily be spoken about. Songs also help cultures without writing traditions (and sometimes even cultures with writing traditions) to continue to preserve and remember their collective history and identity. Singing, in these cultures, represents ways in which they keep reminding themselves of past events and more importantly, on how their ancestors have survived predation and enslavement. The ability to communicate the traumatic events of the past through songs ensures the survival and continuity of the memories of enslavement and more significantly of triumph and survival.

What do the songs under review reveal about strategies of Black resistance and identity within these communities, and in what forms do these occur? Are there ways in which the peoples' actions and reactions have shaped their present identity? These are the main examples of forms of resistance that the songs address. Cultural adaptations, resistance and the preservation of identity as revealed through these songs, thus promise to add to our store of knowledge and enhance our understanding on how cultures that became victims of slave raids often negotiated, adapted and survived their enslavement and oppression.

The Bulsa and Kasena are neighbours in terms of proximity and are found in the Upper East Region of Ghana. They share a common border with Burkina Faso. The Bulsa speak a language known as Buli, while the Kasena speak Kasem. Both ethnic groups are believed to have migrated to their present settlements from different locations. The Bulsa for example are believed to have migrated from Mamprusi Land in the Northern Region of Ghana, while the Kasena are believed to have descended from an ancestor called Butu and came from Zeko beyond Bukina Faso to settle in various settlements in the Northern Region.

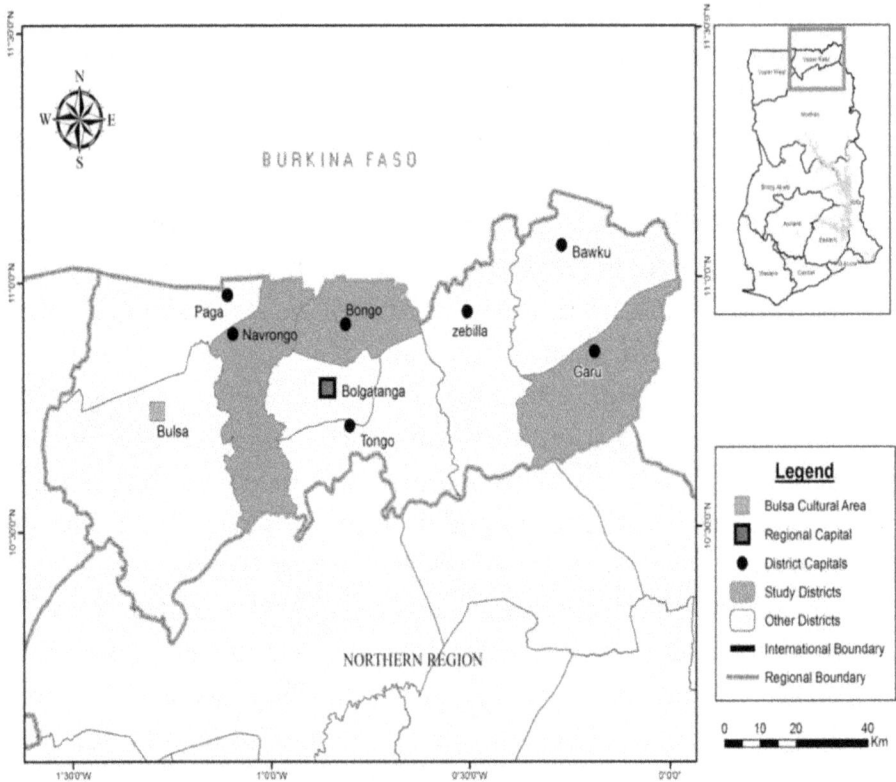

Map of Ghana showing the Northern Region: Source: Geography Information Systems, Cartography and Remote Sensing Section, Department of Geography and Regional Planning, University of Cape Coast, Ghana 2016

Northern Ghana is an important cultural and geographical location relative to the history of slavery in Ghana because of its strategic place in the three different, but inter-related slave systems; the trans-Atlantic, trans-Saharan and the indigenous African slave systems, which occurred at different times in the history of the region. Although memories of these distinct slave systems are often blurred within most northern communities, the legacies of enslavement and resistance still resonate within their oral traditions. Der (1998) has suggested that northern Ghana was originally not part of the network of the trans-Atlantic slave enterprise until the nineteenth century. The nineteenth century, according to Der, was when northern Ghana became part of the infamous slave trade through the activities of Zabarima and Asante slave raiders when they began a series of systematic plundering and pillaging within certain communities and capturing people to sell as slaves.

Indeed, images of the Zabarima and Asante slave raiders are captured within the oral traditions of the people. Principal slave raiders often mentioned among the Bulsa and Kasena are Babatu, Samori, Gazare and Bagao, although the latter is relatively unknown (Der, 1998; Saboro, 2013). Indeed, oral accounts from among these communities in Ghana refer to these slave raiders as major predators who terrorised these areas with constant raiding and the threats of captivity and enslavement. In the section that follows, the focus is specifically on songs that convey the themes of warfare and others that celebrate communal victory over predation.

Memorialising war as a resistance strategy

The songs which deal with resistance to enslavement within these communities reveal in very subtle ways, attempts by these cultures to rewrite their collective history and to carve out a new identity for themselves. The songs discussed below provide a window into how these cultures often responded to their plight of enslavement by fighting back. Since slave raiding was always carried out through the use of some degree of violence, fighting back became a significant cultural response mechanism and this is portrayed in the songs through images of war.

Photo showing the chief of Doninga (Bulsa) in his war regalia: Photo courtesy of Saboro 2013

Although war songs are not entirely exclusive to these cultures, and not all of the songs about war relate to slavery and enslavement, there are songs with very specific references to the slave raiders and their activities within these cultures. Some of these become evident in the examples which are discussed below.

In an interview with a clan elder in Navrongo about slave raids, this is how he conceptualised communal responses to the threats of enslavement within the Kasena collective consciousness:

> When the slaver raider came, he could not penetrate here. The raids were intense in areas such as *Prata*, *Bassisem*, *Bonor* and *Liu*. He captured people around those areas but because we are hunters or fighters, we fought back. The slave raider came with guns but we resisted with bows and arrows so they could not defeat our people like others (Wemegura, 2012).

Although it appears this elder had a rather romantic view of community resistance by insisting that the slave raider could not penetrate their community, his stance reflects a common theme that runs through some of their songs. One obvious strategy this informant mentions is fighting back. In the aforementioned interview, the elder further relates to the experience of slave raiding and resistance by alluding to the fact that:

> During the *Fao* festival celebrations, we re-enact the experience of resistance and use the occasion to remind ourselves that we are not afraid of the slave raider. We dress in war dresses during the festival because of the slave raider. We have a song that goes like this: *Miatu, Miatu, Nam yein se de jeiri Chena bwolo ne,* strongman, strongman, let us meet each other on the battle field. This song reflects bravery. The song says to those who are firing guns that we are not afraid of gun shots or war (Wemegura, 2012).

Another interviewee said that 'our people were warriors' and that 'although the slave raiders had weapons, our people defended themselves by fighting back' (Anasemyen, 2016). These images of fighting back are carried very forcefully in the song below. The song Wemagura earlier alluded to in the interview was later recorded from a male singing group within the community. The words of the song are as follows:

Miatu Miatu
Miatu miatu
Nam yein se de jeiri
Chena bwolo ne
Miatu miatu
Nam yein se de jeiri
Chena bwolo ne
Kanbonga lɔge peo
Debam ba peo kwori cheiga

Nasara lɔge peo
Debam ba peo kwori cheiga
Miatu miatu
Nam yein se de jeiri
Chena bwolo ne
Strong men, strong men,
Strong men, strong men,
Let us meet on the battlefield.
Strong men, strong men,
Let us meet on the battlefield.
The slave raider has given a gun shot;
We do not listen to gun shots.
The Whiteman has given a gun shot;
We do not listen to gun shots.
Strong men, strong men,
Let us meet on the battlefield to know who is who.

This song was performed by men in Navrongo and its performance was accompanied by drums. In this song, we are presented with a call and a challenge to battle. The expression of emotion in calling forth strong men, 'strong men let's meet each other on the battle field' reinforces the fact that war was a significant response pattern among these cultures that became prone to the constant harassment and threats of enslavement. The song reflects the ways in which the people's ancestors were not deterred by the gun shots of the slave raiders but confronted their oppressors head-on. In this song reference is made to the 'white man' and 'guns' and this is particularly significant. Although there is, no evidence to suggest that the Europeans were involved in slave raids within these cultures, associating them with guns is an indication that communities were often aware of European influence in the enslavement process.

Communal memories about the slave experience among these two ethnic groups suggest that violence was a necessary and legitimate response to the threats of predation and enslavement. This is seen in how some of the songs articulate the themes of violence and aggression. Reflecting on the nature of enslavement within Africa, Lovejoy has pointed out that, 'the legitimisation of enslavement ... reinforced a tendency towards war and other forms of violence.' This observation by Lovejoy finds validation within the context of this discussion, as the songs articulate the themes of war and violence rather forcefully. The songs often evoke images of bloodshed, shooting of arrows, and violent battles (Lovejoy, 2000, p. 35).

Wemegura, in the extract below, provides a strong and clear indication of the extent through which African communities often understood what was at stake in confronting the threats of their communal territories. When he was asked whether slavery was a common feature among the Kasena before slave raiding by the Zabarima and Asante, and how they responded to such slave raids, he had this to say:

> In our land, we were not used to selling people. What we have come to meet and appreciate is the fact that everybody is his brother's keeper. Nobody has the right to sell his fellow brother outside as a slave. The slave raider brought about slave trading/selling. Our ancestors usually fought and secured the freedom of the slaves and left them in his house where they became members of the household. Slave raiding/trading has made us wiser and more conscious of ourselves. When you hear any cry (alarm), nobody sits down. Everybody gets up with axes, bows and arrows to help each other so that no situation is able to overwhelm us (Wemegura, 2012).

Here Wemeguru was extremely emphatic about a communal response to the threats of enslavement: fighting back and the insistence that 'nobody sits down' reinforces the degrees to which communal efforts were harnessed in resisting the slave trade in most parts of Africa. Reference to 'bows and arrows' is a pointer to how cultures who lacked sophisticated weapons, were yet still able to challenge their enslavement through open confrontation. They were, as the title of this book suggests, fighting for the freedom and their cultural identity.

In 2005 while collecting oral evidence of the slave experience among the Bulsa, I recorded a number of songs dealing with strong images of violence and warfare. One particular song alluding to a resistance strategy conveying the theme of war says: 'let someone be deceived to raise an axe'. The song says:

> *Ba paasi waai te wa zak liak*
> *Ba paasi waai te wa zak liak*
> *Liak nya zimm*
> *Ba paasi waai te wa ga yeri*
> *Ga kum baliŋ cheŋ be*
> Let someone be deceived
> To raise an axe
> An axe stained with blood
> Then he will be deceived, go home,
> Cry and get lost

This song is usually performed by men with accompaniment provided by drumming. The drum is used to produce a time line (a recurring rhythmic pattern of fixed duration or time span). The significance of this time line is to clarify the regulative beat which is a common feature of rhythmic organisation in most African traditions. In the song, the slave raider is challenged to initiate war if he dares, and should he choose to do so, he would surely regret it. The central animating metaphor in the song is the overriding image of bloodshed and violence. The image of 'an axe stained with blood' is of great symbolic significance. Blood within the context of this song connotes violence and aggressive resistance suggesting that resistance was predicated on great individual and collective sacrifice.

photo of the Nakong chief's Palace within the Kasena cultural area, showing some slave relics believed to have been left behind by slave raiders. Photo courtesy of Saboro (2013).

In articulating the subject of communal bravery and resilience, we are reminded in the Kasena song which celebrates the fighting spirit and valour of the people of Achaanea and Ayaara, that these were people who did not remain passive but fought to redeem themselves from the yoke of slave raiding and oppression. The song says:

Ba na nɔn nɔn ba baa nuŋi gwala pasaa ne
Ba na nɔn nɔn ba baa nuŋi gwala pasaa ne
Nɔn nɔn yeiri Achanea

Debam mo vere taa de jaa vu kukula
Ba vere paare ba tane de pεεro naa
Ayaarania ganε wo laŋa ne
Ba tan de fera maa ke mare mare nee
Sam yiga gwala maa ke mare mare nee
Debam mo mage naa de jaa vu kukula
Ayaarania ganε wo laŋa ne
When they move out and meet the slave raider inside Pasaa
When they move out and meet the slave raider inside Pasaa
No one knows Achaanea
We fought them through to Kukula
We took over titles and confiscated their guns
The people of Ayaara are buffalos on the battlefield
They and the fra are in readiness
The distant slave raider is in readiness
We fought them till Kukula
The people of Ayaara are buffalos on the battlefield

This song is performed by women in Kayoro which is located in
the Kasena area. The song expresses a militant tone and articulates
clearly the ways in which people were brave enough to challenge
their threat of capture and enslavement. The song alludes to the
'moving out to meet the slave raider.' Moving out suggests three
significant variables of fighting, taking of titles and the confiscating
of guns. These variables clearly define the ways and context in
which resistance over oppression was undertaken, through
aggressive warfare. The emphasis on the collectivity expressed
in the sentiments 'we fought,' and 'we took over titles' reveals
ways in which collaborative efforts were necessary in resisting
oppression. Taking of titles and confiscating guns is suggestive
of valour and bravery even in the midst of overwhelming odds.
The allusion to Kukula in the song is significant. Kukula is a
significant sacred space within the Kasena cultural landscape: a
river deity located in Kayoro. This deity is held in great reverence

because of the belief in its ability to help anyone who comes to it with a problem ranging from childlessness, the desire for material prosperity and so on. When slave raids became intense within these areas, oral narrative accounts suggest that the local people who were pursued by slave raiders, often ran to Kukula to seek protection from enslavement. In the song, the people allude to fighting all the way to Kukula where titles and guns were confiscated thus suggesting a kind of redemptive role played by this deity in securing their freedom.

These communal memories expressed in the songs thus repudiate the arguments that Africans either willingly gave themselves up to be enslaved or were passive. The preponderance of evidence within these subaltern groups is overwhelming. In another Bulsa song for example, we are reminded of how the Bulsa challenged slave raiders to an open confrontation. The song that follows for example, is usually performed by men and during its re-enactment, especially during the *feok* festival, one would notice the men dressed in war regalia, and brandishing war implements accompanied by war drums. The audience is often drawn to its emotional and warlike feeling through the lead singer's dignified steps and the call and response pattern which some of the stanzas normally assume. The song says:

A Boni Chaaba, Ti Boni Chaab Yoo
A boni chaaba, ti boni chaab yoo
Fidan chiiba zaani ti boni chaab
A boni chaaba, ti boni chaab yoo
Fi dan chiib zaani ti boni chaab
Nankoŋbaliiuk la nak ku a chali
Naara katuak, fi dan togsi
Yegyega, ku gebi keribi, tama
Me siaya, ni dan chiib zaani ti boni chaab
Let's chop each other into pieces
If you are brave and stand
We will chop each other into pieces

> If you stand we will chop each other into pieces
> We are like the millipede, even if we
> Are wounded, we will fight on and not surrender.
> We are like vinegar made from the stalks of early millet
> If you put so much in your soup, it will be too
> Concentrated and you will not be able to eat it
> We have agreed that if you are brave
> To fight us; we will chop each other into pieces

The overriding theme in the song is centred on violent confrontation as a means to challenge oppression. The image of 'chopping' each other into pieces conveys very strong emotional associations to warfare. The song expresses a simile carved in animal symbolic behaviour expressed in the lines:

> We are like the millipede,
> Even if we are wounded,
> We will fight on and not surrender.

The song's use of the millipede as a metaphor is significant. The significance of the millipede is revealed in its associated images of slow movement, adeptness, and impregnability and hence its reference in the songs suggests a resistance strategy rather than weakness and vulnerability. The millipede is a medium to large sized invertebrate found under rocks and in decaying logs all around the world. When under threat from predators, the millipede would normally recoil and resurface after the perceived threat is over. The outer skin of the millipede is also covered in a thick layer making it impregnable to external predators. By comparing themselves with the millipede, the people are actually using this song, to allude to the positive attributes of the millipede to themselves. These are the qualities of impregnability and skill.

The Bulsa people's association with the slow movement of the millipede should not, however, be misconstrued as a weakness but rather, as a strategy over their oppression. The song also expresses an awareness of the possible consequences of violent resistance and awareness that there may be causalities in the cause of fighting for freedom. The line 'we will fight and not surrender' is once again indicative of the collective will and resolve to challenge oppression at all cost. This song thus adds to existing body of knowledge and emphasises the 'legitimisation of violence' as Lovejoy has suggested. The song also projects and sheds light on communal values of self-sacrifice and resilience even in the midst of tragedy. A people may suffer indignities and oppression but remain resolute and their spirit not broken. Communal memories of resistance to the indignities of enslavement are often accompanied by the collective remembrance of victory over the forces of slave raiding. Indeed, these communities are often proud that their ancestors not only fought battles, but that they also won. That slave raiding and enslavement may have succeeded in reducing some of them as prey, others still stood, fought and eventually triumphed. This sense of communal victory is reflected in some songs.

Celebrating Triumph over Tragedy

Reflecting upon the context of the impact of the history of slaving in northern Ghana, Hartman has suggested that, a people's history is a battle royal, a contest between the powerful and the powerless in what happened as well as in the stories we tell about what happened; a fight to death over the meaning of the past (Hartman, 2007, p. 7).

In Hartman's view, 'the narrative of the defeated never triumphs' therefore leading to the question of whether '...the story of the defeated must always be a story of defeat'. Hartman wonders if it is too late to imagine that their lives (victim communities) might be redeemed. The songs indeed suggest that their struggles cast a shadow into a future in which they eventually won. One of such songs that convey a sense of communal pride and sense of victory is seen in the Bulsa song, 'our fathers drove away the slave raider.'

Taa koma yiak kanbong kaa

Taa koma yiak kanbong kaa
Kanbong kai le nyini taa teng ka la
Taa koma yiak Kanbongka te kaa chali
Ya yee aye yee yee aye yawi yaa
Taa koma yiak kanbongka
Ta koma yaik kanbongka te ka chali
Ya yee yee yoooo
Our fathers drove away the slave raider
Our fathers drove away the slave raider and he run away
The slave raider who entered our land was driven away by
our fathers
Our fathers drove away the slave raider and he run away
Can't you see how our fathers could shoot arrows?
Our fathers drove away the slave raider
Can't you see how they are coming out with arrows?

In this song, we see how a community articulates communal resistance and celebrates the collective efforts of their forebears in the resistance struggle. The emphasis on the slave raider being driven away does not in any way suggest acquiesce, docility or victimhood. The song's reference to the shooting of arrows is significant. The shooting of arrows is resistance and not passivity. It takes only the brave to fight back even in the midst of sophisticated weaponry. This collective resolve to fight and win is reinforced in another song. This song's primary focus is on the role of their forebears who fought and won. The song says:

Ba Toŋ Ba De, Pelim Toŋ Ba De
Ba toŋ ba de, pelim toŋ ba de
Ba yaa kala ayen ba toŋ nab pein
Ba be le de
Ba toŋ ba de, pelim toŋ ba de
Ba yaa kala ayen ba toŋ nab pein
Ba be le de
They fought and won

They fought and won again
They are now going to shoot a cow's arrow
And they will surely win too

This song celebrates a group's collective achievement. In its performance, the lead singer repeats the first two lines several times, while the rest of the women respond to succeeding lines, which normally serve as the chorus. The central animating metaphor in this song is fighting and winning. Fighting and winning is certainly not a feature of a people who were apathetic. The emphasis that they are now going to shoot a cow's arrow and they will surely win too, attests to the confidence of a brave and resilient people.

In the song, 'Kanbonsa nalema, yie za be?' the sense of communal triumph is again projected. This song is performed accompanied by drums, gongs and pieces of metal played by a few members of the adult male group members leading the song while the rest act-sing the chorus. During its performance, especially during the *feok* festival among the Bulsa, one would usually notice the brandishing of bow and arrows and bodily movements signifying courage and defiance which stir up warlike feelings among the audience. The song is sung in a call and response pattern and begins with a rhetorical question. The song says:

Kanbonsa nalema, yie za be?
Kanbonsa nalema, yie za be?
Kanbonsa nalema baa yiri yaa
Kanbonsa nalema, yie za be?
Kanbonsa nalema, yie za be?
Kanbonsa nalema baa yiri yaa
Where are the houses of the slave raiders?
Where are the houses of the chiefs of the slave raiders?
The chiefs of the slave raiders have fled.
Where are the houses of the chiefs of the slave raiders?
Where are the houses of the chiefs of the slave raiders?

The chiefs of the slave raider have fled

In its aesthetic form, we see a set of rhetorical questions marked by repetitive structures. Repetition is a basic principle of oral art and can be viewed both as a stylistic and fundamental grammatical form. Repetition in these songs take varied forms, and in this particular song, we see a lexical and structural repetition of 'kanbongsa nalema yie za be?' The essence of this verbal repetition is not only intended to mark emphasis but to contribute immensely to the musical quality of the song. During performance, the drum accompaniment together with other para-linguistic modes of communication such as facial expressions and dignified steps by the war dancers, enhances the performance and elicits audience response. The second line of the song is more forceful:

Kanbongsa nalema baa yiri yaa
The chiefs of the slave raiders have fled.

The song is a pointer to the fact that resistance led to the fleeing of the *kanbong*. On the metaphoric and symbolic level, the song challenges the very institution of the slave raiding hegemony by the use of the rhetorical question, where are the foundations of the slave enterprise? Or in other words, where are the power structures of the enslavers? This song re-echoes the fact that the very foundations of the institution of enslavement have been challenged through open confrontation.

The ultimate reward of a fierce resistance over the forces of enslavement was that victory was eventually won. The excitement and emotion associated with this military confrontation and positive outcome is reflected in some songs which usually reveal a triumphal procession after war. The song below is an example of a song celebrating a successful military combat. The song says:

Tigurika ya nueri ate vuusi
Kanbong ka yaa nueri a te vuusi
Kanbong ka yaa nueri a te vuusi

Yee-yee yee-yee
Kanbong yaa nueri ate vuusi
Tigurika ya nueri ate vuusi
Tigurika ya nueri ate vuusi
Yee-yee yee-yee
Tigurika yaa nueri ate vuusi
We are free at last
Victory over the slave raider has brought us a sigh of relief
Victory over the slave raider has brought us a sigh of relief
The battle is ended and we are free at last
The battle is ended and we are free at last
Victory over the slave raider has brought us a sigh of relief
Victory over the slave raider has brought us a sigh of relief
The battle is ended and we are free at last
The battle is ended and we are free at last

The song is performed by men accompanied by metal gongs and drums in which they produce a very powerful rhythmic pattern. Given the context in which slave raiding and captivity often occurred within these communities, with its attendant violence and aggression, the defeat of the slave raider produced an exhilarating effect on both individuals and the collective society. The song suggests that victory over the forces of enslavement was achieved as a consequence of warfare. The end of this warfare brought freedom at last.

Conclusion

This chapter has examined the centrality of the experience of enslavement and resistance to the slave trade among the Bulsa and Kasena who became victims of systematic plunder and pillage through the activities of slave raiders. The chapter focussed on examples of public culture that sought to reveal how the memory of the threats of violence and enslavement continue to shape public representations of identity in these societies and especially the ways in which resistance is presented today as a dominant metaphor in public and private representations of local identity.

The songs examined here as texts reveal the attempt by communities hitherto perceived as victim communities, to carve out new identities for themselves. The songs suggest that while slave raiding and enslavement may have diminished the central communality that had bound communities together, the forces of enslavement were never able to destroy them or to leave individuals and communities atomized and physically defenceless. In this sense, therefore, from the moment Europeans started their interaction with Africans, resulting in Africans engaging in slave raids, Africans fought against such attacks. Whilst these attacks were centred upon fellow African slave raiders, these were European inspired raids. Whereas these peoples of northern Ghana used the medium of songs and oral testimonies as vehicles with which to resist, reflect and reconstruct their own forms of Black identity, the next chapter by Botchway demonstrates how the Black people used religion as another medium with which to challenge the Euro-centric forms of control which were being imposed upon them.

References

Anasemyen, E. K. (2016). Community Elder, interviewed by E. Saboro at Nakong, Near Navrongo 2 February.

Bah, Thierno M. (2003). Slave-Raiding and Defensive Systems South of Lake Chad from the Sixteenth to the Nineteenth Century in Diouf A. Sylviane eds. *Fighting the Slave Trade: West African Strategies,* Athens, Ohio University Press.

Cordell, Dennis D. (2003). 'The Myth of Inevitability and Invincibility: Resistance to Slavers and the Slave Trade in

Central Africa, 1850-1910' in Diouf A. Sylviane eds. *Fighting the Slave Trade: West African Strategies,* Athens, Ohio University Press.

Cressida, H. (2012). "Identity Politics", *The Stanford Encyclopedia of Philosophy.* Edward N. Zalta eds. <http://plato.stanford.edu/archives/sum2012/entries/identity-politics retrieved on 03/03/2016 @ 7:48 p.m.

Der, Benedict. (1998). *The Slave Trade in Northern Ghana,* Accra, Woeli Press.

Genovese, Eugene D. (1979). *From Rebellion to Revolution: Afro-American Slave Revolts in the Making of the Modern World,* Baton Rouge.

Halbwachs, Maurice. (1925). *Les Cadres Sociaux de la memoire,* Paris, F. Alcan.

Hartman, Saidiya. (2007). *Lose Your Mother: A Journey along the Transatlantic Slave Route,* New York, Farrar, Straus and Giroux.

Howell, Allison, M. (2007). 'Showers of Arrows: The Reactions and Resistance of the Kasena to Slave Raid in the 18th and 19th Centuries', in Aquandah, J. K., Opoku-Agyemang N.J., and Doormont, M. eds. *The Trans-Atlantic Slave Trade: Landmarks, Legacies and Expectations,* Accra, Sub-Saharan Publishers.

Joachim, Agamba, J. (2005/2006). 'Beyond Elmina: The Slave Trade in Northern Ghana' *Ufahamu: Journal of the African Activist Association,* Fall 2005/Winter 2006; 32, 1/2.

Johnson, Marion. (1986). 'The Slaves of Salaga' *Journal of African History Vol. 27 Issue 02July, pp.341-362.*

Klein, Martin A. (2003). 'Defensive Strategies: Wasulu, Masina and the Slave Trade', in Diouf A. Sylviane eds, *Fighting the Slave Trade: West African Strategies,* Athens, Ohio University Press.

Klein, Martin A. (1989). 'Studying the History of those Who Would Rather Forget: Oral History and the Experience of Slavery' in *History in Africa, Vol.16 (1989).* 209-217.

Klein, Martin. (2001). 'The Slave Trade and Decentralised Societies' in *Journal of African History,* Vol. 42. 49-65.

Levine, Lawrence W. (2007). *Black Culture and Black Consciousness: Afro-American Folk Thought from Slavery to Freedom*, 30th Anniversary Edition, Oxford University Press.

Lovejoy, Paul E. (1982). 'Polanyi's "Ports of Trade": Salaga and Kano in the Nineteenth Century' in *Canadian Journal of African Studies, 16 (1982)*. 245-277.

Moore, Niamh and Whelan Yvonne eds. (2007). *Heritage, Memory and the Politics of Identity: New Perspectives on the Cultural Landscape*, USA, Ashgate Publishing Ltd.

Saboro, E. (2016). 'Remembering Enslavement through Oral Expressive Culture: Animistic Metaphors Contesting Notions of Victimhood among the Bulsa of Ghana' *International Journal of Humanities and Cultural Studies*. Vol. 2 (4), 921-933.

Saboro, E. (2013). 'Songs of Sorrow, Songs of Triumph: Memories of the Slave Trade among the Bulsa of Ghana' in Alice Bellangamba, Sandra Greene and Martin Klein eds. *Bitter Legacy: African Slavery Past and Present*, Princeton, N.J., Markus Wiener.

Thompson, V. B. (1987). *The Making of the African Diaspora in the Americas,1441-1990*, New York, Longman Publihers.

Okon, Uya, E. (1992). *African Diaspora and the Black Experience in New World Slavery*, Lagos, Third Press Publishers.

Opoku-Agyemang, Naana J. (2007). 'The Living Experience of the Slave Trade in Sankana and Gwollu and the Implications for Tourism', in Anquandah, J.K., Opoku- Agyemang, N. J., Doormont, M. eds. *The Trans-Atlantic Slave Trade: Landmarks, Legacies, Expectations* Accra, Sub-Saharan Publishers.

Price, Richard eds. (1979). Maroon *Societies: Rebel Slave Communities in the Americas*, Baltimore, John Hopkins University Press.

Lovejoy, Paul, E. (2000). *Transformations In Slavery: A History of Slavery in Africa*, Cambridge, Cambridge University Press

Wemegura, Puawuveh. (2012). Community Elder, interviewed by E. Saboro at Navorongo on 10 March.

CHAPTER THREE

In the Name of God Resist! -Prophet Jemisimiham Jehu Appiah and African Religious Nationalism in Twentieth Century Gold Coast

De-Valera N.Y.M. Botchway

'We refuse to be what you want us to be. We are what we are. That's the way it's going to be' (Robert Nesta Marley 1979)

Introduction

This chapter focuses on the phenomenon of Black (African) leaders using religious idioms to negotiate various kinds of resistance to foreign domination of Blacks. It pays particular attention to the twentieth century case study of Joseph William Egyanka Appiah in the Gold Coast (now Ghana). In the 1920s, Appiah who was working as a teacher-catechist for the England-controlled Wesleyan Mission Methodist Church in the Gold Coast colony, left the Church and established the Musama Disco Christo Church (lit. Army of the Cross of Christ, hereafter MDCC, as a new 'true' African church). He left the Methodist Church, as a teacher-catechist, because it opposed his personal stance, and established the first 'indigenous' African church – Musama Disco Christo Church (MDCC) – in the Gold Coast. He initiated nationalist philosophies and liberation theologies to reform Euro-centric Christianity into an Afro-centric one to salvage aspects of indigenous African cultural beliefs and practices. Historically, Euro-centric Christianity provided ideological and institutional support to European enslavement and colonialism of the African peoples, and psychologically alienated many from their original mental and cultural personality.

In this way, Appiah conceptualised and reconsidered religion as a force of social change. Religion, therefore, had to be used in African nationalism, because it was not just a matter of personal worship and spiritual salvation, but a potent tool for the physical redemption of the African. He then became known as Prophet Jemisimiham Jehu-Appiah. Appiah viewed his church as Afrocentric, born and controlled by Africans, and instituted to restore the lustre of Afrocentricity to Christianity, which was a universal religion of freedom and self-determination. Europe had made it Eurocentric to serve European cultural and political interests and to control African societies.

Much of his action was motivated by his personal disagreement with the Eurocentric nature of Christianity in colonial Africa, and his rejection of the tradition where European clerics, not Africans, had been the actual controllers and real managers of the administration of the church in Africa. Africans were regarded as just auxiliaries within this structure. He found this to be a product of the colonial order, which gave privileges and political, economic and religious power to Europeans over Africans. The irony was that the church in Africa, was largely populated by Africans and it purported to serve their interests, yet Christianity was being used as an appendix of the colonial order. Appiah was thus discontented with this discrimination in the Methodist Church in particular and the Christian Church in general. By extension, he was unhappy with the colonial order. Accordingly, he sought to initiate some reforms into the liturgical and political structure of the Methodist Church, and hoped that the reforms would remove some of the issues which he had problems pertaining to the ecclesiastical arrangements in the colonial churches in general. His requests for reforms were, however, opposed by the colonial status quo of the Methodist Church administration. Unable to withstand that opposition, he founded the MDCC, which assumed a nationalist stance against the illegitimate notion and practice of European and foreign control of the Gold Coast and Africa in general. Thus, the religious arena became a place where Appiah initiated certain activities and innovations, and ideas and philosophies, as intellectual resistance techniques, which challenged European religious paternalism in Africa and European colonialism.

The Methodist Church deemed him a truculent rebel and heretic, and a menace to the church's political and ecclesiastical bureaucratic status quo, and excommunicated him. Was Appiah a rebel with a cause? He saw himself as a prophet of God, mandated to use religion to bring not only spiritual salvation to his people, but to resist all nuances of colonialism which Eurocentric Christianity had promoted in the Gold Coast and among African peoples. He saw himself as an envoy tasked to sermonise and adduce reason and philosophies of Black theology of liberation and Afrocentric liturgical innovations, within the context of Christianity, and to inject a sense of nationalism and racial pride in African Christians and encourage them to assert their humanity and control their political and cultural destinies, because they are divinely and naturally mandated to do so.

Conceptualising Black Nationalism in Religions in Africa and the African Diaspora

In separate times and places within the African continent and African Diaspora, Black people, via the use of religious, political and economic spheres, responded to the loss of their individual freedom, and collective sovereignty and national independence which were associated with Western slavery and European colonialism. Black leaders emerged as rebles, intellectuals, nationalist activists, and religious authorities who claimed to be priests or priestesses, or prophets or prophetesses, or mediums, or God incarnates, and considered themselves divinely mandated to restore the dignity and welfare of the African and their institutions. They often employed different means such as intellectual physical and spiritual, methods to resist the exercise of Western hegemony and overthrow all forms of foreign control of African personalities and institutions. For the leaders who operated in the area of religion, they felt that it was a good place to attack the injustices within the political and economic spheres of the world. Black leaders such as Gabriel Prosser, Denmark Vesey, and Nat Turner, declared at different times, during the first half of the nineteenth century that God had sent them to lead their fellow enslaved Africans in the U.S.A. to freedom because they were the lost Hebrews, the so-called God's chosen of the Bible (Azevedo and Davis, 1998, pp. 405-424). They were using religious language and imagery to move their people to act politically and rebel against the institution of slavery in the U.S.A. When Boukman, an enslaved African in the French colony of Saint Domingue, invoked Vodun, an African deity also spelt as voodoo, he said:

The god who created the sun . . . who rouses the wave and rules the storm . . . watches us. He sees what the white man does.

The god of the white man inspires him with crime, but our god calls upon us to do good works. Our god. . . orders us to revenge our wrongs. He will direct our arms and aid us. Throw away the symbol of the god of the white who has so often caused us to weep, and listen to the voice of liberty, which speaks in the hearts of us all, (James, 1963, p. 87)

He was using sentiments of religion to move the enslaved people to act politically, an effort and act which contributed to the start of the Haitian Revolution and ultimate triumph of the Black insurrection against slavery and the birth of the free Black republic of Haiti.

To many of the African leaders who established and operated resistance campaigns to foreign domination within the sphere of religion, the key issue was that Black people should be in charge of their religious destinies as well as their affairs in the secular space. Black religious campaigns, therefore, could not be divorced from the so-called secular affairs of the world, because religion was more than worship, morals and spiritual salvation. For them, the essence of religion was the imparting of Black Nationalism, race pride, self-determination, and self-reliance. A significant end product of this notion of challenge and resistance to the subjugation of Blacks was the rise of Afrocentric redemption religious movements and sects and churches in the diaspora, and independent African churches on the continent, of which the MDCC was a classical case in the Gold Coast in Africa.

The African Diaspora is replete with many examples of such groups, like the Candomble in Brazil, Vodun in Haiti, Santeria in Cuba, changô in Trinidad, the secret Black church services of enslaved African alias "invisible Church", the African Methodist Episcopal Church, the Marcus Garvey Universal Negro Improvement Association affiliated African Orthodox Church, the Nation of Islam, the Black Jews, and the African Hebrew Israelites in the U.S.A., and the Revivalist and Poccomina groups, the Native Baptists movement popularly known as Bedwardism, and Rastafari in Jamaica. This helps to explain why some of these Black religious systems are also briefly examined in the chapter by Beckford and Charles on Jamaica and also discussed in Talburt's chapter on Pan Africanism. Some of the initiators of some leading independent churches in Africa in the twentieth century were William Harris, of Liberia, Garrick Braid of Sierra Leone, Simon Kimbangu of the Belgian Congo, Elliot Kamwana of Malawi, and Isaiah Shemba of South Africa. Many of such leaders were condemned and persecuted by some of the traditional European churches. Some like Kimbangu and Elliot Kamwana were imprisoned by the colonialists.

In the context of Christianity, such Afrocentric groups and churches were the products of a long process of incubation and results from the mixture of Christian ideas and African indigenous beliefs. Christian ideas were grafted on indigenous African cultural roots and concepts. The Christian God was seen as a redeeming Black/African deity who was ready to listen and save his people. The message of Christianity based on the Bible was, for the subjected African, the message of salvation, deliverance and equality of all persons regardless of race.

The founders and leaders of such groups realised that religion, especially when it was controlled by Blacks, was a tool that could be employed as a notion and institution to get people to act as patriots and nationalists. The rise, creation and existence of certain Afrocentric churches and religious sects, which refused to be subjects of White religious groups, were an assertion of African nationalism and racial self-determination. As challengers to the European leadership in religion, especially Christianity, these leading individuals indirectly and directly encouraged other Africans to question the illegality of European political and economic leadership in the affairs and lives of the African. They encouraged them to question the European appropriation of their land, destruction of their prestige, prohibition of their ancestral religious and cultural world views, and introduction of an exploitative economic system that deprived Black people in their African homeland and in the African Diaspora. Whether the churches were founded because of leadership issues or ideological and doctrinal differences between Whites and Blacks, the fact is that, they signalled the African determination for their voices to be heard as equal and rational beings. Furthermore, there was a need for their ideas to be taken into consideration by the European missionary, who by and large, had been a direct or indirect factor of European imperialism and colonialism which frustrated Africans and their aspirations.

In Africa, independence in the church was an early step on the path to political autonomy in the twentieth century. In the Gold Coast, which became Ghana and a beacon of African independence struggle and Pan Africanism when it attained independence from the British in 1957, the tradition of schism was manifested through the early efforts of people like J.B. Anaman, who established the Nigritian Church (1907), and Appiah who instituted the MDCC. Both their efforts in the twentieth century formed part of the history and continuum of the global Black resistance efforts against non-Black, i.e. European slavery and colonialism.

The rest of this chapter examines the anti-colonial ideas and activities of Appiah and his efforts in the Gold Coast to give Africans the right and power of religious redefinition of Christianity. It pays attention to his Afrocentric cultural innovations which he injected into the fabric of the Eurocentric liturgy of the Methodist Church. It discusses his ultimate production of the MDCC Church as a Blackman's church with its own Black religious leaders, which did not need any authorisation from England or Rome or Jerusalem. It also highlight the actual and symbolic significance of his struggle and the church that he established to campaign for Black leaders to manage the affairs of their peoples and their communities. Appiah's story of religious reformation and schism was part of the early manifestations of African reactions of resistance to colonialism in the religious field in Africa. Despite Appiah's death in 1948, his church has remained alive and active today.

The man and his work: Appiah and the birth of MDCC

Appiah was born in 1892 or 1893 to parents who were illiterate peasant farmers in the village of Abura Edumfa, near the coastal town of Cape Coast (known by its indigenous Fante people as Oguaa). Cape Coast was the colonial capital of the Gold Coast until 1877. Thus, Appiah belonged to the Fante section of the larger Akan ethnic group in the Gold Coast. He spent his early days as a pupil in the Methodist primary school at Abura Edumfa, in the Abura state, within the Cape Coast District of the then Central Province. He later joined the Methodist Middle School in Cape

Coast in 1907. Cape Coast was the starting point and key centre of Wesleyan Methodist missionary activities, and the main training ground of catechists and teachers, especially Wesleyans, and a renowned bastion of the western formal school system in the Gold Coast. Reverend Joseph Rhodes Dunwell who arrived at Cape Coast on 31 December 1834, was the one who started Wesleyan missionary work there on 1 January 1835, with the mandate of the Missionary Committee of British Methodist Conference (Bartels, 1965, p.1).

Appiah was baptised at birth as a Christian, but his parents, who were nominal Christians of Methodism, trained him to understand and respect the cultural mores and values of his people. He completed middle school and received the Standard Four Certificate in 1911. Whilst in Cape Coast as a student he stayed under the home-stay care of Reverend S.R.B. Attoh Ahuma who was a member of the Aborigines Rights Protection Society (ARPS), which was an African nationalist and land protection group in the Gold Coast. It was Appiah's father and senior brother who made that residential arrangement for him. Attoh Ahuma was the author of various nationalistic articles and books. He edited some nationalist newspapers including the *Gold Coast Aborigines*, and *Gold Coast Leader*, which often promoted antigovernment ideas. These included *Memoir of West African Celebrities*, *Cruel as the Grave*, and *The Gold Coast Nation and National Consciousness*.

He was an unrepentant and articulate political critic of colonialism and westernisation. The Wesleyan authorities sacked him as a Wesleyan minister because of his political activism in the 1890s, especially for publishing "Colony or Protectorate: Which?", which was a critical article against British imperialism in 1897, and he joined the African-American inspired African Methodist Episcopal Church when it was established in the Gold Coast in 1898.

Appiah's stay in Cape Coast occurred at a time when the region was a hotbed of anti-colonialism activities, street and neighbourhood corner meetings of political agitators, and nationalist rhetoric, and the base of several nationalist newspapers and societies which were influenced by a very active and dynamic corpus of literate and professional African elites. These exposed Appiah to information and popular discussions about colonial policy and the prevailing nationalist atmosphere during the early years of the twentieth century (Enison, 2004). He became familiar with the nationalist rhetoric and philosophies of his guardian Attoh Ahuma, and those of other nationalists like J.M. Sarbah, , J.E. Casely-Hayford, Reverend Ossam Pinanko, Kwegyir Aggrey, and Kobina Sekyi. Kobina Sekyi became the lawyer and personal friend of Appiah when he became the founder and prophet of the MDCC. Appiah therefore became exposed to abundant anti colonial ideas and revolutionary notions of Cape Coast nationalists that filtered through the various nationalist newspaper and local homes, market places, pulpits and street corners (Sagoe, 2004).

By the time that Appiah completed his education at the age of eighteen, he was familiar with the growing local dislike for certain alien policies of the colonial regime, and the tension between Africans and Europeans over leadership in administrative offices in the colony, even in the Methodist Church, which was a dependent Overseas District of British Methodism. He obtained a job as a pupil-teacher at the Wesleyan Primary School in the village of Abakrampa, near his hometown in 1911. When the village's teacher-catechist died he was appointed by the Wesleyan supervisors as teacher-catechist. Perhaps the supervisors gave him that post because of his gift and talent as a good orator and preacher, which he exhibited during students' evangelisation work and church services when he was a student in the Methodist school in Cape Coast. In any case, his talent was useful to Methodist evangelism in Abakrampa. He worked in Abakrampa for three years as an enlightened well-read liberal who tolerated some of the short-comings of his congregants and enthusiastically evangelised (Ennin, 2004). Still enamored by the nationalist activities and environment of Cape Coast, he occasionally made time to attend meetings of the ARPS there. He later became a member of the APRS till his death.

Appiah found the teacher-catechist work to be financially unrewarding and he abandoned it. From 1914 to 1917 he worked as a self-employed cocoa purchaser at Osino, in the Eastern Province, and petty trader and farmer at Agona Abodom, the Central Province, but he was not successful in these ventures. He did some occasional lay preaching sessions in the local Methodist society at Agona Abodom where he lived and impressed the local congregation with his flair. Soon, Reverend Ernest Bruce, the new Methodist superintendent of the Gomoa circuit, heard about Appiah's state of near unemployment and his occasional service to the local church, and offered to re-employ him as teacher-catechist in Gomoa Dunkwa. Appiah took the job, but he soon realised that the church needed to undergo some fundamental reforms, especially with regard to the centrality of the individual and also some recognition and acceptance of the needs of the African.

He also pondered over the leadership position of Europeans in the Church and its affairs in the Gold Coast. He thought about why Africans occupied auxiliary positions in both the secular and religious spaces in the colonial period. He saw a disguised colonialism present in the Methodist church, which was very much in common with the mission churches. This was, as far as he was concerned, the spiritual arm of political colonialism. He mused over why the church did not provide an outlet for African Christians to engage the spiritual power of Christ to heal, and why women leadership, miracles, and respect for certain African cultural values were not promoted in the church. He realised that it was because the church was not owned by Africans, so they could not dictate how it should be structured to serve their unique spiritual, cultural and economic needs. Recognising that the Eurocentric church had not tolerated such norms because they would be similar to indigenous religious practices and spiritual ideas, Appiah thought of introducing some of these ideas into the Methodist church, and thereby sought to implement reforms within the church's organisational structure and liturgy. By doing so, he hoped to disprove colonial missionary paternalistic views and mentality that African cultures were inferior, immoral and doomed to collapse. Maybe, at this time, he heard about Prophet Harris, the itinerant Liberian Methodist preacher, who, not bound to any mission, performed exorcism and cured diseases in Christ's name in the Gold Coast. Grace Tani and John Nackabah, and a third person, John Hackman, who followed Harris later constituted Harris's followers into the Church of the Twelve Apostles in Ghana (Baeta, 1962, p. 9).

Without planning to break away from the church but seeking instead to bring some Afrocentric reforms into the Methodist Church in the African society of the Gold Coast, Appiah secretly desired and had 'the intuition to fast and pray for the faith of miracles' (Jehu-Appiah, 1959, p. 2). He particularly wanted to be able to heal, exorcise and take care of other spiritual needs of the local people and meet the local aspirations of the African congregants. By wanting to infuse African ways and ideas into the church in the African terrain he was resisting the dominance of European ways and notions in Christianity, which did not belong to Europe but to all humanity.

He established a special 'prayer group': *Egyedzifo Kuw* (trans. Faith Society) within his Methodist congregation in 1919 (Musama Disco Christo Church Diamond Jubilee Celebration Programme, 2000, p. 2). This small exclusive group, which held early secret meetings of contemplation and prayers for miracles, also attracted a few of Appiah's teacher-catechist friends from the neighbouring villages of Gomoa Tarkwa, Gomoa Brofun, Gomoa Mumford and Gomoa Dawurampon (Sagoe, 2004). Appiah took long retreats for meditation in the bush. Soon his group became known to the local church as he introduced some novel activities and ideas into to the congregation. Unique to his ministry was the introduction and extensive use of vibrant African singing and drumming and dancing techniques and musical instruments in the church's service in order augment as well as enliven it, and his performance and instances of miraculous healing with water through faith. Many members of the congregation and the town flocked to hear him and to receive answers to their health and social problems.

His Circuit's superintendent at Apam heard about his unorthodox innovations and cautioned him and his congregants to disband the Society of the Faithful (Eghan, 2004). His overseers warned him to not neglect his duty and to stop spreading and practising what they called 'curious magical rites and customs', which contradicted Methodist tenets (Baeta, 1962, p. 30). Consequently, he confidently claimed that an angel of God had ordered him to advocate revival and continue his reformatory activities within the framework of the Methodist church and by extension the existing mission churches, and not to dismantle the doctrinal basis of the churches. With the purpose of disrupting what he had started, his superiors transferred him to the village of Gomoa Ogwan (Oguan) in 1920. He carried his 'unorthodox' activities there and intensified the spiritual activities such as speaking in tongues, ecstatic African-style singing and dancing, falling into trances, laying-on-of-hands faith healing, and exorcism in the church and among the local people. Even though he explained the Biblical legitimacy and the socio-cultural usefulness and implications of his innovations and actions to the local community and African society in general, his bosses, especially Reverend Gaddiel Acquaah (OBE), a Gold Coaster, who were auxiliaries to both the mother Methodist church in England and the few European missionaries in the Gold Coast, disagreed and re-cautioned him. Appiah then parted ways with the Methodists, moved to the village of Onyaawonsu where he declared himself a prophet and married a women by the name of Hannah Barnes, whom he shared his prophethood with, and formed the MDCC. Hannah Barnes became known as Komhyenibaa (Prophetess) Nathalomoa Jehu-Appiah.

Appiah, established a religious commune, which he named as Mozano (My Town), and made it the headquarters of the MDCC. Mozano, in the Gold Coast, was considered by Appiah and members of the MDCC as an African holy city, the 'New Jerusalem, of their African church, which was not inferior to places like England and the Vatican in Rome, which were revered by European Anglicans and Methodists, and Catholics respectively. At Mozano, Appiah became the *Akaboha* (a traditional religio-political authority) and *Komhyeni*, (lit. prophet or seer) of the town and church, which he stated was accessible to all religious traditions, despite the sectarian nature of many churches. Appiah's example of religious reformation and schism couched in African nationalism inspired several independent Afrocentric churches to subsequently emerge in the country both in the colonial and post-colonial periods. His African church supported the Convention Peoples Party-dominated mass struggle for political autonomy in the country from 1949 to 1957. The church's population grew. Some other 'orthodox' churches in Ghana during this period subsequently borrowed some of his reform practices. The MDCC has numerous branches in Ghana and the global African Diaspora (Botchway, 2004).

At this juncture, it is important to consider whether Appiah's actions and beliefs were justified, and whether his intention were predicated on a selfish distortion of the rules of a European religious order, and a purely personal hubristic promotion of his hermeneutics of scripture and ecclesiastical tradition. We can tell from the intellectual ideas and rationalisations that he provided for his rebellious ways, i.e. the innovations and the Black church that he built, that he was a visionary of his times. His reactions as a reformer emphasised a new Christianity to advance Black

Nationalist cultural consciousness in the Gold Coast and other colonies. His actions reflected the frustrations of colonialism during the early decades of the twentieth century when he lived. What was significant is that he intellectually explained his actions as part of a conscious African resistance to European cultural hegemony and religious colonialism. He came to bear some of the key characteristics of the early Gold Coast nationalist politicians. According to Kimble, 'the [early twentieth century Gold Coast] nationalist politician[s] played many parts: newspaper editor, lay preacher, platform orator or petition drafter; as champion of native customs . . . or defending the Chiefs' jurisdiction in their own domain' (Kimble, 1963, pp. 555-556). Appiah was a preacher, champion of 'native' customs and defender of traditional authority. His reformatory activities in Christianity meant to endorse several African traditional beliefs, values, customs and norms, and produce . . . [an] offering [of] what it regarded as a new perspective and new solutions to problems of traditional as well a contemporary nature in the Gold Coast (Clarke, 1986, p. 189). He advanced his intellectual responses in sermons and wrote some down. He, in a nationalistic fervour, sermonised and wrote in the local Fante language, even though he could speak English. He reasoned that it was better to address his followers in an African language and not that of the coloniser.

In his rationalisations for some of his innovations, these were drawn largely from the African experiences expressed in a distinctly African way. In this way, these Africans were resisting European cultural domination and influence in attempts to assert their own identity. Some of the African strategies of these Black religious resistance involved the use of African music and musical instruments and dance in Christian worship, promotion of faith healing, miracles and spirit possession, acceptance of polygyny as African and Christian, the legitimation of speaking in tongues, and the right of women to be church leaders in the Christian church in Africa, and the justification that he gave to the imperativeness of the creation of made-in-Africa churches, which brought about the MDCC example. We shall draw examples of his ideas from our translated excerpts of his not so well-known small book, *Christ Mbiamudua Hu Dom Asorn Hu Abakosem* (lit. History of the Army of the Cross of Christ), published in 1943 (Jehu Appiah, 1943). All his innovations found free expression in the MDCC. He used common sense, practical examples from the indigenous African cultural tradition, and his creative hermeneutics of the Bible, to issue his Black liberation theology philosophies, to support his reactions and actions.

Legitimisation of African Musical Instruments, Music and Dance in the Church

Contrary to the Methodist custom, Appiah encouraged the use of African musical instruments like the donno, mpintin, akasa, totorubento and mfiritwuwa, and energetic un-hymn-like singing, including the abibinwom (lit. Black African Songs) genre which carried Fante lyrics, and vigorous clapping and dancing within his Methodist congregation. Such items had commonly been deemed objectionable by the mission churches because they also featured in African traditional religious ceremonies (Sagoe, 2004). Generally the Methodist mission did not permit members to go near indigenous drumming groups and dance to their music. They were permitted to:

> march, or shuffle along, in a . . . column, to . . . Sankey
> and Moody tunes played by a village brass band.
> [W]omen . . . sway[ed] a little to . . . the tune . . . while
> the men stepped out with dignity bringing up the rear
> (Bartels, 1965, p. 234).

But this arrangement was quite alien to the indigenous religious terrain and worldview, because, to the African, religion is, apart from the belief in and expectation from the supernatural, a medium of self-expression, entertainment and even enjoyment, which is deeply rooted in his culture (Nukunya, 1992, p.131). Missionaries were not the only persons who condemned indigenous music and dance expressions. A governor like F.M. Hodgson remarked in 1896 that a mark of 'advancement towards enlightenment and civilised character' was when natives abandoned their performances and adopted "drum and fife band with English instruments' (Dispatch From Hodgson, 1896).

Appiah disagreed with the notion that indigenous instruments and singing and dancing were heathen and uncivil and should be excluded from church services (Prophet M.J. Jehu-Appiah (Akaboha III, 2004). He argued that they injected new meaning and dignity to African Christianity and cultural pride, and allowed an inclusive type and procedure of worship. They could also invoke the Holy Spirit, who channels healing, miracles, and divine messages through tongues and spirit possession (Antobam, 2004). He intellectually rebutted this irrational rule in the church, a rule which his senior, the eminent Gold Coast nationalist and lawyer, J.E. Casely-Hayford – a Methodist himself, earlier interrogated in 1903, that:

> Why . . . should not the . . .convert sing his own native songs, and play his native airs in church? Why should he not attune his horns, his adziwa, his gomey, or . . . his adankum, to the praise of God, much as the Israelites of old praised Jehovah upon the cymbal and the harp? . . . Why, indeed, except that the simple missionary has, from the beginning ruled that all these things are against the letter, if not the spirit, of the Gospel? (Casely-Hayford, 1903, p.105).

Appiah opined that the playing of African traditional musical instruments and dancing in the church was not un-Christian. He argued that African ancestors used indigenous instruments such as mpintsin, mfuaba or adziwa, mbenson, and nsenkuto worship and glorify God. However, he argued that due to the so-called:

> modernisation, Europeanisation and doubt many people now deem it wrong for Christians to play these instruments

and dance to them. [W]e (MDCC) dispel the lie and ignorance to bare the truth. God does not forbid the playing of musical instruments and dancing . . . to glorify His name (Jehu-Appiah, 1943, pp. 41-42).

He charged that European instruments were not more appropriate for Christian activities than African ones:

Most European musical instruments are un-Christian and used for worldly functions. For example the Baan [sic] (Side Drum/Brass Band) are mainly played on the battlefield by European soldiers. However, they can play the same to accompany Christian songs to glorify God. This is deemed proper [by them]. By the same token . . . people (Africans), use traditional African musical instruments like the Kyin, etumpan, and kyinsin to worship God. Such is pleasant in the sight of God (Jehu- Appiah, 1943, p. 42).

He creatively invoked scriptural evidence like Psalms 68:25, 81:2-4, 150:3-6 and 149:3 to Biblically legitimise his argument (Jehu-Appiah, 1943). He also identified how 'in Exodus 15:20 . . . . 'Miriam the prophetess . . . and the women went out . . . with timbrels and with dances', and how in 2 Samuel 6:14 and 15 David danced and all Israel shouted and sounded trumpets when the Ark of the Covenant of the Lord was brought. He also pointed out how in 1 Chronicles 15:16 and 19, 'David spoke to . . . the Levites to appoint . . . musicians to make a joyful sound with musical instruments: lyres, harps, and cymbals (Jehu-Appiah, 1943).

The legality of Faith Healing, Miracles and Spirit Possession in Christianity in Africa

When he tackled the issue of faith healing, he argued that God was a God that saved souls and also met the material needs and health problems of people (Jehu-Appiah, 1959, p. 10). The church in Africa was therefore to relate the Gospel to the notion of the importance of spirit backed miracles, faith healing, prosperity and fertility as desired in, and expressed through, the traditions of Africa. Aware that in the epidemiological universe of Africa, disease was attributed to both physical and spiritual causes, he argued that the church in Africa should logically promote healing through faith:

> God (Nyankopon) is the Healer of humankind. Traditional priests, healers and herbalists even acknowledge that God heals, thus: 'God is our Helper'. Biblical[ly] . . . is written . . . 'I am the Lord who heals you' (Exodus 15:26). . . . Jesus Christ . . . healed . . . with the spiritual powers within Himself. . . He asked his disciples to preach . . . and baptise. . . . 'And . . . in my name [Jesus] they will cast out demons; . . . speak . . . tongues . . . lay hands on the sick, and they will recover.' Mark 16:15-18 (Jehu-Appiah, 1943, p. 37-39).

He emphasised that Jesus Christ engaged in faith healing and the Holy Spirit permitted it so it was wrong and hypocritical for the mission churches to prohibit its use by Africans in the church in Africa. 'Invoking Matthew 17:14-21 into his argument for faith healing, Appiah pointed out that Jesus Christ once restored a boy's good health by rubuking a demon within him; and that Christ told his amazed disciples that if their faith was as a mustard seed they could have healed the young man and say to a mountain to a mountain, 'move from here to there,' and it will move and nothing would be impossible for you' (Jehu-Appiah, 1943). Appiah also made reference to James 5:14-15 which said 'Is anyone among you sick? Let him call for the elders of the church, and let them pray over him, anointing him with oil in the name of the Lord', to support his rationalisations. Undercutting the authority of the missionary dominance, he cautioned African Christians who 'obeyed' the scepticism of the missionary church that:

> [Y]ou are that one's slaves whom you obey, whether of sin leading to death, or of obedience leading to righteousness' (Romans 6:16). . . . . [L]et us [African Christians] . . . thrive in faith and dedicate our souls and bodies to Him (God) (Jehu-Appiah, 1943).

With regard to the issue of polygyny, he argued that even though the orthodox churches excommunicated polygynists and compelled converts to be monogamous because polygyny was deemed sinful and unacceptable in the Eurocentric church, because European society was mainly monogamous, the institution of polygyny in Africa was important to the building of family and society. Arguing that it was from ancient times, and not a sin that should disqualify any African polygynist from Christianity, he argued that even Abraham, who according to the Bible was God's faithful friend, and other patriarchs like Jacob, Moses and King David, whom Christianity venerates, married many women (Jehu-Appiah, 1943). He pointed out the God's law stipulated that: 'thou shall not commit murder and thou shall not commit adultery', but did not say that thou shall not practice polygyny. He consequently declared that:

> [W]e, [Africans] today, are not obliged . . . to marry just one woman; because the worship of God did not start in these modern days. . . Many of our forbearers and predecessors were priests and prophets whom God spoke with, and yet no law barred them from marrying a number of wives (Jehu-Appiah, 1943).

He added that: marriage is a physical, social and cultural institution and contrary to missionary churches' intolerance of African polygyny, intolerance inspired by a European monogamous worldview, Matthew 22:29-30 showed that Jesus Christ never made a law to sanction only monogamy. Appiah further argued that the imposition of foreign laws that forbade polygyny had made many African Christians pretend to be monogamous but to have affairs with several women in secrecy. 'Is this practice not adulterous before God? he asked (Jehu-Appiah, 1943). He interpreted the Pauline declaration on monogamy in 1Timothy 3:2; 12, that it was for bishops and deacons and not for everybody. He added that the same Paul, who wished that men would be celibates, also said in 1 Corinthians 7:7-9, that if men could not exercise self-control, then let them marry . . . than to burn with passion. Appiah charged that some men were unable to keep one wife, and went against God's law by fornicating. Hence, the stance of the MDCC on polygyny was valid. He declared that God instructed the MDCC not to forbid polygyny like other churches. Consequently, he stated that 'The Holy Spirit has revealed its desires concerning marriage to mankind' (Jehu-Appiah, 1943).

Appiah deemed the Holy Spirit a vital instructor and ally and edifier of the MDCC, and Christianity as a whole. He opined that the Spirit could possess Christians and reveal God's desires and perform wonders through them. The notion that spirits of ancestors or deities could possess people and create communion between humans and the spirit world, was part of the indigenous African worldview. Appiah therefore argued that 'holy' spirit possession should be legitimate in the context of the church in Africa, and Biblically justifying it, he cited Acts 19:2-6 where Paul laid hands of a group of Christians who had not received the Holy Spirit and the 'spirit came on them, and they spoke with tongues and prophesied.' He argued that belief and encouragement of the phenomenon of Holy Spirit possession in the Christian worship pattern of the MDCC, like the days of old, should not be a new phenomenon to many since John 14:16-17 declared that:

> He (God) will give you another Helper . . . forever – The Spirit of truth, whom the world cannot receive . . . but you know Him, for He dwells with you and will be in you (Jehu-Appiah, 1943).

God's Holy Spirit, unlike and Satan's Evil Spirit:

> possesses . . . through faith . . . mostly Godly people who fast and pray. They [can] perform miracles . . . shout out the name of Jesus Christ. . . . Other signs include falling down, speaking in tongues, and prophesying. . . . [T]he Spirit . . . even came . . . upon Saul . . . and he walked along prophesying. . . . (1 Samuel 19:23-24). [I]gnorance . . . in modern times, has shadowed the truth about spirit possession. Remember . . .

[a]lso . . . the Day of Pentecost . . . they were all filled with the Holy Spirit and began to speak . . . tongues, as the Spirit gave them utterance. Others mockingly said, They are full of new wine.' (Acts 2:1-4 and 13) (Jehu-Appiah, 1943).

In the case of the MDCC, an African church, he observed that: 'Now ignorance makes people to mock at the members of the church because of their relationship with spirit possession' (Jehu-Appiah, 1943). God, he argued, had not authorised some groups, in reference to missionaries and mission churches, to monopolise the Holy Spirit because, as John 12:32 and Acts 2:39 showed, the Spirit and its gifts of wisdom, knowledge, faith, healing, performance of miracles, prophecy, discerning of spirits, speaking in tongues, and interpretation of tongues was promised to humankind. Referencing Mark 3:28-30, he confidently declared: [D]o away with all doubts, and work with the power of the Holy Spirit . . . [H]e who blasphemes against the Holy Spirit . . . is subject to eternal condemnation . . . . He rehearsed Jesus Christ's statement in John 14:12 that: '[H]e who believes in me . . . greater works than these he will do, because I go to My Father,' to further legitimate spirit possession in the MDCC and Christianity in general (Jehu-Appiah, 1943).

The Need for an African Church with African Leaders Including Women

His innovations were wise to a mind that could understand and tolerate indigenous African cultural mores and values. They were strange to the Eurocentric minded Christians and churches. Therefore, he finally argued that the creation of an autonomous African church, which would easily accept functional African beliefs and practices such as polygyny, was logical. The Methodist and orthodox churches restrained Afro-centric innovations because paternalistic European missionaries captured Christianity, and traditionally monopolised the leadership and policy making power in the church. The reason for this monopoly was the imperialist false notion that Europeans were superior to Africans. Racism and prejudice, found in the colonial politics of Appiah's time, also shaped inequalities in the Christian religious arena. Europe still dictated the paradigm and form of Christianity. Appiah claimed that an African controlled church was necessary to be instituted to awaken the African to be self-determining, and repudiate the White supremacy myth and augment the wider Black struggle against European hegemony in African affairs. He used history, logic and his Biblical hermeneutics of liberation for this. Challenging the tradition where the seat of administration of the Christian Church had been cited outside Africa, for example in Rome, England and Jerusalem, he, who had instituted Mozano as the Holy city of his African church, argued that the Gold Coast and Africa could also incubate the Divine:

> [S]ceptics ask whether the Musama Disco Christo Church was introduced into the Gold Coast (Africa) from elsewhere. It is the same as asking whether 'any good thing can come out of Nazareth?' (John 1:46) . . . [W]e (MDCC) believe that something good can come out of Nazareth. . . . 'With men this is impossible, but with God all things are possible (Matthew 19:26) (Jehu-Appiah, 1943, p. 29).

In the sense of Ethiopianism, he questioned why Europe and Europeans should lead the church in Africa thus:

> [H]as the time not come for the African also to see God . . . [and] to see himself as a human being? Is it not time for an African leader to emerge? (Jehu-Appiah, 1943).

This opposed the age-old European missionary subtle intolerance of the labours of African clerics to have equal status in church leadership and administration in both Africa and the African Diaspora. Racial discrimination and the notion of Social Darwinism had long been present in the Methodist Church in the Gold Coast (Bartels, 1965, p. 139). In 1894, Reverend Dennis Kemp, who worked in Cape Coast from 1887-1897 as the General Superintendent of the Gold Coast Methodists, claimed that a

Synod which was exclusively European was desirable and better. Kemp further articulated a Social Darwinist view, a notion that other European missionaries shared, that 'the Negro was not built 'so as to be on an equality – intellectually – with the White race', and that his African friends in Cape Coast were 1500 years behind England in Christian influences' (Bartels, 1965, p. 14). Even though this incident energised some African clerics' wish for religious self-assertion, by the time Appiah worked as a teacher-catechist, his African supervisors were still auxiliaries to European missionaries. Thus, they followed orthodox Wesleyan life in terms of doctrine and liturgy. Many African clerics were still subordinates of a leadership order, which Europe primarily exercised because of a colour line problem and Social Darwinist notions. Conversely, Appiah commented:

> The time has come for us (Africans) to know that Jerusalem is with us in Africa. Africa is our Nazareth. It is here, that we have to . . . take our rightful place before the throne of God, instead of crawling before others for them to direct us. Please think about this because you are a human being (Jehu-Appiah, 1943).

In a bid to show the practicability and necessity of an African church he referenced the example of the MDCC and declared that it was 'not from overseas.'

> [S]ceptics, God . . . has power to use an African to establish a Christian Church . . . an African Church . . . in Africa. Africa is the land of our birth . . . we have to search here . . . we shall find.' The 'ladder of Jacob' is everywhere. The . . . Church is a genuine Christian Church . . . we are not afraid of any disorders. Doubters should read 1 Corinthians 12:5 – 'There are differences of ministries, but the same Lord' (Jehu-Appiah, 1943).

It was in the context of the logic of differences in ministries, that he accentuated and integrated facets of African customary practices and beliefs into the cosmology of the MDCC, which was a church that was 'never a carbon copy of any imported Church . . . [but] purely an African Church' with members who love it because they are Africans (Opoku, 1969, p. 13). He sought to revive the ancient lustre of true religion through his church. For example, he proscribed the use of footwear in the Church's building because it was God's, and a Holy Place. This was related to the African indigenous prohibition of footwear in ritualistic worship places and hierophanic spots like shrines and sacred groves. Additionally, he emphasised that women should have equal access to leadership in Christianity, because they performed leadership functions as priestesses and ritual specialists with moral and spiritual authority in the indigenous setting. His wife was the co-leader and *Akatitibi* (Queen) of the MDCC. Many women became ordained prophetesses, priestesses, mediums, pastors, and healers. This improvement in Christianity in the Gold Coast opposed the androcentric nature of the traditional sacerdotal leadership structure in the mission churches then.

Jehu-Appiah's Legacy

This study has demonstrated that Prophet Jemisimiham Jehu-Appiah was as an example of the many manifestations of Blacks/ African resistance to foreign control, and reassertion of rights and aspects of their African culture. He initiated African culture-friendly revolutionary ideas and reformatory practises into the Europeanised Methodist Church, and startled people with his supernatural powers. He launched a crusade to Africanise, indigenise and contextualise Christianity, and founded the MDCC to represent, and give grounding to this crusade. His image as an African cultural nationalist leader, does not only come from his charisma, and membership in the nationalist group of the ARPS, and his church's association with the popular Convention Peoples Party, but most importantly from his successful defiance of an established church which largely served the idiosyncrasy of a foreign culture and rule.

A number of key individuals interviewed for this study have asserted that the polemical tone that the Methodist authorities used to describe him as a heterodox has almost disappeared in Ghana (Acquah, et al, 2004). Many leaders and theologians of the 'old' churches in Ghana today, including Catholic Archbishop Emeritus Peter Kwasi Sarpong of Kumasi, who has supported the idea of Africanizing the liturgy of the Catholic Church in particular (Sarpong, 2002), have advocated for the inculturation of Christianity in Africa and adaptation of some of his innovations.

It has been 97 years since the saga of Appiah's nationalism and his image as a historical figure started to take shape. This story of courage, hope and perseverance has continued to acquire different features even after his death. Nevertheless, his story reminds Africans to make Christianity meaningful to their culture. He was a phenomenal embodiment of diverse images: visionary, nationalist, politician – traditional leader, and father. As a religious and cultural reformer he inspired the development of other African churches. He was a reformer, because his actions sought the 'modification of existing institutions, the introduction of new ideas and new ways of doing things, a determination to achieve certain definite ends through planned action' (Ikime 1974, p. xiv). His reformation was a resistance campaign against Eurocentric Christianity, the spiritual arm of colonialism. Appiah realised that colonialism, had contributed to the demolishing of African community structures, including rituals, religious concepts, and languages, and the destruction of laws and taboos, and the absorbing of African land and the wealth to a foreign economy, and the European subjection of the African. The missionary churches played a complimentary role in this framework of colonial interference. The churches' agents, the missionaries in, most cases, were the first instruments of colonial dominion and contempt (Fernandez, 1964, p. 533). Their churches imposed Eurocentric Christianity on Africans "lock, stock and barrel" and contributed to the disruption of African ethnic cultural complexes and turned Africans into followers instead of leaders.

Conclusion

Appiah's conscious awareness of the exploitation present in the Christian churches in the early twentieth century in Cape Coast led to a broad dissatisfaction and disaffection for the Methodist and the westernised church's activities in the Gold Coast. He recognised a religious void within the context of the local Christian landscape because he saw a church that was alien and was not fulfilling the organic aspirations of the society, hence his innovations and call for made-in-Africa churches. He detected discrepancies between the Bible and what the Europeanised churches taught and promoted in Africa. He discovered that the Bible, the Christian constitution, bequeathed blessings to miracles, spirit possession, love for and protection of one's land, fertility, leadership of women, veneration of ancestors, self-determination, equality of humankind, and polygyny, all of which were legal notions within the African indigenous worldview. This awareness about the misrepresentation of the Bible by the churches as well as the adding of their own Western biases to create prefabricated dogmas and abstract theologies to suppress aspects of African cultures and people, compelled Appiah to creatively generate his Biblical hermeneutics as liberation theology arguments to oppose such interpretations, dogmas and theologies and point out faults in the structure of the mission church(es). His arguments, liturgical innovations, and establishment of an African church were aimed at signalling, and did signal and animate, the Africans' natural right and desire to control their own destiny by exercising the intellectual and spiritual powers that God had promised humankind through the Holy Spirit. The nuanced and ultimate implication was that the African, by natural, logical and divine rights, had to free him/herself and be free from White political domination. Appiah and his work and church implied a resistance to colonialism and a definite stance in the struggle for Black identity.

References

Antobam, Opanyin Kwame. (2004). a Methodist, 92 years old, interviewed by Botchway on 11 February, at Gomoa Ogwan.

Acquah, Reverend J.E. (2004). Superintendent in-charge of Apam Methodist Circuit, 62 years, interviewed by Botchway, Methodist Manse, Apam, 2nd April, Right Reverend Isaac K. Quansah, B.A., M.A, Bishop of the Cape Coast Methodist Diocese, interviewed by Botchway 59 years, at his office, Standfast Manse, Cape Coast, 2nd April; Reverend Father Linus Zanmwinlaaro, Roman Catholic Father with the Wa Diocese, 45 years old, interviewed by Botchway, University of Cape Coast, Cape Coast, 4th April.

Azevedo, Mario and Davis, Gregory. (1998). 'Religion in the Diaspora', in Mario Azevedo (ed.) *Africana Studies: A Survey of Africa and the African Diaspora* (2nd Edition), Durham, North Carolina: Carolina Academic Press, 1998, pp. 405-424.

Baeta, C.G. (1962). *Prophetism in Ghana: A study of some 'spiritual' Churches*, London: SCM Press.

Bartels, F.L. (1965). *The Roots of Ghana Methodism*, Cambridge University Press.

Botchway, De-Valera N.Y.M. (2004). *Prophet Jemisimiham Jehu-Appiah: The Man, His Vision, His Work*, Unpublished M.Phil Thesis, Department of History, University of Cape Coast

Casely-Hayford, J.E. (1903). *Gold Coast Native Institutions*, London,.

Clarke, P.B. (1986). *West Africa and Christianity*, London, Arnold Publishers Ltd.

Dispatch From Hodgson to Chamberlain. (1896). 29 September C.O/96/277, Nos. 386 in Kimble, David. (1963). *A Political History of Ghana*, Oxford, Clarendon Press.

Eghan, Mr. (2004). Senior teacher, Abura Abakrampa Methodist School, 57 years old, interviewed by Botchway on 12 January, at Abura Abakrampa.

Ennin, Peter Kwame. (2004). a Methodist, over 80 years old, interviewed by Botchway on 9 January at Abura Abakrampa.

Enison, Samuel, K. (2004). MDCC member since 1946, and Elder of MDCC at Abura Abakrampa, 67 years old, interviewed by Botchway on 9 January at Abura Abakrampa.

IKime, Obaro eds. (1974). *Leadership in 19th Century Africa*, London: Longmans.

Fernandez, James. (1964). "African Religious Movements: Types and Dynamics", *Journal of Modern African Studies*, Vol.2,No. 4,.

James, C.L.R. (1963). James, *The Black Jacobins: Toussaint L'Ouverture and the San Domingo Revolution*, 2nd rev.ed. New York: Vintage, 1963, p. 87.

Jehu-Appiah, M.M. (1959). *The Constitution of the Musama Disco Christo Church*, Accra: Guinea Press Ltd.

Jehu-Appiah, J. (1943). *Christ Mbiamudua Hu Dom Asorn Hu Abakosem*, Koforidua, Fanzaar Press.

Kimble, David. (1963). *A Political History of Ghana*, Oxford, Clarendon Press.

'Musama Disco Christo Church Diamond Jubilee Celebration and Peace Festival Souvenir Programme', (2000). Accra: Billy-Ham Press Limited.

Nukunya, G.K. (1992). *Tradition and Change in Ghana*, Accra, Ghana University Press.

Opoku, K.A. (1969). 'A Brief History of Independent Church Movement in Ghana' A paper presented at the Annual Meeting of the Historical Society of Ghana, Ghana.

Jehu-Appiah Prophet M.J. (Akaboha III), (2004). interviewed by Botchway, 2 February, Mozano.

Sagoe, Coodiasney Cobbah. (2004). Retired Minister and Instructor of MDCC Pastoral Seminary, 78 years old, interviewed by Botchway on 29 January, at Mozano

Sarpong, Peter K. (2002). *Peoples Differ: An Approach to inculturation in Evangelisation*, Legon – Accra: Sub Saharan Publishers.

CHAPTER FOUR

Local Black Resistance Against Colonial Integration of Ewedome (British Trust Territory) 1951-1956

Wilson Yayoh

Introduction

The purpose of this chapter is to examine the nature of a local Black resistance campaign by the Black-led Togoland Congress against the British Colonial Office, working in tandem with local political parties and officials in Ghana, over attempts to integrate the Trust Territory within the Gold Coast. The completion of new local government structures in Ewedome (British Trust Territory of Togoland) in 1953 coincided with the gradual devolution of power to the Convention People's Party (CPP) dominated Cabinet and Legislative Assembly in the Gold Coast. This development had a direct bearing on the trusteeship status of the territory. The CPP, supported by the British colonial officials, was determined to integrate the Trust Territory into the Gold Coast. The Togoland Congress vehemently opposed such moves and sought, instead, the unification of the two Togolands as an independent entity. This chapter, therefore, analyses the politicisation of local Black councils over the issue of the status of the Trust Territory at the local, national and international levels. In doing so, the chapter re-examines the existing narrative of the Ewe unification question, as it unfolded in Ewedome, in order to illuminate our understanding of the impact of the resistance against integration of Ewedome into the Gold Coast. In the end, therefore, this struggle was carried out between two groups of African nationals who, similar to the slave resistance we saw in chapter two, were caught up in a wider colonial resistance involving a more powerful European country actually using one group of Africans against another to satisfy its own interests.

Ewedome has had a chequered history. It was part of German Togoland that was partitioned between Britain and France after the First World War. A tentative definition of the boundary between Britain and France was made possible following the work of the Anglo-French Boundary Commission and the issuance of a Boundary Protocol in 1929. The British share of Togoland, of which Ewedome was a part, was administered under the provisions of the Togoland Agreement under the British Mandate Order-in-Council which was signed on 11 October 1923 by the Governor of the Gold Coast (UN Trusteeship Report, 1947). Thus Ewedome, and for that matter British Togoland, remained under the mandate system conferred by the League of Nations for 25 years. When, in 1946, the British Foreign Secretary told the United Nations General Assembly that his country would welcome the Trusteeship Council which was to replace the mandate system, it marked yet another political change in the history of Ewedome and British Togoland as a whole (UN Trusteeship Report, 1946).

A key provision in the trusteeship agreement, was that the administering authorities had to constitute their respective territories into customs, fiscal or administrative unions or federations with adjacent territories and to promote the political advancement of the inhabitants (UN Trusteeship Report, 1946). Henceforth, various policies and ordinances passed in relation to the territory, as well as innovations in the Native Authority (NA) system of local government were largely informed by the provisions of the trusteeship agreement and post-war developments in the Gold Coast. It is important to note that the mandate to administer part of former German Togoland was given to Britain, with the hope that ethnic groups that had been divided by the Anglo-German partition of 1890 could be re-united. Following the expulsion of the Germans in 1914, and the subsequent partition of former German Togoland between Britain and France, attempts were made to form an ethnically coherent boundary between the British and the French spheres of Togoland. This resulted in the unification of the Dagomba kingdom in the present-day Northern Region of Ghana; but in the southern section of British Togoland, dominated by the Ewe sub-group, no such unification was achieved.

This became a source of resentment, disenchantment and agitation among the Ewe, who came under the British-controlled Togoland (Yayoh, 2013). It was also one of the factors that led to the development of Togoland/Ewe Nationalism. Togoland Nationalism can be seen as 'the growing awareness among the different ethnic groups in the former German Togo, of their shared colonial experiences and, for that matter, a common identity' (Yayoh, 2013). Furthermore, Togoland Nationalism was a discourse that sought to mobilise the collective identity of the inhabitants of the former German colony as a basis for promoting Togoland unification. The British Colonial Government's solution to the problem was to integrate British Togoland into the Gold Coast so as to kill off any agitation for Togoland unification. It was, therefore, this strategy on the part of the British Colonial Government, which the local people of Ewedome sought to resist, by attempting to reclaim and also assert their own political and cultural autonomy.

Post-war labour militancy, riots and a surge in anti-colonial sentiment in the Gold Coast Colony in 1948 led to major constitutional reforms in the colony, with ramifications for the Trust Territory. At the centre of the reforms, was part-two of the Coussey Report of 1949, that had made far-reaching recommendations that would change completely, the structure of local administration in the colony and the Trust Territory, by replacing Native Authorities with local councils. By 1953, all the local councils in Ewedome had been established and they were seen as new, increasingly democratic systems of rule, eventually leading to full self-government. But abolishing the NA system was part of the decolonisation process which Nkrumah and the CPP leadership believed would be controlled by the party, through the new local government structures, thereby actually bolstering central control by the new nationalist government. Inadvertently, therefore, Nkrumah and the CPP were indirectly helping to carry out the wishes of the British Colonial regime over the interests of the local Ewe community.

In Ewedome, the emergence of Ewe national consciousness, the trusteeship status of the territory and the agitations for the unification of British and French Togolands set the whole process of decolonisation apart. Thus the dynamics of decolonisation in Ewedome became more complex, assuming more of an international dimension, than the cases which were witnessed in the Gold Coast colony, Asante and the Northern Territories. What is of significance here is the way inhabitants in the Ewedome area of British Togoland were able to use the colonial state structures, such as local councils to resist, though unsuccessfully, the diarchy government's resolve to integrate the Trust Territory into the then Gold Coast.

Political Re-organisation

The creation of the Trans-Volta Togoland Region in 1952, needed to be given more meaning by bringing Togolanders (British Togoland) and the Gold Coasters together in a regional administrative body. The plan was first mooted in 1948, when Sir Thorleif Mangin, Chief Commissioner of the Colony, toured the southern section of British Togoland and discussed with the chiefs and their subjects, the need for a representative of Togoland on the Joint Provincial Council (JPC) as the first step towards Togolanders having a representative on the Legislative Council in the Gold Coast. The JPC was, for over 30 years, the body of chiefs in southern Ghana, with its headquarters at Dodowa, the capital of the Eastern Province of the Colony. It was dissolved in 1958 by the CPP Government to give way for the Houses of Chiefs in the regions it had previously covered (*West Africa*, 29 November 1958, p. 1129).

It was subsequent to this, that the 1949 Native Authority Ordinance for the southern section of British Togoland was passed, in order to harmonise the NAs in the territory in line with that of the Gold Coast Colony to facilitate the admission of southern Togolanders into the JPC (Chief Commissioner's Report, 1948). This proposal was responsible for the increased agitation for Togoland unification. The Ewe chiefs of Ewedome were not sure how their membership of the Joint Provincial Council would affect their status as a Trust Territory as well as a possible unification with Ewes in French Togo. Meanwhile, the failure of the Southern Togoland Council, established in 1949, was due in part to the feeling of uneasiness by a large concentration of Akan strangers to the north of Ewedome, that they would not be easy associates with the more numerous Ewes on a regional body. Nonetheless, Mangin, the key British colonial official and staunch supporter of the old indirect rule system at this time of rapid move towards reform, thought otherwise. He felt that, for further progress to be made in the development of local government, this interest in ethnic identity must give way to the general interests of larger political units, such as the Joint Provincial Council or a regional body (Chief Commissioner's Report, 1949). In this way, the British Colonial Office official was ignoring the local political wishes and desires of Black people. This would, understandably, pave the way for a series of resistance campaigns against this British colonial policy. It would also result in local resistance against the CPP which, for their own reasons of political power and control, also shared similar sentiments with the British colonial regime.

After careful consideration, the Gold Coast Government decided to shelve the idea of Togolanders taking seats on the JPC, on the grounds that it would only be a matter of time before they were naturally drawn into closer contact with the JPC. This decision stemmed from a concern that the Togoland Union, one of the groups agitating for Togoland identity and Unification, could capitalise on the issue and cause a split in the territory, especially as the union was composed largely of members of the more educated class. Furthermore, a considerable amount of work had to be done on the various legislative amendments required to carry this decision into effect. Consequently, the matter became the subject of a series of correspondences between the District Commissioner of Ho, and the office of the Chief Commissioner of the Gold Coast until 1950, when major constitutional developments were set in motion in the Gold Coast. The Southern Togoland Council opposed the creation of a Trans-Volta Togoland Council because it was thought that it was not in the interest of the special status of the Trust Territory.

In 1953, the regional reorganisation was completed with the creation of the Trans-Volta Togoland Council. Its members were drawn from local and district councils including Anlo and Peki sections of the Gold Coast and it was to support and supervise the new local councils in their bid to increase the pace of economic and social development. As a deliberative and advisory body, it had no executive or legislative functions (Togoland Report, 1952). Government only needed to consult it in formulating policies regarding important issues such as constitutional matters or development programmes. A regional officer was to be appointed to coordinate all government activities in the region and to be responsible directly to the central government in Accra. Many Ewes of the Trust Territory continued to show resentment against the establishment of Trans-Volta Togoland Region and its Council, which they claimed would be dominated by Ewes from the Gold Coast (Minutes of the Southern Togoland Council, 1950).

Since the British took over Togoland from the Germans, the area had witnessed the influx of Gold Coast Ewes mainly from Peki and from Anlo, the coastal region to the south. G. O. Awuma, one of the leaders of Togoland Union, observed that it was difficult to see how Togolanders could be given education in self-determination when all the key positions in the local councils, the schools, commerce, and even the churches were filled with 'adventurers' from the Gold Coast Eweland (Coleman, 2013). It seemed, therefore, to the Togolanders that the British government, the missionary societies and the merchant houses seemed to have conspired to support Gold Coast Ewes to dominate Togolanders. Consequently, the feeling among the inhabitants was that the new regional council was going to operate to the advantage of Gold Coast Ewes, who were not only more educated than the Ewes in the Trust Territory, but also more inclined towards supporting the diarchy government's design to integrate British Togoland into the Gold Coast. In this way, the Ewedome community felt powerless and potentially exploited. This further supports the claim that some degree of organised resistance campaign was necessary for their very existence as an autonomous people with a history and culture to be respected and preserved.

There was no doubt that Ewedome and the entire Trust Territory, was in a backward state of economic development. It is also a fact that although the region was administered as an integral part of the Gold Coast, its trust status conveyed special assistance from the British Government and the responsibility towards the UN rested on the shoulders of the British Government (Colonial Office to the Governor, 1950). This position was supported by the Treasury in London, which felt that there was a pre-eminently strong case based on strict economic grounds, for a measure of further [financial] assistance to Togoland and the Cameroon. The effective administration of such a fund in the territory, made a strong case for a regional body that could oversee its implementation. The Togoland Congress, which became the umbrella organisation spearheading Togoland Unification, opposed the creation of the regional council, on the grounds that the identity of Ewe Togolanders would be subsumed by external groups in such a regional body, and thereby run the risk of eroding important aspects of its history, culture and influence.

The action of uniting the Ewes in the Colony and those in the Trust Territory, was designed to further the long-held objective of the colonial administration, and later that of the CPP, of attempting to fully integrate Togoland into the Gold Coast. This would make it easier to resist pressure in the future for the unification of the British and French Trust Territories. Indeed, the UN Trusteeship Council observed that the plan to create the Trans-Volta Togoland Region, conceived in 1949, 'appeared to have the effect of strengthening the integration of the southern section of the Trust Territory with the adjoining part of the Gold Coast' (Report of the Trusteeship Council to the General Assembly, 1949-950, p. 44). Through this system, the governor retained powers over Togoland, as there was a gradual devolution of power, both executive and legislative, to the CPP from 1951, although, the governor never actually used his reserved powers as regards Togoland (Coleman, 2013, p. 20).

Development Issues

In the past, owing to the slow development of primary and middle-schools, as well as the absence of secondary schools in the Trust Territory, fewer students from Ewedome than from Anlo, Peki and other parts of the Gold Coast, had achieved standards of education beyond middle-school level. Formal education started very late in Ewedome although there had been schools in the Gold Coast areas inhabited by Ewes for more than one hundred years (UN Visiting Missing Report, 1949). It was only at the beginning of 1952 that free primary education was made available to all children. Consequently, very few people from Ewedome occupied positions of importance in the government service, teaching and commercial sectors. This situation had been commented upon by the Visiting Mission in 1950. It was one of the bitterest causes of division between the people of Ewedome (in the Trust Territory) and Ewes in the Gold Coast. It was to hasten the removal of this grievance, that the Trans-Volta Togoland (TVT) Council made its proposal for a special scholarship scheme for the region in 1953. The grant was to cover a seven-year period at an estimated cost of £40,000, and it formed part of the £1,000,000 pledged by the diarchy for the development of the region (Trans-Volta Togoland Council, 1953).

Most inhabitants of Ewedome were disappointed about the combining of the Trust Territory and the Gold Coast areas for the disbursement of the scholarship scheme (Standing Financial Committee Report, 1953). This feeling of animosity was further evidenced by the way in which the local Black people felt they were being disempowered by the British colonialists and the CPP. They had expected the scheme to be devoted specifically to bridging the yawning gap in the education differential between the Trust Territory and the Gold Coast areas occupied by other Ewes. The UK Government's report on education, which was corroborated by the UN report on scholarships, showed that the majority of the most educated people in Togoland were teachers. However, out of twenty scholarships made available to the southern section of the Trust Territory in 1948, only one was awarded to an indigenous teacher. Furthermore, it had been observed by the Trusteeship Council in 1950, that some Gold Coast Ewe teachers were transferred to Ewedome and were given Togoland addresses so that they could benefit from the scholarship scheme (UN Trusteeship Council Report, 1950). This seemed to create the impression of an official strategy of connivance with Gold Coast Ewes to deprive indigenous Togolanders of scholarship which had been specifically allocated for them.

The TVT Council appreciated the fact that extension of the scope of its scholarship scheme beyond the Trust Territory, would not address the imbalance that the people of Ewedome had been yearning to correct since the late 1940s. But the hands of the council appeared to be tied by the joining of the Trust Territory to the Ewe-dominated parts of the Gold Coast. It was, therefore, inadvisable to discriminate in the disbursement of the scholarship grants by excluding the Gold Coast areas, particularly as the Tongu area between Ewedome and the Anlo Region, with one-fifth of the total population, was also considered to be educationally disadvantaged and deprived.

Local Councils and the Question of Integration

This section of the chapter focuses upon the specifically contested issue of Togoland unification. Given the situation pertaining to powerlessness and the gradual erosion of their cultural and historic significance described above, it is little wonder that the local people engaged in resistance campaigns. The post-Second World War era marked the beginning of Ewe cultural consciousness and nationalism, which built up gradually until it reached a crescendo in the early 1950s. Hitherto, the Ewes of Ewedome had been a disunited people who tended to resist any attempt to bring them together. The gradual emergence of a movement towards Ewe unification, however, helped to alter the political and cultural positioning of the people.

From 1953, the Togoland Congress intensified its fight against integrating British Togoland with the Gold Coast, in reaction to political developments in the Gold Coast such as the rise of the Northern People's Party and the National Liberation Movement in 1953-56. There were allegations that Government agents in the Gold Coast were conducting their own campaigns, arising from their fears or beliefs that the UN was not capable of helping Togolanders to realise their aspirations of forming a united Togo. The allegations had their roots in a booklet published in 1953 by the Togoland Congress, which it called a *'Most Secret' document on the future of Togoland*. The document, allegedly written by the British government, was said to have contained plans to incorporate Togoland into the Gold Coast. According to the document, the problem facing the British Colonial Office was how to ensure that the territory emerged from its trust status not later than the same year when the Gold Coast attained full self-government. Furthermore, Skinner has demonstrated how leaders of Togolanders sought to use documented evidence to help shore up their credibility in their bid to galvanise support for the fight against integration (Skinner, 2015).

Meanwhile, the Van Lare Commission had completed the re-demarcation of electoral districts for the second general elections to be held in 1954 (Austin, 1964; Amenumey, 1989). Three constituencies were created in Ewedome: Kpando North, Ho East and Ho West. The Togoland Congress had made a demand to the Commission to ensure that the electoral districts did not overlap the Trust Territory and the Gold Coast (Amenumey, 1989). In addition, the Togoland Congress wanted a separate legislature to be created for Togoland to show its special status as a Trust Territory and to maintain its Togoland identity. The relevance of the 1954 elections was in its objective of establishing a sovereign government that would place the administration of the Gold Coast and the British Togoland in the hands of Africans (Austin, 1964; Amenumey, 1989). By so doing, this further disempowered the local people of Ewedome.

In the elections, S. G. Antor won Kpando North, which included Hohoe, while Rev. Ametowobla, a Togoland Congress supporter from Awatime, who stood as an independent candidate, won Ho West and G. O. Awumah took the Ho East seat, all in the Ewedome area of the Trust Territory. In all, the CPP had seventy two out of the one hundred and four seats in the Assembly, eight of which were from the TVT Region. Togoland Congress participated in all these elections because, according to Amenumey, it feared if they did not, CPP supporters could be elected to speak on behalf of the Trust Territory. The victory of the CPP in the 1954 general elections moved the political development of the Gold Coast and Togoland rapidly towards independence. It introduced significant political advances both at the local and the national levels to the extent that the number of Togolanders on the National Legislative Body had increased from one in 1951 to six in 1954 (Scott to the Trusteeship Council, 1954). As it happened, the United Kingdom Trusteeship Order-in-Council 1954, for all intent and purposes, effectively put and end to any hope of unificationists realising their objectives. What fuelled the consternation of the Togoland Congress most was the 'progressive devolution of real executive power to the CPP component of the Executive and the Legislative Assembly' (Coleman, 2013). The only portfolios reserved for the governor were those of defence, security, external affairs and the responsibility for the administration of British Togoland as stipulated by the Trusteeship Agreement. The reforms also introduced an all-African cabinet, which included two Togolanders: G. O. Awuma from Ho and F. Y. Asare from Buem (Skinner, 2007).

For practical purposes of local government administration, revenue accruing in the southern section of British Togoland was included in the budgets of the Gold Coast as a whole, and expenditures were allocated to the former, based on the needs of the parts of the Gold Coast with which it was administratively integrated. Moreover, the use of the central government services of the Gold Coast in running the administration of the Trust Territory had resulted in an appreciable reduction in overhead administrative costs for the local government institutions since 1951. In addition, for the quarter of a century that British Togoland had been administered as part and parcel of the Gold Coast, the local government and educational systems had been developed on the British model. All the modern ideas, philosophical and political thoughts, institutions, trade practices, monetary policies, and indeed the overall way of life of the people of British Togoland were very much in keeping with British systems and expectations. Anything to the contrary, according to integrationists, could be a retrograde step in the political and economic development of the

Trust Territory. All this fed into the CPP's agenda that focused on the creation of a strong, centralised and unitary independent state, which would include Ewedome, and for that matter the Trust Territory. Federation or outright separation, in the view of the CPP, was associated with the out-dated power of chiefs, especially with regard to the National Liberation Movement (NLM) in Asante. Notwithstanding these issues, the Togoland Congress still felt it had a strong case, for the UK government had no mandate from the UN to transfer its responsibility over the Trust Territory to the new Gold Coast Government.

What is of concern to this study is the way local councils were used as a platform for the struggle between integrationist and unificationist advocates on the overall development of local government in the territory. While the new local government system sought to reduce, according to the nationalist modernisers, the overbearing influence of chiefs, there was the real danger of separatist parties gaining control over local councils. As it turned out, local government affairs became caught up and confused with national politics, as the councils became the platform for canvassing support for or against integration. In Kpando District Council, for example, a ban was placed on the discussion of Togoland politics at its meetings because the district was not exclusive to the Trust Territory but extended into the Gold Coast (Kpando Local Council Minutes, 1954). We noted that Peki, which had been outside the Trust Territory, was incorporated into the Kpando District in 1953. However, this could not insulate the council from the politicisation of its proceedings. Kpando became one of the hottest spots for the showdown between the CPP in league with the British Colonial Government and the Togoland Congress. It seemed ironic, therefore, that the political independence movements of the Gold Coast should be regarded as a colonial vehicle or tool to disempower an entire community in this way.

The leadership of the Togoland Congress toured Ewedome, and specifically called on the inhabitants not to cooperate with councils (Minutes of Asogli Local Council, 1954). Local Councils were labelled as CPP-invented structures that should not be allowed to work. There were demands by the Togoland Congress to move the Trans-Volta Togoland Council headquarters from Ho to Hohoe, on the grounds that the future political position of Ho was uncertain (Minutes of the Ho Branch of the CPP, 1955). But the real reason behind this demand was that Ho was more of a CPP stronghold than Hohoe. It will be recalled, that the Togoland Congress newspaper, the *Vanguard*, which appeared at irregular intervals, had been published by the Togoland News Syndicate at Hohoe until it was suspended in 1954. Hohoe was the *de facto* headquarters of the Togoland Congress. Ho, in contrast, was host to the second national annual conference of the CPP in 1951, where the future strategy of the party was approved (Austin, 1964). In this way, as we shall see in Beckford and Charles' chapter on Jamaica, and indeed, throughout this book, a much larger anti-colonial struggle on a grander scale, had influenced local struggles for Black independence and identity on a local scale. In other words, whilst there was 'big men' politics being played out, the real victims were the local Ewedome people. In the words of an old African proverb, 'whether the elephants make love or make war, it's the grass that suffers.'

Interestingly enough, even though all the councils including those in Ewedome resolved to be integrated into the Gold Coast, it seemed clear from the results of the plebiscite conducted later in 1956, that the local councils in Ewedome were hijacked by CPP activists who were able to whip up support and thereby influence councillors to create the impression that the inhabitants of Ewedome were in support of integration. One interesting development common throughout Ewedome, was the tendency for elected councillors to switch political camp to the side of the CPP once they got onto the local councils, while the wards which elected them remained predominantly pro-Togoland Congress. One cogent reason given by Brown for this trend, was that participation in councils implied support for the TVT administration; positions which were opposed by the Togoland Congress (Brown, 1977). In addition, there were material benefits for councillors to gain from supporting the CPP and the colonial government. All key positions went to CPP supporters. Some Togoland Congress supporters, who resisted the use of coercive apparatus to force them to decamp, boycotted initial council meetings in protest. This was a form of African resistance to their disempowerment, and was further supported by Brown, where he cited the case in which Togoland Congress councillors from Alavanyo, boycotted the first sittings of the Akpini Local Council (Brown, 1977). In this way, the CPP came to have absolute control over the local councils from 1951.

The CPP itself had advantages to gain in seeking the integration of Togoland into the Gold Coast. Its stance emanated partly from the proposed Volta River project. This was an elaborate hydro-electric power scheme which involved the damming of the river. The economic implications of the project on the livelihood of the fishing communities along the river were enormous. An aerial survey conducted in 1957, showed that the artificial dam to be created would displace many of the Togolanders living along the river banks. Togolanders, particularly from Ewedome, had therefore sent a petition to the UN demanding that the Volta River scheme should be looked at as an international project on which Togoland should be 'represented as a nation' (Petition from Togoland Youth Association, 1953; Amenumey, 1989). It would have been unthinkable for the Gold Coast Government to build such a gigantic dam so close to Togoland, and allow the latter to become an independent nation. That would have had serious security implications for the Gold Coast. It was imperative, therefore, that Togoland remain part of the Gold Coast without which the project might have well been abandoned.

In addition, the people in Buem-Krachi District to the north of Ewedome were linguistically and historically linked to the Gold Coast. The Krachis and Nkonyas were said to have migrated from the Gold Coast. The same could be said of Adeles and Nchumurus (in the Nkwanta district of the present-day Volta Region) who traced their origin to the west. In pre-colonial times, the chief of Krachi was said to have served the Asantehene. Similarly, the inhabitants in the northern section of British Togoland had strong ethnic links with people in the Gold Coast, with whom they shared common customs and traditions. Not even the division of Dagomba into two by the Anglo-German partition of 1890 could prevent the Ya Na in German Yendi from continuously exercising authority over the selection of chiefs among the Dagombas in the Gold Coast.

Consequently, they described the whole idea of unification as political madness that sought to exchange the frontier to their east for a new frontier to their west. In a resolution sent to the UN Trusteeship Council, the Buem-Krachi District Council reiterated the point that they were tired of being handed over from one power to another and considered that the progress of their area had been greatly retarded by the frequent changes in the foreign powers who had administered them. The only area where a dissenting view was recorded, was the Biakoye Local Council to the north of Ewedome, made up predominantly of a number of small ethnic groups, which were neither Akan nor Ewe. Certain chiefs in this area declared their preference for unification of the two Togolands on the grounds that the Gold Coast had been their enemies since time immemorial (UN Visiting Mission Report, 1955).

In December 1954, the UN General Assembly observed that the imminent independence of the Gold Coast rendered the continued administration of British Togoland by the UK Government under the Trusteeship Agreement, impossible. A change in the Trusteeship Agreement was also not feasible, for any such change could necessarily affect the interests of the inhabitants of Togoland under French administration. Moreover, no one could guess the exact conditions under which French Togoland would eventually be granted independence, or whether or not those conditions would be compatible with the aspirations of all Ewes. Among the imponderables, was the likelihood of the French Government backing an idea of 'balkanisation as against the creation of a new African state' (Howe, 1977). What made the situation more intricate was the statement by the British Government to the UN in 1954 that if the Gold Coast became independent, it would not be prepared to remain in Togoland (Arden-Clarke to Trans-Volta Togoland Council, 1954).

Although the Togoland problem was first brought to the attention of the Trusteeship Council as far back as 1947, when seven petitions were received from, among others, Mr Augustino de Souza, President of the *Comité de l'UnitéTogolaise* in French Togoland demanding the unification of Ewe people, the problem was allowed to simmer for that long. As the Gold Coast drew nearer to independence, the issue became more complex. The UN Visiting Mission stated in 1953 that:

> it seems clear that a constitution granting full autonomy to the Gold Coast cannot be made to apply also to Togoland so long as the Trusteeship Agreement retains its present form, since the United Kingdom Government would no longer exercise any control over the Gold Coast Government it would not be possible for Togoland to be administered any longer as an integral part of the Gold Coast and still retain the United Kingdom Government as its Administering Authority' (UN Visiting Mission Report, 1953, paragraph 84).

Based on these facts, the UN General Assembly adopted the draft resolution terminating the Trusteeship Agreement in 1954. The Trusteeship Council was then tasked to determine how the wishes of the inhabitants could be ascertained. In pursuance of this task, a special UN visiting mission was despatched to the territory in 1955. Therefore, while the Trusteeship Agreement was emphatic about the need for earliest possible attainment of self-government or independence for the Trust Territory, it was silent on the factors to be considered in deciding on the termination of the trust status (Scott to the Trusteeship Council, 1954).

Local Councils Resistance and the 1956 Plebiscite

After the 1954 elections, the CPP, supported by the British Colonial Government, endeavoured to speed up the integration process by embarking on a vigorous political campaign to open branches in the Trust Territory with the view of integrating it with the Gold Coast 'by the time of Ghana's independence' (Brown, 1977). Interestingly, the slogan of the CPP was 'freedom' while that of the Togoland Congress was the Ewe translation of freedom which is *'ablode'*. Arrangements were made for the leadership of the CPP to meet members of the local and district councils. Nkrumah toured Ho district with Komla Gbedemah and held meetings in such towns as Ho, Hohoe, Kpando, Kpetoe, Kpedze, Vane and Saviefe. Gbedemah, an Ewe from Anlo, was a leading member of the CPP and a key lieutenant of Nkrumah who became the first Finance Minister of independent Ghana. His presence in Nkrumah's entourage was to appeal to ethnic sentiments of the Ewes of Ewedome and to calm fears that integration with the Gold Coast implied the subjugation of Ewe of Togoland, but his Anlo identity did not help matters. The people of Ewes of Togoland section of Ewdome felt that their ethnic, political and cultural identity were being attacked and eroded by the very Gold Coast Government, which in theory at least, was supposed to be integrating them more fully into this emerging new nation.

The local councils became the main field on which the political battle between the CPP/colonial government and the Togoland Congress was fought. Many council meetings frequently broke up in disorder and confusion and there were instances where councillors refused to attend meetings. As the councils were divided into factions, the initial enthusiasm of both councillors and the general populace began to wear off. In some cases, the campaign brought in its trail outright conflict. At Hohoe in August 1954, some people opposed to integration, vandalised a CPP van, destroyed its loud speakers and assaulted its occupants. One person was arrested, charged, convicted and sentenced to two months imprisonment (UN Visiting Mission Report 1954). In Awatime, for example, towns and villages which supported the CPP became targets of abuse (Report, Trans-Volta Togoland House of Chiefs, 1958). In East Dain Local Council, the political differences reached such a crescendo that the council became divided in two, with one half threatening to secede to form a separate council to avoid the political machinations of Antor and the Togoland Congress. In the Asogli Local Council, the disruptive effects of the struggle between unificationists and integrationists led to the resignation of some councillors and a threat by their respective wards to withdraw from the council in 1955. These were, therefore, more than just political struggles by a people to maintain their independence. These were very clear instances of people fighting for their freedom as well as their ethnic and cultural identity.

The situation in the Akpini Local Council, with its headquarters at Kpando, was most deplorable. The relocation of a new market from Togoland Congress-dominated Aloyi to a pro-CPP Tsakpe, led to serious disputes between the CPP group, most of whom were the youth, and the separatists (Brown, 1977). Some councillors walked out in protest at the attempts by the chairperson of the Akpini Local Council to get the full support of the council for the purposes of integration (Amenumey). Brown noted further, that the antagonism between integrationists and unificationists made it virtually impossible for the local council to attempt any revenue collection in the pro-Ablode areas.

Another issue which people used to organise their resistance campaign was through the systems of rate collection. The collection of such rates suffered because many elderly people became reluctant to pay their rate in protest against the move by the government to integrate the territory into the Gold Coast. According to Brown, cocoa farmers supported Togoland Congress while local council and government department employees, who were more educated, younger with less social status or wealth tended to support the CPP (Brown, 1977). This explains how this conflict led to a generational divide which had deteriorating effects on the new councils. In Akpini Local Council areas, CPP supporters were omitted from the nominal roll upon which rate liability was based, and there were several cases where Togoland Congress supporters were harassed for payment, and there were cases where organised raids were made on pro-Ablode villages (Brown, 1977). It became obvious that the resolution of the issue of integration was pivotal for the development of local government in the territory.

On 9 May 1956, the people of Togoland under the UK Trusteeship went to the polls to decide whether their territory should be united with an independent Gold Coast, or whether it should be separated from the Gold Coast and allowed to continue under trusteeship, pending the ultimate determination of its political future. The results of the plebiscite showed 92,775 for union with the Gold Coast and 67,529 for separation. Allegations of rigging were made by the Togoland Congress, though it failed to provide concrete evidence in support of its allegation (*Daily Graphic*, 12 May, 1956). This is significant as it shows that over a third of the voters were clearly opposed to this move. An interesting picture that emerged showed that while Ewedome voted overwhelmingly for separation, the other ethnic groups to the north voted for union with the Gold Coast. Even within Ewedome, the picture was more complicated than the general figures show.

Skinner makes the point that political affiliation with the Togoland Congress/Unificationists or the CPP and voting in the plebiscite operated on 'communal lines' (Skinner, 2007). She notes further that 'local issues, rather than adherence to a broader party manifesto, were crucial in determining voting behaviour. Indeed, the fight for and against integration provided fertile ground for local rivalries and conflicts to be articulated through CPP - Togoland Congress politics (Dunn and Robertson, 1973). In other words, internal feud or stool rivalries between one division and another, often determined the support for or against integration. Amenumey notes that because of an old dispute between Vakpo and Anfoega, the former decided to support unification, while Anfoega was a stronghold of the CPP (Amenumey, 1989). In the East Dain Local Council, the old conflict between Tafi and Logba was revived and articulated with national politics. The political differences reached such fever pitch, that the council became divided into two with one half, most from Tafi, threatening to secede to form a separate council to avoid the political machinations of Antor, a citizen of Lobga.

Results of the 1956 Plebiscite

Section	Union/Integration	Separation
Northern Section	49,119	12,707
Southern Section	93,095	67,493
TOTAL	**142,214**	**80,200**

Results of the 1956 Plebiscite in Ewedome

District	Union/Integration	Separation
Ho	7,217	18,981
Kpando	8,581	17,020
TOTAL	**15,798**	**36,001**

Source Daily Graphic 12 May 1956

Two months after the plebiscite, the third general elections were held in the Gold Coast and the Trust Territory on 17 July 1956 to sort out two very important issues. The first was whether the UK Government should relinquish power to the CPP in 1956. The second issue was whether at independence, the country should be a unitary or federal state (Austin, 1964). The Togoland Congress once again won in its three traditional districts in Ewedome – Ho East, Ho West and Kpando North – but the CPP, which favoured a unitary state, was the overall winner by claiming seventy one out of the one hundred and four seats throughout the country. The results of the plebiscite and the 1956 elections effectively killed off any lingering federalist and separatist inclinations and aspirations of the opposition elements and put and end to the campaign of the Togoland Congress for the unification of the two Togolands. This did not, however, bring to an end the spate of violent incidents in Ewedome. Violence escalated in Kpandu and Hohoe areas in 1956-7. The leadership of the Togoland Congress wanted to salvage something out of the loss they suffered in the plebiscite, by fighting for the recognition and maintenance of southern Togoland identity within the enlarged Gold Coast. This, it hoped to achieve by the creation of a separate region for Southern Togoland (Parliamentary Report, 1957). Although the Togoland Congress got the support of a large number of chiefs in Ewedome, it was frustrated by the Togoland branch of the CPP. The Togoland Congress and the majority of chiefs then decided to boycott the independence celebrations scheduled for 6 March 1957 until their demand for a separate region was met (Parliamentary Report, 1957).

On the 27 February 1957, the Togoland Congress organised a rally of resistance in Kpando to galvanise support for the boycott of the events on March 6. After the rally, unsubstantiated rumours spread alleging that the Togoland Congress had hatched plans to vandalise the local police station, dynamite houses and shoot supporters of the CPP. In addition, the Togoland Congress was supposed to have sent one hundred and fifty young men to Kumasi to train as Action Troopers. It was also alleged that

CPP supporters had a secret meeting at Kpandu Agudzi where guns and gunpowder were distributed to members, and that an assassination plot was being organised at Kpandu Aloi. Finally, it was also alleged that the people were being trained in the bush for subversive activities (Austin, 1964). The government's position on the issue was that while no one was under any obligation to take part in the celebration of the independence, it would not countenance any attempt to prevent those who wished to do so.

The discovery of alleged Togoland Congress camps in the Alavanyo area in the Kpando district and Hodzokofe in the Ho district led to the deployment of four hundred and eighty five police and four hundred troops into Ewedome. To legitimise the presence of the troops, the Governor signed a Peace Preservation Order on 26 February 1957. Searches were conducted to retrieve firearms, cutlasses and other weapons. On 4 March, some supporters of the Togoland Congress in Kpando went to the fore-court of the district and local councils and dismantled buntings mounted in preparation for the independence celebration and broke the windows of the council buildings. They then moved on to vandalise the post office and a petrol station which had also been decorated in preparations for the Independence celebrations. On 6 March, there was an exchange of gun fire between another group of Togoland Congress supporters and the police which left two people dead and several wounded, despite a ban on the use of arms and ammunitions.

Indiscriminate arrests were made by the police, resulting in many innocent people being beaten and arrested. Elderly people, travellers and even members of the CPP who did not oppose the celebrations were mistakenly arrested and severely beaten (Parliamentary Report, 1957). The whole district was mired in utter confusion and chaos, with one hundred and fourty one arrests made. The disproportionate reprisal by the government forces in the run-up to independence created widespread fear, indignation and disquiet throughout Ewedome, which adversely affected the work of local government institutions. Ironically, Kpando tended to benefit most from the Gold Coast government during this turbulent period in the run-up to the 1956 plebiscite. According to Brown between 1952 and 1957, Kpandu received more benefits in the form of development, than at any other time before or since (Brown,1977). Kpando was a stronghold of the CPP in Ewedome and the strategy of the party was to use resource allocation to promote the development of constituencies which were most supportive of the party and its leader. Kpando *borbobor*- a cultural dance performed by the youth of Kpando - became an organ of the CPP. The group attended all CPP rallies and attracted many of the youth. More specific to Kpando's case, was the dominant role played by its CPP activists in the TVT Council, a body responsible for the distribution of government grants and projects in the region from 1952 to 1958.

Examples of projects undertaken in Kpando included: district council offices, community centres, health centres, secondary schools, a library, pipe-borne water, a new market, post office, tarring of the strests of the town, construction of drainage systems and the trade school, which later became Kpando Technical Institute. All these projects were executed within a period of four years. The most disturbing picture was that even within Kpando itself, CPP- dominated areas benefited more than Togoland Congress areas such as Kpando-Aloyi in the allocation of development projects. This explains the decision of *Ablode* supporters to boycott payment of rates to the councils in Ewedome. Brown quoted the Government Agent at Kpando, David Heaton, who had said in 1955, that party politics plays an unfortunately large part in the council's affairs and colours almost all its discussions (Brown, 1977). This problem identified by Heaton became a disturbing feature of local government throughout Ewedome right from the inception of the new councils and well into the post-independent era. Resistance to integration lingered on throughout the First Republic of independent Ghana. Chiefs and leaders of the resistance movement fled into exile in French Togoland as the Nkrumah government moved to clear Ewedome of integrationist elements.

The results of the plebiscite and the subsequent integration of the Togoland into the Gold Coast was no different from what happned in other parts of Africa where partition of the continent forced smaller African entities to dissolve into larger ones. We have seen Makonde divided and absorbed inot Mozambique and Tanzania; the Dan could be found in Cote d'Ivore and Sierra Leone and Somalia people are absorbed into Ethiopia, Kenya, and Somalia. Attempts by the Somali people to create unification failed to materialise. As colonialism began to receed, resistance to integration became wide-spread in Africa. The failed attempt by Katanga province to secede from the Belgian Congo in the early 1960s; the aborted Biafra secessionist in Nigeria in 1967; the unsuccessful resistance by Krio to their integration in Sierra Leone were clear examples of how ethnic groups, wich were divided by colonial boundaries and absorbed into artificially created nations, sought to assert their political and ethnic autonomy (curtin, et al, 1995). One exception to this general observation is the case where Gambia avoided incorporation into a united Senegambia. Although in most cases, resistance to integration failed, it signalled the importance of ethnic identity and 'group consciousness' in the declonisation process (Reid, 2009).

Conclusion

The run-up to the 1956 plebiscite was the most turbulent period in the history of Ewedome and British Togoland as a whole. As the Gold Coast moved towards independence, the trusteeship status of British Togoland brought the issue of integration onto the international stage. The dynamics of Togoland identity, coupled with the diarchy government's determination to integrate the Trust Territory into the Gold Coast, complicated matters. At the heart of this struggle, was the issue of a confrontation between, those wishing to continue their existence as a people, and those seeking to integrate them into a larger whole, which threatened this sense of local community ethnicity and identity.

The political atmosphere of the territory was greatly disturbed. The overall effect was that modern party politics began to impact negatively on local councils. In the Ewedome area, resistance against integration made the new institutions of local government vehicles for the broader party political struggle. The real danger was that any ethnographic state within the southern section of British Togoland would be an anachronism and the resolution of the problem through the UN-sponsored plebiscite came as a breath of fresh air to the CPP and the UK government.

References

Amenumey, D. E. K. (1989). *The Ewe Unification Movement: A Political History*, Accra, Ghana Universities Press.

Arden-Clarke. (1954). Address to Trans-Volta Togoland Council, RAG/H.

Austin, D. (1964). *Politics in Ghana, 1946-1960*, Oxford University Press.

Brown, D. (1977). *Politics in the Kpandu Area of Ghana, 1925 to 1969: A Study of the Influence of Central Government and National Politics upon Local Factional Competition*, Unpublished PhD Thesis, University of Birmingham.

Chief Commissioner's Report. (1949). Chief Commissioner's Office to the District Councils in Togoland, RAG/H D/D 388.

Chief Commissioner's Report. (1948). Address by the Chief Commissioner T. R. O. Mangin, Ho (1948). RAG/H D/D 388.

Colonial Office to the Governor in Accra. (1950). National Archives, London, CO96/826/9 (1950).

Coleman, J. S. (2013). 'Togoland', *International Conciliation*, 509. September 1956, USA, Literary Licensing Publishers.

Coussey Report (1950). Note by the Colonial Office on the Coussey Report, National Archives, London, CO96/824/7.

Curtin, P. *et al.* (1995). *African History from Earliest Times to Independence*, Edinburgh, Pearson.

Dunn, J. and Robertson, A. F. (1973). *Dependence and Opportunity: Political Change in Ahafo*, Cambridge University Press.

Howe, R. W. (1979). *Black Star Arising*: *A Journey through West Africa in Transition*, London, Butterworth.

Kpando Local Council Meetings and Minutes (1954). RAG/H/ HLC 23/SF.4.

Minutes of Asogli Local Council, (1954). PRAAD/D ADM 39/1/511, No. S.0180/SF.30.

Minutes of the Southern Togoland Council (1950). National Archives, London, CO96/827/2.

Minutes of the Ho Branch of the CPP, (1955). Memorandum by the Ho District Branch of the CPP on the Transfer of TVT Council from HO). RAG/H.

Nugent, P. (2002). *Smugglers, Secessionists and Loyal Citizens on the Ghana-Togo Frontier: The Lie of the Borderlands since 1914*, Athens, OH, Ohio University Press.

Petition from Togoland Youth Association (1953). Petition to the Ho District to the Trusteeship Council, RAG/H ACC No. 344.

Reid, R. J. (2009). *a History of Modern Africa, 1800 to the Present*, Malden, Wiley-Blackwell.

Report on the Trans-Volta Togoland Regional Councils of Chiefs, Ho. (1958). RAG/H RAO/C.728.

Report of the Trusteeship Council to the General Assembly, (1949-1950). New York..

Parliamentary Report. (1957). Parliamentary Opposition Fact-Finding Delegation to Southern Togoland, RAG/H.

Scott to the Trusteeship Council, (1954). Mr Scott to the Fourth Committee of the Trusteeship Council, RAG/H ACC 343.

Skinner, K. (2007). 'Reading, Writing and Rallies: The Politics of "Freedom" in Southern British Togoland, 1953-1956', *Journal of Contemporary History*, 39(2).

Skinner, K. (2015). *The Fruits of Freedom in British Togoland: Literacy, Politics and Nationalism, 1914-2014*, Cambridge University Press..

Standing Financial Committee Report, (1953). Trans-Volta Togoland Council Development Plan, PRAAD/D ADM 39/1/532.

Togoland Reports 1952, 1949.

Trans-Volta Togoland Council. (1953). Supplementary Scheme for Scholarships and Bursaries. RAG/H, (1953/53).

West Africa, 29 November 1958.

West Africa, 1 December 1956.

Yayoh, Wilson. K. (2013). 'What is in a Flag? The Swastika and Togoland Nationalism', *Contemporary Journal of African Studies*, Vol. 1. p. 2-3.

UN Trusteeship Reports, (*passim*) 1946, 1947, 1949, 1950, 1951.

United Nations Visiting Mission Reports, (*passim*) 1949, 1950, 1952, 1953, 1955 RAG/H.

UN Visiting Mission to Biakoye Local Council (1954). RAG/H ACC.0012.

UN Visiting Mission Report. (1953). (Document No. T/1040).

CHAPTER FIVE

Black Radical Tradition and Resistance in Jamaica

Orville W. Beckford and Christopher A.D. Charles

Introduction

In the beginning there was Africa. Black resistance to White oppression was recorded in Africa when Europeans went there in the sixteenth and seventeenth centuries to capture Africans for use as forced labourers in the Americas. There was ongoing armed resistance in Africa against European captors which took place along the rivers; in the interior and along the coast; in the barracoons holding the captives; against the crew of the ships docked in the harbour and, on the voyages across the Atlantic, later known as the Middle Passage and, which continued in the plantation societies of the Americas (Beckles, 2013; Hall, 2005). The captors viewed such slave resistance as an occupational hazard and the cost of doing business. Some of the African leaders who resisted the European captors were assassinated. Despite the various forms of resistance, an estimated eleven to fifteen million Africans were forcibly removed from Africa during the trans-Atlantic slave trade from the sixteenth to the nineteenth centuries (Beckles, 2013; Eltis, Lewis & Richardson, 2005; Hall, 2005; Warner-Lewis, 2003), and an estimated one hundred million Africans were killded because of this trade (Hall, 2005). As was previously mentioned in part one of this book, Black resistance continued during slavery in the Americas as captured Africans not only brought aspects of their culture with them to the Americas, but continued to resist European domination whenever and wherever possible, and thereby also ensured that many components of Black culture survived to the present day (Hall, 2005; Warner-Lewis, 2003). This chapter on the study of Black reistance in Jamaica is, therefore, particularly instructive as it helps to contextualise the myriad of Black resistance strategies that were employed throughout most of the Americas, encapsulated within one particular country, from the onset of European slavery and colonialism to the present time.

The Europeans' desire for African labour followed Christopher Columbus' arrival in the Caribbean in 1492. The majority of these indigenous peoples, described as Indians by Columbus and then later adopted by the Spanish, were exterminated by European diseases, forced labour, and war, which created the huge demand for labour (Williams, 1970). It was this labour shortage to supply the demands of the Caribbean plantations, which eventually resulted in Europeans acquiring African labourers from essentially West and Central Africa. As soon as these Afrians arrived in the Caribbean, they embarked upon resistance campaigns.

Africans taken to Jamaica resisted their oppressors, and African descendants continued this in what is known as the Black radical tradition. Black resistance, therefore, as used in this chapter, denotes Africans and their descendants challenging colonial and neo-colonial oppression, respectively by fighting for their rights, as well as to ensure aspects of their own cultural identity. The Black radical tradition indicates that there is a history of Black resistance that links the past with the present. Resistance, which takes several forms, is a core feature of the Black radical tradition. This resistance was previously carried out by Maroons who had escaped from Spanish slavery and continued their resistance through rebellions against the British. Captive Africans, working on commercial plantations, as well as the effects of the Maroon wars created serious problems for the colonial militias. The Black radical tradition manifested itself in the 1865 Morant Bay

Rebellion and was also observed in the subversive preaching of Reverend Alexander Bedward, in the Black Nationalism of Marcus Garvey, the 1938 labour protests, and the rise of Leonard Howell and other Rastafari founders who promoted Ethiopianism and Garvey's conception of Black Nationalism. The resistance continued through Reverend Claudius Henry's suspected coup, and the Walter Rodney protests of the 1960s. Black resistance also manifested itself over the brutality of some Chinese merchants, and through the controversial and conscious lyrics of popular songs, especially those belonging to the genre of reggae music. These are the major themes which form the basis of this chapter.

The Maroon Wars

The Maroon wars were one one of the earliest forms of organised Black resistance in Jamaica. The Spaniards started colonialism in Jamaica when they arrived in 1494, which continued until 1655 when the British attacked them and captured the colony. The indigenous people were exterminated by starvation, forced labour and diseases the Spaniards brought to the Americas, such as small pox among others (Crosby, 2003). This loss of labour influenced the Spaniards to import captives from Africa. Some of these captive Africans subsequently attacked their captors and escaped into the mountains and became the first Maroons. These violent acts of liberation were some of the early forms of Black resistance in Jamaica. Spaniards could not defeat these runaways and liberated peoples, who became a constant threat to the colonialists. These free Africans practiced guerilla warfare, and became known for their hit and run attacks, backed by the element of surprise. The Maroons decided that they would never again become captives and violently defended their freedom. The resistance of these original Maroons was a continuation of the Black resistance started in Africa and laid the foundation for the Black radical tradition in Jamaica, where Black people challenged the system in various ways for their right to freedom (Greggus, 1981; Wilson, 2009).

The Maroons violently clashed with the British in defense of their freedom from 1665 when the British took over the control of the island. There were several groups of Maroons which were called the Western or Leeward Maroons and the Eastern or Windward Maroons because they resided in the mountainous interior of the Eastern and Western sections of the colony respectively. These Maroon communities, like their fore-parents, were skilled guerilla fighters who constantly defeated and out-smarted the British regiments employed to pursue the Africans who fled the plantations to join the Maroons. The Obeah worldview and the military prowess of the Maroon leaders gave them the ability to maintain loyalty among their followers. The Maroons fought major battles against the British in the First Maroon War (1729-1739) and the Second Maroon War (1795-1796). These Black freedom fighters successfully resisted the British, who had one of the most powerful military forces at the time (Greggus, 1981; Wilson, 2009).

The British Government was eventually forced to make peace with them in 1739. The Maroons gained several concessions from the British in the successful defense of their freedom. They gained the right to bear arms, perpetual freedom and land. However, Maroons in turn agreed to defend the colony on behalf of the British if it was attacked by rival European powers. They also agreed to return captive Africans who fled the plantations. The two sides, over time, interpreted the treaty to suit their own interests. Occasionally, the Maroons violated the treaty by raiding the plantations for fighters and women when they needed human capital. The Maroons had an uneasy peace with the British because of their twin strategy of accommodation and resistance. The colonial authorities, over time also sought to reduce the powers of the Maroons through their reinterpretation of the treaty in an attempt to get more concession to suit their own interests.

Two Maroons who stole sheep from a plantation were caught and flogged by the overseer. The captive Africans jeered the Maroons before they were taken to jail. The insult and humiliation felt by the Maroon communities over the incident triggered the Second Maroon War. The captive Africans hated the Maroons because they honoured their treaty obligations with the British, particularly the issue of capturing and returning captive Africans who fled the plantations (Greggus, 1981; Wilson, 2009). This hatred is still felt by some Afrocentric Jamaicans today who argue that the Maroons were traitors. However, there is a counter view by Lewis (1989) who argues that the Maroons saw themselves as a separate ethnic group and did not think in racial terms, so they were willing to return runway captives in return for their own freedom. Moreover, Jamaica was a colony and not a state, so there wasn't a Jamaican national identity that would emotionally connect the Maroons to their fellow Africans. Despite the ill feeling that some Jamaicans hold for the Maroons of the past and the present, it is an undeniable fact that the Maroons were major players in the Black radical tradition.

Rebellions of the Captive Africans

Maronage was one major form of resistance, but the rebellions of the captive Africans in Jamaica were extensive and relentless. The British developed commercial plantations in the 1700s which increased the demand for African labour. The majority of the commercial plantations cultivated sugar, which was labour intensive. The captive Africans engaged in non-violent resistance such as refusing to work, working slowly, pretending to misunderstand work instructions, feigning illness, deliberately breaking tools, sabotaging the work and destroying crops. Other forms of non-violent resistance used by the captives were publicly participating in African rituals, displaying African symbols, cursing their captors, attending the church of their choice, marrying without the permission of their captors, dictating the terms and content of their education in the schools they were allowed to attend a few years before emancipation, challenging their captivity in the courts and running away from the plantations (Dunkley, 2013).

The Africans also engaged in violent resistance such as poisoning their captors, individually attacking their captors, and rebelling collectively. Jamaica experienced more captive rebellions than other British colonies in the Caribbean. Primordial ethnic loyalties divided the Africans when they arrived in Jamaica. However, the different African ethnic groups over the years developed a radical Black identity because they intermingled on the sugar estates and the other areas of the plantation economy. The continuation of the resistance and the development of a Black identity, led to more organised revolts which occurred with tedious frequency in Jamaica. The stand out rebellion, however, was the one which occurred in 1832, known generally as the Christmas Rebellion led by Samuel Sharpe, a deacon in the Baptist Church. This rebellion had a significant impact both in Jamaica and in Britain regarding the eventual fate of Caribbean slavery as an economic and political system. This was because it was a very organised, integrated and much larger collective resistance that indicated to the planters that African captivity could not continue for much longer because of the increasing violent resistance. The threat of the captives to the colonial system was one of the major factors that influenced the British Government to emancipate the captives in 1834 (Robotham, 1988; Williams, 1966).

The Morant Bay Rebellion

Precisely beause the legal emancipation of slavery in the British Caribbean, was not accompanied by any degree of political or economic freedom, within a generation, a major rebellion took place in St Thomas in the easern part of the island. The Morant Bay Rebellion of 1865 continued the tradition of resisting White domination in the emancipation period. The demise of African enslavement in 1834 and the end of the apprenticeship in 1838 led to economic turmoil. The majority of Africans left the plantations and became small peasant farmers. The decline of the plantation system and its effects on the colonial economy continued for decades. The 1860s saw rising prices and rising unemployment and the deteriorating economic situation was made worse by drought. This situation and grievances the people had with the colonial government, such as inequality and the injustices they faced influenced the Baptist deacon, Paul Bogle to lead a group of people from St. Thomas to Kingston to meet with the Governor in 1865. The Governor refused to meet with the people (Dick, 2010; Post, 1978; Robotham, 1984).

The people were persistent. On their return to St. Thomas, the petitioners were accused of disrupting a courtroom trial in Morant Bay on October 7, 1865. The police issued warrants for the arrest of the petitioners. The militia that was sent to execute the warrant could not find the people in their village. The militia destroyed the village. The people were enraged by the destruction of their village. These angry people under the leadership of Paul Bogle armed themselves and proceeded to the Morant Bay Courthouse. Paul Bogle admonished his followers to cleave to the Black. This radical call for Black unity fueled the resolve of the people. The militia at the courthouse attacked the people. In the violence that ensued, the courthouse was set ablaze, and fifteen White officials and three planters were killed. This attack of the system was the most violent since the 1832 Christmas rebellion. The British sought the help of Maroon trackers who captured the rebel leaders and turned them over to the British. The British hanged the leaders of the rebellion without a trial. The Crown Colony Government, which was established in response to the rebellion removed the limited suffrage and increased the power of the governor (Fullweiler, 2000; Post, 1978 Robotham, 1984; Zeidenfelt, 1952).

The help of the Maroons was not localised in St Thomas. It was part of a larger assistance given to the British during the period of unrest in 1865. According to one of the Jamaican newspapers of the period:

> It having been ascertained that the main body of the rebels who had committed the outrages at Morant Bay had moved on to Port Antonio, in the parish of Portland, and seized a lot of ammunition by the Bay, His Excellency the Governor at once proceeded to that place with Troops and artillery, and issued an address, calling upon the loyal Maroons, who quickly answered the call to come out and aid the authorities to put down the Rebellion. The honorable Alexander Gordon Fyfe, member of the legislative council, and the colonel of the Maroons, was dispatched towards them (*The Colonial Standard and Jamaica Despatch*, 1865, October 24: p. 4).

The Maroons seemed eager to assist the governor to put down the rebellion as the writer of the newspaper article described, 'his reception by this loyal and well affected people' as 'most enthusiastic' (p.4). The newspaper article went on to note that, 'The Maroons crowded him and professed their devotion to the Queen and to him. They assured the governor of their readiness to aid in suppressing the rebellion, on being furnished with arms, and to protect Portland' (*The Colonial Standard*, October 24, 1865, p.4). The conclusion could be drawn that the Maroons wanted to get their hands on ammunition for their own protection and not ostensibly to help the British Governor. However, the same newspaper article further noted that, 'four hundred Maroons volunteered their services to the governor at Port Antonio for the protection of the place' (*The Colonial Standard*, October 24, p. 4).

The support from the Maroons enabled the maintenance of British rule (*The Jamaica Guardian*, 1865, November 15, p. 2). The resistance and concomitant fighting tactics of the Maroons were therefore praised by the British, who noted that 'This bush fighting is the speciality of the Maroons, who were great hunters, quick of eye, fleet of foot, and, are learned, in all the tortuous and winding shifts that bush warfare demands. Their manner consists of covering themselves with branches of leaves so as to seem as part of the surrounding foliage, and by such means, throw the pursued off their guard (*The Jamaica Guardian*, 1865, November 15, p 2). The Morant Bay Rebellion, therefore, was a major event in the Black radical tradition which was remembered three decades later by Alexander Bedward, whose religious ideas challenged the colonial system (Fullweiler, 2000; Post, 1978 Robotham, 1984; Zeidenfelt, 1952).

Alexander Bedward

The Jamaica Native Baptist Free Church which was founded in 1889 by H.E.S Wood in August Town, St. Andrew, became an institutional conduit for the Black radical tradition. The church was transformed by one of its elders, Alexander Bedward, into a social movement with ideas that challenged British colonialism. A popular ritual at the church was a bath in the Mona River dubbed the healing stream. Black people came to the church from all over the country to be baptised. Some Bedwardites believed that their leader was Jesus Christ. This belief challenged the doctrine of the status quo that God is white. Bedward further alarmed the colonial authorities when he asked his followers to remember the Morant War. This call on Black historical memory rejected the colonial framing of the Morant Bay Rebellion as the "notorious riot" and embraced it as a war that should be celebrated and honoured because it was waged against the White oppressors. Bedward's call broke the law (Post, 1978).

The warrant that was issued for Bedward's arrest by the colonial authorities was instructive. Quoting Bedward, the warrant read in part:

> We (meaning thereby the Black subjects of our said lady the Queen in this island) are the true people; White men are hypocrites, robbers and thieves; they are liars. Hell will be your portion if you do not rise up and crush the White men. The time is coming, I tell you the time is

coming. There is a White wall and a Black wall, and the White wall has been closing around the Black wall; but now the Black wall has become bigger than the White wall, and they must knock the White wall down. The White wall has oppressed us for years and now we must oppress the White Wall (cited in Post, 1978, p.7).

Bedward refused to recant and repeated the same statement at his 1895 trial. He pleaded guilty on the grounds of mental disorder and was freed. However, the Governor committed Bedward to the mental asylum on the Queen's pleasure. Bedward's lawyer intervened and he was freed on a legal technicality (Post, 1978).

The religious doctrine and rituals of the Free Native Baptist Church became established beliefs and practices among Bedward's followers, which spread because the social movement grew rapidly from 1895 to 1921. There were several confrontations between the government and Bedward in 1921. In one of these incidents Bedward announced that on April 27, 1921 he and his followers would march to Kingston. Following the announcement the government issued a warrant for Bedward's arrest. The Royal Sussex Regiment and the police intercepted the marchers who were dressed in white robes and carried a white cross and a palm tree. The police arrested Bedward and six hundred and eighty five marchers who were brought before the court. The followers were convicted of vagrancy while their leader was found to have a mental disorder. Bedward was committed to the asylum and died there in 1930 (Campbell, 1987; Post, 1978).

The ideas and activities of Bedward were non-violent but the governor would not tolerate rhetorical challenges to White supremacy in the colony because he feared it would mobilise Black people to engage in organised forms of sustained resistance against the colonial authorities. Therefore, Black leaders who challenged British oppression in the early twentieth century were deemed to be mentally ill and psychiatrically incarcerated.

At this point it is important to briefly address a contemporary myth about Bedward. This myth states that before Bedward was arrested in 1921 he gathered his followers in August Town where they would ascend to heaven. A search of the online archives of the *Daily Gleaner* during the period of Bedward activities did not yield any articles about the plan to fly to heaven. In response, to the harassment from the colonial establishment including the *Daily Gleaner*, Bedward summoned his followers from all over the country for a mass service in August Town. He told his followers to sell their sins and that his spirit would ascend to heaven which was common parlance among people of this religious tradition. The mobilisation of his followers, some of whom sold their possessions, was a show of political power. Bedward did not say he and his followers would fly to heaven. However, the story about flying to heaven suddenly appeared in the *Gleaner* in the 1960s (Harris, personal communication, 2001). The important point to bear in mind is that the liberating ideas of Bedward did not die with him in 1930 but found new expressions in the philosophy and activities of Marcus Garvey.

Marcus Garvey

The philosophy of Marcus Garvey is at the zenith of the Black radical tradition. Garvey experienced colourism and racism as the supportive ideologies of British colonialism while growing up in Jamaica. Garvey, looking at the history of Black people and their continued oppression and miseducation in the West, felt that it was important to raise the racial consciousness of Blacks globally. He was influenced by Black Nationalism and Ethiopianism, which had its genesis in the 1870s in South Africa when the Africans started their own church because of the White racism they experienced in the Dutch Reform Church. The leaders of Ethiopianism argued that African redemption was at hand and Africa was for the Africans. Garvey embraced Ethiopianism. This embrace by Garvey triggered the development of a radical Black identity, which he used to interpret Black oppression in Jamaica in particular and the world in general. He was bothered by the fact that White domination could not be challenged peacefully because of the low level of racial consciousness among Blacks which prevented peaceful collective resistance (Campbell, 1987).

Garvey assessed the racial situation in Jamaica in 1916 thus:

> Jamaica is unlike the United States where the race question is concerned. We have no open race prejudice here, and we do not openly antagonise one another. The extremes here are not between White and Black hence we have never had a case of lynching or anything so desperate. The Black people here form the economic asset of the country, they number six to one of Coloured and Whites combined and without them in labour or general industry the country would go bankrupt. The Black people have seventy -eight years of emancipation but all during that time they have never produced a leader of their own, hence they have never been led to think racially but in common with the destinies of the other people with whom they mix as fellow citizens. After emancipation, the Negro was unable to cope intellectually with his master and perforce he had to learn at the knees of his emancipator. He has therefore grown with his master's ideal and up to today you will find the Jamaican Negro unable to think apart from the customs and ideals of his old slave masters. Unlike the American Negro, the Jamaican never thought of race ideals much to his detriment, as instead of progressing generally, he has become a serf in the bulk and a gentleman in the few (Cited in Lewis, 1998a, p. 229).

The extensive quotation from Garvey above reveals that he analysed the social control of Black people in Jamaica by the colonial institutions and articulated the absence of lynching as an extreme form of racism in Jamaica. The absence of lynching does not mean that White racism did not exist. The difference Garvey alluded to was that Jamaican Negroes were the numerical majority and American Blacks were the numerical minority, so there were differences in the dynamics of oppression and collective consciousness that guided their behaviour. However, both groups were the oppressed sociological minority. Garvey was also concerned about the absence of a Black leader who could mobilise Black Jamaicans around their racial identity and not so much that there were no Negro leaders.

With this kind of in depth analysis Garvey saw the need for organising Blacks, raising their racial consciousness and pride with a view to Black liberation and economic empowerment. Garvey therefore formed the Universal Negro Improvement Association (UNIA) in Jamaica in 1914. His central arguments were race first, economic empowerment through self-reliance, Black Nationalism, the centrality of Africa and the liberation of Blacks from mental slavery. Garvey also ran for a seat in the 1929 Local Government Elections and was elected as a Parish Councilor in the Kingston and St. Andrew Corporation for the Allman Town division in Jamaica. He also formed the People's Political Party in 1927. He mobilised among the masses and held weekly meetings and activities at Eldeweis Park where he articulated his philosophy and held cultural activities. Garvey's Headquarters in Jamaica was at Liberty Hall in Downtown Kingston. Each division of the UNIA was required to have a Liberty Hall, which was the administrative, political, cultural and financial centre of the UNIA (Lewis, 1988, 1998a).

His ideas influenced some of the leaders of the 1938 labour protests, the black feminist movements and the establishment of the Peoples National Party (PNP). Garvey further argued that Blacks should rise up as one nation. To this end he used the slogan of Ethiopianism, 'Africa for Africans both at home and abroad,' though as chapter nine of this study discusses, this phrase had previously been used by some Black people in the nineteenth century, but was made universally popular by Garvey in the twentieth century. This philosophy of Black Nationalism was economic and psychological. Garvey used his experience as a printer to spread his message of Black unification within the UNIA, which was aimed at developing Black pride and inculcating Black self-identity. The UNIA also provided a forum for the galvanising of Black people on the road to Black Nationalism. The philosophy of Garvey included repatriation of Blacks to Africa, the owning of Black businesses and a swelling of Black pride through marches and mass meetings. These activities were aimed at undoing the damage caused by slavery and continued racism against Blacks in the United States and elsewhere (Lewis, 1988, 1998a).

Although Garvey was more successful in increasing Black pride by his resistance to White domination and the integration of Blacks as a dominant force in American and Jamaican society, his business skills were not quite as successful. In the early years of the UNIA it had a membership of almost one million people worldwide with almost five hundred thousand in the United States alone. The UNIA grew rapidly in the United States in 1921 and was in decline by the 1930s. In the first half of the twentieth century the UNIA was the largest and most successful Pan-African movement in the world. The movement initially captured the imagination of Blacks as a viable alternative to their sufferings and lack of racial identity in countries in which they were relegated to the role of sub-altern groups. Garvey's philosophy became a rallying cry for the oppressed Blacks and brought a belief in Black mass movements as a way of righting some of the wrongs of racism through racial unity and racial pride (Lewis, 1988, 1998a).

Garvey congratulated His Majesty *Ras Tafari* when he ascended to the Ethiopian throne in 1930. *Ras Tafari* was also congratulated in the *Negro World* (New York edition) and Garvey penned an article for the *Blackman* newspaper in Jamaica. Garvey also challenged the European argument that Ethiopia was not a part of Africa and highlighted the many European political leaders and royalties that attended the coronation of *Ras Tafari*. Garvey also started the Black Star Liner Shipping Company in the United States. The many business ideas such as the Blackman newspaper, Black Star Liner, the UNIA, and *Negro World* newspaper were all intended to be the economic force behind his Black Nationalist philosophy. Garvey was not a good businessman and the shipping company failed. Despite Garvey's huge popularity in the United States among Black Americans he was at odds with some Black American leaders because he preached racial separation and a return to Africa and these leaders were fighting for Black Americans' acceptance and racial integration in the United States. Therefore, when the shipping business failed and many UNIA members were angry about losing the shares they had bought in the company, Garvey never got the support of many Black American leaders. The complaints by shareholders led to the arrest and conviction of Garvey for mail fraud in the United States in 1923. He was deported to Jamaica when he was released from prison in 1927 (Lewis, 1988, 1998a). Despite his demise in the United States, Marcus Garvey, and not Bob Marley, is the most popular and loved Jamaican among Blacks in that country. Even in the establishment of Rastafari in Jamaica, Garvey's influence could be felt, even though he was not a Rastafari.

Leonard Howell and Rastafari

It can be argued that Leonard Howell was the first Rasta and thereby a crucial figure in the establishment of Rastafarianism. The early 1930s saw the manifestation of Rastafarianism because Garvey inspired Jamaicans challenged the colonial system and institutions that were oppressing them. Rastafarianism arose in response to the oppressive socioeconomic and racist political system. The early Rastafarians who developed an anti-systemic identity or radical Black identity critiqued the colonial system and affirmed the African self and presence. Encounters that the early

Rastafarians had with colonialism and the existential questions they had, triggered a process of becoming Black through religious conversion. This Black religious identity or moral blackness vehemently rejected colonialism and publicly displayed African ideas, symbols and sociocultural traditions (Price, 2009).

The Rastas used the Bible as a basis to declare the divinity of Emperor Haile Selassie of Ethiopia. They drew heavily on Revelation chapter 5 and in particular verse 5 which read thus, 'And one of the elders saith unto me, weep not: behold the Lion of the tribe of Judah, the Root of David hath prevailed to open the book, and to loose the seven seals thereof' (King James Version, 2000). The Rastafarians interpreted the Lion of the Tribe of Judah to be Emperor Haile Selassie who was the two hundred and twenty fifth King in the ancestral lineage from King Solomon and the Queen of Sheba. Since Selassie was from King Solomon's lineage he received the title "Lion of the Tribe of Judah." King David was Solomon's father so Emperor Haile Selassie came from the Root of David. The Rastafarians also ascribed the title of Kings of Kings to Emperor Haile Selassie. Selassie's coronation as the Emperor of Ethiopia in 1930 made him Ras of all the Rases. He was deemed the Emperor of all the Emperors (King of all Kings) in Ethiopia. These titles helped to cement the divination of Emperor Haile Selassie in the Rastafarian worldview (Campbell, 1987; Lewis, 1998a).

The statement by Garvey that Blacks should look for the Black King that would be crowned in the East because this King was the Black redeemer and deliverer were interpreted by the Rastafarians as prophecy fulfilled by the crowning of Ras Tafari Makonnen in 1930 as Emperor of Ethiopia. This prophecy was backed by Psalms 68, 31, which states that 'Princes shall come out of Egypt, [and] Ethiopia shall soon stretch out her hands unto God' (King James Verson 2000). The coronation of Emperor Selassie was also buttressed by his success in holding off the invading colonial forces of Italy led by Mussolini even before the Italian invasion of Ethiopia in October 1935. Although forced into exile in May 2,

1936, Emperor Haile Selassie continued his resistance against the occupying forces and eventually re-entered Addis Ababa in May 5, 1941, when the Ethiopian forces were able to defeat the army of Mussolini and regain control of Ethiopia in 1942 (Campbell, 1987; Lewis, 1998a).

The first person to reportedly hold public meetings where he preached that Rastafari was the King of Kings and Lord of Lords was Leonard Howell. Howell also sold the picture of Rastafari to the people. There were other early Rasta preachers such as Joseph Nathaniel Hibbert, Archibald Dunkley and Robert Hinds. Howell's doctrine challenged the colonial system because he preached that God is Black, which refuted the establishment doctrine of a White God (Campbell, 1987; Lewis, 1998a). He argued that the allegiance of Jamaicans was to Emperor Haile Selassie of Ethiopia and not the British Monarch. Howell at the end of one of his street meetings asked the crowd to sing 'God save the king' and after the completion of the song Howell told the gathering that the king was Emperor Haile Selassie. The new revelation articulated by Howell and the other street preachers were inspired by Garveyism (Campbell, 1987; Lewis, 1998a). The early Rastafarians used Afrocentric hermeneutics to counter the Eurocentric interpretations of the Bible. These early preachers read documents such as *The Promised Key, The Living Testament of Rastafari* and *The Rastafari Manifesto*. The interpretation of these books contradicted the Eurocentric interpretations of the Bible (Campbell, 1987; Lewis, 1998a).

Today there are three main Mansions or Houses of Rastafari. These are the Nyabinghi, Boboshanti and the Twelve Tribes of Israel. Not all Rastafarians are members of these Houses. Generally Rastafari from its inception in the 1930s have rejected Babylon (spiritual wickedness) and they have articulated racial consciousness and racial pride with the centrality of Africa. Rastafarians, with their radical aesthetic physicality, have also replaced the European worldview with an African cosmology, the White God with a Black God, and heaven with repatriation to Ethiopia. This repatriation is now mostly a spiritual one. Word sounds or the use of words to navigate their social world is very evident among Rastafarians. For example, marijuana is called 'herb' and not 'weed,' they do not 'understand but 'overstand,' they do not speak of 'next week' but 'next strong', there is no 'oppressor' but a 'downpressor' and so on. They have also replaced the title 'Mr' with King and My Lord, and 'Miss' with 'Empress' because these titles herald the majesty of the Black race. Rastafarians in their expression of the Black radical tradition have influenced language, diet, music and the racial consciousness of Blacks people globally. Similarly, the ideas of Rastafarians and Marcus Garvey influenced the grassroots leaders of the 1938 labour protests.

The Labour Riots of the 1930s

Black Jamaicans continued their quest and struggle for personhood, economic justice, and civil and political rights. These quests and struggles led to the 1938 riots because of the crises of inadequate social integration, economic distribution, and political participation. The Black majority was not integrated into the society because it was socially marginalised. Black workers received starvation wages under poor working conditions. Also, Black peoples' hope of political participation was blocked by the White political hegemony associated with the Crown Colony Government. These three crises were contested by Garvey's economic nationalism and Ethiopianism that increased the racial consciousness of the masses. The situation was made worse by the fall in wages caused by the economic depression of the international capitalist system during the period 1929-1932 and its lingering consequences during the rest of that decade. Hunger marches occurred in the early 1930s. Banana workers rioted in Oracabessa, St. Mary, in May 1935, when the planters imported labour from Port Maria to keep wages low. In the same month, dock workers rioted in Falmouth and the banana loaders of ships at Kingston's wharf went on strike. The Jamaica Development Convention created by Garvey became the Workers and Labour Association in June 1936. The Jamaica Workers and Tradesmen's Union was also formed in 1936 because the masses were applying pressure from below in an attempt to resolve the crisis of economic distribution by creating new institutions with positive meanings (Campbell, 1987; Hart, 1989; Post, 1978).

Two years later, in 1938, on the 100th anniversary of Emancipation, the Black Jamaican sufferers once more revolted against the White sugar barons and the colonial state. On January 5, 1938, about one thousand four hundred workers of the Serge Island Sugar Estate in St. Thomas armed themselves with machetes and sticks, and went on strike against the starvation wages and the semi-slavery working conditions. The repressive colonial authorities unleashed the police on the workers and sixty were arrested and thirty four injured. In Westmoreland, on April 28, 1938, workers on the Frome Sugar Estate challenged the conglomerate Tate and Lyle by rejecting their wage offer of 2 shillings and 6 pence per day and demanded 4 shillings per day. The police shot at the protesting sufferers, four of whom were killed, including a pregnant worker. A further one hundred and five workers were arrested. In Kingston, Alexander Bustamante co-opted the striking dockworkers and street protesters by articulating their grievances to the colonial authority. Bustamante's intervention restored calm to the Frome Sugar Estate. Bustamante and labour leader St. William Grant were subsequently arrested for inciting an unlawful assembly (Campbell, 1987; Hart, 1989, 1999; Post, 1978).

The lawyer, Norman Manley, a cousin of Bustamante, who built his legal career on the defense of the local and international capitalists, mediated between the workers and the colonial authorities. The workers refused to end their protest until their arrested leaders were released. The workers relented only after the colonial authority established procedures for the inspection and enforcement of safety standards in the sugar factories, legalised trade unionism through labour legislation, and created the Workers' Compensation Law and the Servants' Law. The Jamaican peasantry did not reach the level of class consciousness required to effectively overthrow British rule. These two Mulatto (dual or mixed heritaged) middle class leaders, as the historical social buffer between Whites and Blacks, negotiated between capital and labour, thereby assuming leadership of the labour movement and blunted the radicalism of Black labour (Campbell, 1987; Hart, 1999; Post, 1978).

The colonialists thanked Manley for his intervention in which he articulated the grievances of the masses within the structures of the rule of law. In this way, Manley and Bustamante became leaders of the Black masses because of their involvement in the 1938 protests. Manley and Bustamante's co-optation of the nascent labour movement (and subsequently the nationalist movement) was a function of their intermediate social position in the society defined by their light complexion and their normative colonial socialisation. This socialisation led to the socially shared belief that the Mulatto social group was ordained at Emancipation to govern Blacks. However, many Black leaders rejected this belief system (Campbell, 1987; Hart, 1999; Post, 1978).

Riding on the momentum of the 1938 protests, Bustamante, in response to the crisis of distribution, used his personality and organisational skills to merge several trade unions to create the Bustamante Industrial Trade Union. Bustamante concentrated on unionism and left agitation for political participation to Manley. The People's National Party (PNP) led by Norman Manley was formed in September 1938, in response to the crisis of political participation. Alexander Bustamante became a member of the PNP. In April 1939, the PNP at its first convention demanded universal adult suffrage and full self-government. The British felt that pluralist electoral competition (in particular, the values of Westminster democracy) was best served by two competing political parties, and encouraged Bustamante to form the Jamaica Labour Party (JLP) which was launched on June 8, 1943 (Hart, 1999; Zeidenfelt, 1952). Thus, in an indirect manner, the social unrest and Black resistance movements of the masses resulted in the formation of the country's major political parties.

The British granted constitutional changes under the aegis of the Moyne Commission in 1944. The constitutional changes went beyond what both Bustamane and Manley anticipated because their limited expectations were constrained by their colonial worldview and socialisation. There was universal adult suffrage and internal self-government in which the Mulatto leaders became Westminster apprentices under a diarchy (Hart, 1999; Zeidenfelt, 1952). These events marked a retrogressive turning point in Black resistance in Jamaica. Electoral competition pitted JLP and PNP supporters against each other. Many Black Jamaicans were no longer interested in attacking the political system. They were caught up in fighting rival party members on behalf of their political party to give it the electoral advantage so that it forms the government. However, there were still Afrocentric Black people who continued to challenge the system (Lacey, 1977). One such individual was Claudius Henry.

Claudius Henry

Claudius Henry, a returnee from the United States in 1957, was not content with the status quo. He became impressed with the liberating ideas of the Rastafarians and joined the movement and established the Africa Reform Church. Henry dubbed himself the Repairer of the Breach, particularly in relation to the Rastafarian demand for repatriation to Africa. Some of Claudius Henry's supporters led by his son, Ronald Henry, believed that the oppressive conditions of the Black masses could only be solved by armed struggle similar to that which had occurred during the Cuban Revolution. Ronald Henry called on Black Jamaicans to violently rise up against the divisive and manipulative political system led by the JLP and the PNP. The younger Henry and some supporters were killed in a confrontation with the Royal Hampshire Regiment in 1963. Claudius Henry was accused of supporting these militant activities and was convicted of treason in 1963. Henry was released from Prison in 1968 and the police targeted his New Creation Peacemakers Association (Campbell, 1987; Gray, 1991). The Late Rastafarian Patriarch, and mentor of Bob Marley, Mortimo "Kumi" Planno rejected the assertion that Claudius Henry was a Rastafarian (Niaah, 2005). However, what is certain is that the ideas of Claudius Henry, and the actions of Roland Henry and his followers violently resisted the colonial establishment.

The Coral Garden incident

In the independence period Black people in Jamaica continued to press for greater levels of recognition and acceptability within the society. The country received political independence from Britain in 1962. The challenge to the system continued with the Rastafarians' consistent affirmation of the spirituality of the Black self, their nonconformist aesthetic physicality, and their critique of the socio-economic inequalities of the Brown and White hegemony in 'Babylon'. A major demand of the Rastafarians as mentioned earlier was their repatriation to Africa, which clashed with the Eurocentric values of the neo-colonial state. In 1963 some Rastafarians in the resort town of Montego Bay refused to stop walking across the Rose Hall property (which was later renamed Coral Gardens) that was being developed as a tourist attraction (Campbell, 1987).

The Rastafarians argued that they had a right to walk across the Half Moon property to get to their community, but the developers countered that the presence of the Rastafarians horrified the White tourists. The disagreement led to an altercation. The state accused the Rastafarians of setting a petrol station ablaze and killing two policemen. The Rastafarians vehemently denied these accusations. The state, in their response, unleashed the army and the police on the Rastafarian community. Eight people were killed, and men, women, and children who were not involved in the initial incidents, were arrested. The power elite in the newly independent Jamaica were not prepared to accept any challenge to the status quo as the fledgling nation embarked on creating its national identity, which meant continued economic and cultural marginalisation of the Black majority (Campbell, 1987).

The Anti-Chinese Riots

Black people were not only staging resisance campaigns against White colonialists, but also some Chinese employers in the country, some of whom engaged in extreme brutality towards their Black Jamaican workers. A brief background of the Chinese in Jamaica is necessary to understand the nature of the protests against two Chinese entreprenueurs. The unwillingness of the Africans in 1838 following the end of slavery and the apprentichsip system in the British Caribbean to work on the plantations, forced the planters to import indentured labourers from India and China to save the plantation economy. In 1854 some four hundred Chinese indentured labourers came to Jamaica, six hundred and ninety six arrived in 1884, and a further two thousand one hundred and eleven arrived between 1891 and 1911. The Chinese came as agricultural labourers, but by the 1900s they had become a commercial group involved in trading, grocery retailing, and rural banking. Within the Jamaica society, the Chinese and Indians fell into the middle strata of the racial hierarchy along with with the Mulattoes. The social consensus of the middle strata based on their common interests was that they were superior to Blacks. The colourism of the Mulattoes and the racism of the Chinese and Indians led to racial and ethnic hostilities between the Africans and these competing groups. However, there was some degree of miscegenation between the newly imported labourers and the

Black population because of the shortage of Chinese and Indian women (Alleyne, 2005; Ha, 1970).

Colourism, racism, and increasing inequality, which were the simmering antecedents in the early 1960s, led to increasing Black consciousness and the violent protests against some physically abusive Chinese employers in downtown Kingston in 1965. Three Chinese brothers reportedly beat a Black female employee in their store because of a disagreement about the payment installments on a radio. Versions of the incident spread rapidly among the masses who became enraged. Blacks retaliated against the flogging of the woman by looting and fire-bombing several Chinese stores because the representation embedded in the reported behaviour of the Chinese brothers, had a common oppressive meaning among Blacks that they would no longer tolerate the whipping which started with the captivity of their African ancestors. This incident and the increasing inequality after Independence increased the frustrations of the people and set the background for the increasing popularity of the Black Power Movement and the Rodney Riots (Lacey, 1977; Lewis, 1998b).

Walter Rodney

The Guyanese Walter Rodney was an icon of Black Power struggle in the Caribbean region and beyond. Rodney got his first degree with first class honours in history from the University of the West Indies in 1963. He graduated from the School of Oriental and African Studies in London in 1966 with a PhD in African History. Rodney travelled all over the globe including Africa, where he researched slavery in the Upper Guinea Coast. He had a strong sense of Black pride, which went beyond the narrow confines of racial prejudice (Lacey, 1977; Lewis, 1988b).

Rodney's sojourn in Jamaica escalated racial and ethnic tensions when he started the 'groundings' with his brothers, the Rastafarians and the urban poor. Walter Rodney taught that Black Power was not Black supremacy, but a counter to White oppression, which was required for Black liberation. Rodney argued that Black Power was against all those who were oppressing Blacks, including other Blacks (Campbell 1987; Lacey, 1977; Rodney, 1990a). Rodney's ideas and activities created tension with the privileged racial and ethnic groups and it should come as no surprise, therefore, that the government banned American Black Power activists from the country. Rodney (1990a, p.13), speaking with reference to the JLP Government's ban of American Black Power activists from Jamaica in the 1960s, stated:

> More recently, and at a time when the Black liberation struggle taking place against White racist American society is fiercest, these same political bandits felt sufficiently threatened by the power of the example of struggle to carry through the banning of Brothers Stokely Carmichael, H. Rap Brown, and James Forman. Even more damming has been their prohibition of the liberation literature of Carmichael, Malcolm X, and Elijah Mohammed, at a time when the world is celebrating International Human Rights Year, piously sponsored by the Jamaican government (Rodney, 1990a, p. 13).

He also criticised the police as state agents of Black oppression because of their activities in the 1960s. He said:

> Since independence, the Black police force of Jamaica have demonstrated that they can be as savage in their approach to Black brothers as the White police in New York, for ultimately they serve the same master. The Prime Minister has not concealed his determination that the police should be used to maintain the present system of social oppression, and he has given them full authority to utilise whatever brutal methods they think necessary to carry out their mandate (Rodney (1990a, p. 13)

On October 16, 1968, the government, in response to the perceived Black Power threat, banned Walter Rodney, who was a lecturer at the University of the West Indies, from returning to Jamaica after he attended the Congress of Black Writers in Canada. The Minister of Home Affairs, in defending the government's action, declared, 'In terms of my office and reading the records of problems in this country, I never came across a man who offers a greater threat to the security of this land than does Walter Rodney' (cited in Campbell, 1987, p. 132). However, Rodney did not advocate violence in the national polemic because he was killing ignorance and liberating minds as a 'guerilla intellectual.' The banning of Rodney triggered a protest march by students of the University of the West Indies who were subsequently joined by urban malcontents, who sympathised with Rodney. The protestors clashed with the police and in the ensuing riot some public busses and stores were damaged (Campbell, 1987; Charles, 2005b; Lewis, 1998b; Rodney, 1990b). The opposition leader in parliament, Norman Manley, criticised the banning of Rodney. Manley, as he did in 1938, strategically co-opted the Black Power social movement with the declaration 'I salute Black Power, which conveniently critiqued the status quo (Lacey, 1977, p. 35). Manley's declaration gained support for the PNP among Black radicals. However, Manley was deeply troubled by the ideas of Black Power, the Rastafarians' worldview and their desire to repatriate to Africa (Manley, 1996).

The White and Brown cultural sections attacked Black Power in the societal debate over national identity. The groups argued vehemently that Marcus Garvey should not be made a national hero because he had not contributed to national development. Black intellectuals influenced by Black Power countered that Garvey's work raised the dignity and the self-respect of the Black majority in Jamaica. This consciousness-raising meant that Garvey had, even if indirectly, contributed to national development (Charles, 2010). These debates and resistance struggles have continued not only within academic circles in Jamaica, but also in Jamaican popular music especially during and after the 1970s.

Jamaican Popular Music

The period of modern popular music dated back to the increasing inequality and the political wars of the 1960s, their escalation in the 1970s with democratic socialism coupled with economic decline, the heyday of the Cold War. These culminated in hundreds of Jamaicans being killed in 1980 because of the violent general election fought between the PNP and the JLP supporters. Political violence has declined significantly since 1980 but still occurs. The divisions, experiences and orientations of political tribalism, the development of a subculture of violence, the reduction in informal social controls in the society, corruption and chronic underdevelopment, have turned Jamaica into one of the most murderous countries in the world. The homicide rate reached a high of 63 per 100,000 of the population in 2005 (Harriott and Katz, 2015). The forgoing is imperative in providing a useful background to understanding the lyrical wailings in some of the Jamaican popular songs.

Regae music is sometimes called resistance music although not all reggae artistes engage in resistance work. Although the focus in this section is on reggae music, resistance work has occurred in the various genres of Jamaican popular music such as mento, ska, rocksteady, roots nyahbinghi, reggae, dub, dancehall and one beat. Cultural studies scholar, ethnomusicologist and Grammy nominated reggae producer Dennis Howard after interviews with Ras Michael and others, have argued that roots nyahbinghi and dub are also Jamaica musical genres. Howard has also added the genre one beat after dancehall because dancehall has changed several times since its inception in the early 1980s and the current sound has one beat. The music is a reflection of the daily struggles of the marginalised, which is documented in songs, dub-poetry, dancehall, and sound clashes. The lyrics are drawn from the imaginative space where, according to Nettleford (1993) speaking about some of the modern influences on Caribbean society, noted that, 'The battle for space continues – between the mass of the population and an oligarchic few who would wish to freeze their current occupation of political and economic space into timeless legitimacy' (Nettleford, 1993, p.83). The lyrics of songs reflect the need of these marginalised people to change this societal status quo of which Nettleford spoke so eloquently to one in which they have a voice, hope, justice and equality. Just as we saw in chapter two of this book, their lyrics respond to their conditions as well as their call for attention to their plight. In the many themes and tropes used by some reggae artistes is an underlying resistance against the current system that leaves them marginalised and hopeless. Bob Andy (Keith Anderson) wrote the following lyrics that describes the lot of the poor and what awaits society if they are constantly marginalised:

My people, you're meeting hell
Brothers have turned to crime
So they die from time to time
We'd like to ask you leaders
What have you got in mind.
I see the fire spreading
It's getting hotter and hot
The haves will want to be
In the shoes of the have-nots
If the sign is on your door
Then you will be saved for sure
But if you are in pretense
You're on the wrong side of the fence

One of the many skills possessed by reggae artistes and in particular the writers of lyrics, is the ability to resist, protest and predict all at once within the same spatial confines of a song, which is the conduit of literary expression. Resistance and protest are born out of a long history of social malfeasance, which conditions the mind. Nettleford spoke about the extent to which 'abuse or denial of personal space by various means of social control, torture and miseducation has now become the norm in the Caribbean. He opined that 'this was a normal feature of Caribbean life under slavery and colonialism and continues, albeit in modified and subtle form(s), in Independence with the new perpetrators to be found among the native governors, the mimic men, and/or the neo-colonial superpowers brought in as allies in pursuit of hegemonic control of geographic spheres' (Nettleford, 1993, p. 82).

These marginalised people of Jamaican society who were engaged in musical creations and expressions did not confine their outlook and experiences to social issues in Jamaica. Although some were unlettered at the time of musical production, their sociological view of the world was organic. Their lyrical dialectics reflected the integrated view of injustice anywhere is injustice everywhere. They sang and toasted about the plight of marginalised people all over the globe through icons such as the Wailers, Burning Spear, The Abyssinians, Third World, Pabo Moses, Culture, Wailing Souls, Israel vibrations, Ras Michael and the Sons of Negus, Jacob Miller and Big Youth, just to name a few. Their consciousness touched the plight of disadvantaged peoples in South Africa, Namibia, Eritrea, Lesotho, Angola, Zimbabwe, Mozambique, Europe, North, South and Central America, and the Caribbean. The weight of their history of suffering and exploitation expanded their creative minds to empathise with subaltern peoples everywhere. Their lyrics were the weapon that they used to fight hegemonic systems such as Apartheid, colonialism, neo-colonialism, communisim, capitalism, genocide and other worldwide injustices.

Bob Marley in the song *War*, taken from Emperor Haile Selassie's speech in 1934 at the General Assembly of the League of Nations, showed his resistance to oppression globally. Marley stated in part:

Until the philosophy which holds one race superior
And another
Inferior
Is finally
And permanently
Discredited
And abandoned
Everywhere is war
Me say war.

Marley's solidarity with the oppressed was universal but in *War* he also spoke to Black oppression and suffering in Mozambique, Angola and South Africa in the 1970s and declared that there would be war until these countries were free from White rule. Similarly, it can be argued that the political wars and high levels of crime in Jamaica will remain high until injustices and oppression are abandoned by the JLP and PNP and their collaborators in the church, the private sector, and their masters in Washngton and London.

Burning Spear in *Slavery Days* says in part, 'Do you remember the days of slavery…And how they beat us…And how they worked us so hard.' Spear is continuing the resistance work of the ancestors by reminding us of the brutality and inhumanity of African captivity in the Americas. Spear, in the song *Marcus Garvey* stated that, 'Marcus Garvey's words come to pass.' He is reinforcing the Rastafarian worldview that Marcus Garvey is a prophet whose message has been fulfilled so this message should be heralded and celebrated.

The group Culture in *Capture Rasta* rejects the racist misinformation that Christopher Columbus discovered Jamaica. Columbus could not have discovered Jamaica when there were people living there before he arrived. They state in the first verse of the song:

Christopher Columbus him come from Spain Sah (Sir)

> When him sail him ship then him come a Jamaica
> Send go tell de (the) queen say him come – come discover
> But when mi (I) tek (take) a stock there was Red Indian

Culture declared in the chorus that 'Him a boast, say him capture Rasta. Him gone boast say him capture Rasta.' They sarcastically state Columbus (symbolic of the White downpressors and their Black allies) is boasting that Rastas have been captured which is impossible because the essence of Rastafarianism is Black liberation and redemption.

Anthony B in *Fire pon (on) Rome* harshly criticises and denounces the prime ministers of Jamaica and prominent private sector leaders for robbing Blacks after their African ancestors were dehumanised and exploited in captivity for centuries by Europeans. The chorus states:

> "Fire pon Rome
> Fi Pope Paul an (and) him scissors and comb
> Black people waan (want to) go home
> A mount Zion a di righteous throne"

Rome is symbolic of Babylon in the worldview of Rastafarians, which needs to be cleansed with the spiritual fire of righteousness. Rastafarians will not retreat from their Nazarene vow to grow their locks so they also burn the scissors used to cut hair and the comb used to groom it. Many Rastafarians in Jamaica continue to face discrimination in employment and positions of power because of their locked hair. Anthony B also argues that Blacks in the West want to return home to Mount Zion, which is Africa. The song in the tradition of Rastafarians lyrically and spiritually connects Blacks in the West to their ancestors and ancestral homeland, Africa. This push is a strident challenge to Afro-phobia in Jamaica where European values and symbols continue to be elevated above Afrocentric ones which are denigrated.

Chronixx in *Capture Land* attacks European colonisation. He states in part:

Lord America a capture land
Di whole a Jamaica a capture land
A long time dem (they) wah (want to) trick the Rasta
man
Like dem nuh (don't) know say man a real African
Yuh tink me nuh memba (you thought I did not
remember) King Ferdinand
And teifing (theifing) Columbus have a Golden plan
Dem make a wrong turn and end up in the Caribbean
One rass (rarce) genocide kill nuff (a lot of) Indian
Lord fi (to) turn paradise in a plantation
And bring cross one ship load a African
Now hear comes the teifing (thiefing) Queen from
England

Chronixx like Bob Marley, Bob Andy, Burning Spear and Anthony B among many others, continues to highlight and denounce the injustices in the past and present. So in *Capture Land* Chronixx argues that the West is captured land and called out some of the major perpetrators and symbols of European colonisation such as Christopher Columbus, King Ferdinand and the crooked Queen of England. The genocide of the Indians in the Americas and the traumatic transatlantic slave trade and their consequences were also denounced. Some one hundred and seventy seven years (1838-2015) after the end of African captivity in Jamaica, the descendants of the Africans, the singers and players of musical instruments continue the resistance work against neo-colonial domination started by the captive Africans. They resist by lyrically denouncing past oppression, current injustices and raising Black pride, consciousness and identity.

Conclusion

This chapter has demonstrated that much of the political, social and cultural history of Jamaica has been concerned with campaigns of Black reistance against European colonial systems of control or influence. These forms of resistance were clearly evident from the era of initial European contact until the present period. Violent and non-violent forms of African resistance were used to challenge African captivity, British colonialism and White supremacy in Jamaica. In fact, the chapter has demonstrated that Black resistance in Jamaica is part of a historical continuum because this resistance started in Africa and continues to this day. This resistance can be divided into the period before 1944 with universal adult suffrage and thereafter. The Black resistance up to 1944 was vertical or anti-system violence because the Africans sought to liberate themselves from captivity and colonial oppression. This violence of liberation became intra-system or horizontal violence, which was retrogressive, tribal and inward after 1944 because the supporters of the JLP and the PNP started fighting political wars and homicides peaked in 2005. Roland Henry's insurgency did not receive the support of the people. The anti-Chinese and Rodney riots were never meant to over throw the system because they were localised violence to protest perceived injustices. Rastafarians and other Afrocentric Blacks have continued with lyrical resistance against injustices and oppression in the society through Jamaican popular music despite the pro-system stance and justification of some Eurocentric Jamaicans.

References

Alleyne, Mervyn C. (2005). *The Construction and Representation of Race and Ethnicity in theCaribbean and the World,* Kingston, Jamaica, University of the West Indies Press.

Andy, Bob. (1974). *Fire Burning,* Kingston, Jamaica, Harry J label.

Austin, G. (2009b). *Cash Crops and Freedom: Export Agriculture and theDecline of Slavery in Colonial West Africa. IRSH, 54.*

Beckles, Hilary. (2013). *Britain's Black Debt: Reparations of Caribbean Slavery and Negative Genocide*, Kingston, Jamaica, University of the West Indies Press.

Campbell, Horace. (1987). *Rasta and Resistance: From Marcus Garvey to Walter Rodney.* Trenton, Africa World Press.

Charles, Christopher A.D. (2005). *Skin Bleaching, Race and Political Identity in Jamaica*, Unpublished manuscript.

Charles, Christopher, A.D. (2010). Skin Bleaching and the Representations of Skin Colour in Jamaican Culture, PhD dissertation, City University of New York.

Colonial Standard. (1865). *The Rebellion in St. Thomas in the East,* 24 October.

Crosby Jr. and Alfrew W. (2003). *The Columbian Exchange: The Biological and Cultural Consequences of 1492.* Santa Barbara, CA: Praeger.

Curto, Jose, C. (2008). Experiences of Enslavement in West Central Africa, *Social History, 41,* 381-415.

Dick, Devon. (2010). *The Cross and the Machete: Native Baptists of Jamaica, Identity, Ministry and Legacy*, Kingston, Jamaica, Ian Randle Publishers.

Dunkley, Daive. (2013). *Agency of the Enslaved: Jamaica and the Culture of Freedom in the Culture of Freedom in the Atlantic World*, New York: Lexington.

Eltis David. Lewis, Frank and Richardson, David. (2005). Slave prices, the African slave trade, and productivity in Caribbean, 1674-1807, *Economic History Review, LVIII,* 673-700.

Fullweiler, Howard, W. (2000). *The Strange Case of Governor Eyre: Race and the Victorian Frame of Mind, CLIO* 29:119-134.

Gertz, Trevor R. (2004). *Slavery and Reform in West Africa: Towards Eemancipation in the Nineteenth Century Senegal and the Gold Coast,* Athens, Ohio University Press.

Gray, Obika. (1991). *Radicalism and Social Change in Jamaica, 1960-1972,* Knoxville, University of Tennessee Press.

Greggus, David. (1981). Jamaica and the Saint Domingue Slave Revolt, 1791-1793, *The Americas,* 38, 219-233.

Hall, Gwendolyn, M. (2005). *Slavery and African Ethnicities in the Americas: Restoring the Links,* Chapel Hill: University of North Carolina Press.

Harris, Duane. (2001). *Personal Communication,* Former research assistant to Professor Monica Schuler.

Harriott, Anthony and Katz, Charles. (2015). Gangs in the Caribbean, Kingston, Jamaica, University of the West Indies Press.

Hart, Richard. (1999). *Towards Decolonization: Political, Labour and Economic Development in Jamaica, 1938-194,* Kingston, Jamaica, Canoe Press, University of the West Indies.

Ha, Jagdish C. (1970). Indentured Indian Migration.*Journal of Indian History* 48: 335-343.

Lacey, Terry. (1977). *Violence and Politics in Jamaica, 1962-1970,* Manchester University Press.

Lewis, Rupert. (1988). Garvey's Perspective on Jamaica, in *Garvey: His Work and Impact,* edited by Rupert Lewis and Patrick Bryan, Kingston, Jamaica, Institute of Social and Economic Research.

Lewis, Rupert. (1998a). Marcus Garvey and the early Rastafarians: Continuity and Discontinuity, in *The Rastafari Reader: Chanting Down Babylon* edited by Nathaniel S. Murrel, William D. Spencer and Adrian A. McFarlane, 145-158. Philadelphia: Temple University Press.

Lewis, Rupert. (1998b). *Walter Rodney: 1968 Revisited*, Kingston, Canoe Press.

Lewis, Rupert. (1989). Personal Commuication.

Lindsay, Louis, G. (1981a). *The Myth of Independence: Middle Class Politics and Non-Mobilisation in Jamaica*, Kingston, Jamaica, University of the West Indies, ISER.

Lovejoy, Paul. (2006). The Children of Slavery-the Transatlantic Phase, *Slavery and Abolition*, 27, 197-217.

Manley, Rachel. (1997). *Drumblair: Memories of a Jamaican Childhood*, New York, Vintage/Random House.

Martin, Tony. (2011). *Caribbean History: From Pre-Colonial Origins to the resent,*NewYork, Pearson.

Nettleford, Rex. (1993). *Inward Stretch Outward Reach: A Voice from the Caribbean*, London and Basingstoke, Macmillan Press.

Niaah, Jahlani. (2005). Personal Communication.

Perbi, Akosua A. (2004). *A History of Indigenous Slavery in Ghana: From the 15th to the 19th Century*. Accra: Sub-Saharan Publishers.

Post, Ken. (1978). *Arise ye Starvelings: The Jamaican Labour Rebellion of 1938 and its Aftermath*. London, Marinus Nijhoff.

Price, Charles R. (2009). *Becoming Rasta: Origins of Rastafari Identity in Jamaica*, New York, New York University Press.

Robotham, Donald. (1984). *The Notorious Riot: The Socio-economic and Political Base of Paul Bogle's Revolt*, Kingston, Jamaica, University of the West Indies, ISER.

Robotham, Donald. (1988). The Development of Black Ethnicity in Jamaica. In *Garvey: His Work and Impact* edited by Rupert Lewis and Patrick Bryan, 23-38, Kingston, Jamaica, University of the West Indies, ISER.

Rodney, Walter. (1990a). *The Groundings with My Brothers*, London, Bogle L'Ouverture Publications.

Rodney, Walter. (1990b). *Walter Rodney Speaks*, Trenton, Africa World Press, Inc.

Sertimer, Ivan Van. (2003). *They Came Before Columbus*, New York, Random House.

The Colonial Standard. (1865). *The Rebellions in St. Thomas in the East*. 24 October, p.4.

The Holy Bible. (2005). KJV large print compact bible. Nashville, Tennessee, Holman Bible Publishers.

Warner-Lewis, Maureen. (2003). *Central Africa in the Caribbean: Transcending Time, Transforming Culture*, Kingston, Jamaica, University of the West Indies Press.

Wiener, Leon. (1922). *Africa and the Discovery of America*, Philadelphia, Innes & Son.

Williams, Eric. (1966). *Capitalism and Slavery*, New York, Putnam..

Williams, Eric. (1970). *From Columbus to Castro*, New York, Vintage Books.

Wilson, K. (2009). The Performance of Freedom: Maroons and the Colonial Order in Eighteenth Century Jamaican and the Atlantic Sound. *William and Mary Quarterly*, LXVI, 45-86

Zeidenfelt, Alex. (1952). Political and Constitutional Developments in Jamaica, *The Journal of Politics* 14: 512-540.

CHAPTER SIX

Maryse Condé's *Heremakhonon* and the Fight for Caribbean Female Francophone Identity

Moussa Traoré

Introduction

Heremakhonon, written by the Guadeloupean writer, Maryse Condé and first published in 1976, can be perceived as the beginning of an important watershed within the history of Francophone Caribbean women writers. *Heremaknhonon* is the story of a young Black Gadeloupean who, in the twentieth century suffers from 'unhomliness' because she does not know, feel, and see where she belongs. That state of confusion and identity conflict leads her to embark upon a physical journey to Guinea, in Africa where she hopes to find her roots. Once in Guinea, she falls in love with a young man who is a minister in the Guinea Government and her search for identity then becomes a real romantic adventure. Her initial love for a romanticised Africa—which she thought would also be her home—ultimately becames a love affair with an African young man. This chapter is therefore the scrutinisation of the search for identity by a Caribbean Black young woman and beyond that, the chapter demonstrates that the Black Caribbean woman suffers from an identity crisis which some of them (like Veronica in this case) boldly attempt to cure by relocating to Africa. Unfortunately in the novel, Veronica's serach for her roots is not completely fulfilled, since she is not understood by the

Guineans (especially the young man whom she falls in love with, who simply sees in her a sex object). In the novel, Veronica realises that in Africa too, she does not 'fully' belong, since she is seen as a foreigner or Westerner because she came to Guinea from the Caribbean via France. The second reason that explains the 'failure' of her search for her roots is the fact that she landed in a continent and a country where the identity crisis she suffers from does not exist. She is, therefore, frustrated and misunderstood.

Although Condé had published a couple of plays before, *Heremakhonon* launched her character as a novelist who, within the next three decades or so, would explore in extremely novel ways, the intersections of colonialism, history, race, class, gender, identity and resistance within her work. *Heremakhonon* is undoubtedly a conventional 'return to Africa' story - a theme which has concerned writers and artists of the African Diaspora in important and interesting ways. Drawing upon her own experiences of spending time in Guinea, Condé's novel complicates the well-known trope of locating an unproblematic homeland within continental Africa. In several ways, her protagonist, Veronica Mercier, a Guadeloupean researcher and academic, reaches an unnamed nation, which by all accounts looks like Guinée in West Africa, via travelling to Paris. This becomes an embodiment of Condé's own admission that she was determined and prepared to 'encounter' Africa. Written in a first person narrative, Veronica's experiences as a teacher of philosophy in a local school, forms the backbone of Conde's novelistic narrative. While working as a teacher, Veronica becomes friends with Saliou, the director of the school and shortly afterwards, becomes the lover of Ibrahim Sory, the Minister of Defense and Interior. It is through these two relationships, that Veronica begins to witness postcolonial Africa, or more specifically, the ideological and political character of the post-colonial African state.

It will not come as a surprise, especially to readers of Frantz Fanon, that much of the representations of Africa in the works of the Caribbean Francophone writers have been influenced by Eurocentrism or Western modernity's construction of Africa. This chapter examines the extent to which this Eurocentric influence informs even some of those works that strive to be assertively and authentically 'Afro-Caribbean' for example, Maryse Condé's *Heremakhonon* (2000) and how such a Eurocentric influence tries to silence the brave resistance of Caribbean women who were opposed to the institution of slavery. Condé's novel is particularly interesting and useful to teach because it stays away from the platitudes of ethnicity. The purpose of this chapter is, therefore, to examine how the protagonist in the novel under study, Veronica Mercier, resists Eurocentrism and the derogatory qualifiers and treatment these earn her, and then fights to reconnect with her roots which she is convinced are in Africa. That gesture in itself is a fight for freedom and a genuine form of resistance. In this way, the chapter discusses how *Heremakhonon* is an example of a literary work which rides on one of the themes of Pan African resistance to Eurocentrism through a search for a feminist Black Caribbean identity. The condition from which Veronica is trying to escape is part of the general identity crisis of the Francophone Caribbean, which Fanon examines in *Black Skin White Masks (1967)*. The crippling nature of that alienation which is caused by physical and mental displacement and accentuated by Eurocentric indoctrination, is obvious when she refers to herself as a patient in *Heremakhonon*: 'I'm an invalid, Mr. Minister, seeking therapy. I could tell you a lot' (p.26) and the new stage, or the target in this quest is the stage of the 'Veronica who is healed' and 'reconciled with Africans and with herself' (p.56). The sickness to which Veronica refers, resonates with one of the general characteristics of the female rebel Caribbean slave. Thompson (2006) writes that one of the reasons behind the departure from the plantation or the world of slavery was fear and sickness. These two factors help to explain Veronica's desire to escape and her eventual departure to Africa.

Caribbean Women Caught Between Afrocentrism and Eurocentrism

Heremakhonon succeeds to some extent in discarding the Afrocentric myth, which is also one of the key features of some of the Diasporan writings. *Heremakhonon* shows the limits of Afrocentrism through two mediums: the first one is Veronica's treatment as a sex object at the hands of an African man, Ibrahima Sory, and the second one is the portrayal of socio-economic and political difficulties faced by African countries as portrayed in the example of Guinea in *Heremakhonon*. Jean Price Mars's *So Spoke the Uncle* (1983) to a minor extent, and Molefi Asante Kete's *Afrocentricity: The Theory of Social Change* (2003), present Africa as the incontestable cradle of humanity, the origin of the Black Diaspora and the location of the panacea to all the troubles that Black people currently face. Molefi Asante Kete's *Afrocentricity* especially, clearly adopts that stance. *Heremakhonon* adopts an opposite position and presents an image of Africa, that is confronted with ordinary daily challenges which are related to the socio-economic and political exigencies of the modern world. In that respect, *Heremakhonon* strips Africa of the Afrocentric myth of invincibility, although it is the continent where this main character of Veronica goes to, in her search for a home. She heavily relies on life on the African continent as a return to her roots and an escape from domination, neglect and the subaltern state of the subhuman into which she has been confined in the Caribbean and in Europe. However, it is equally important to point out that this chapter reveals that *Heremakhonon* is evidence that Africans made deliberate and free choices in their interactions with Europeans during the period of the post colonial era, and in doing that, the novel succeeds in the removal the foundations of Eurocentrism and Afrocentrism which have prevented the expression of individual and personal Francophone Caribbean identities.

As mentioned in the introduction to the chapter, in her self-discovery efforts, Veronica finds herself in Guinea, which is presented as an ordinary post-independence African country where newly elected African leaders try to establish a third way or non-aligned approach between the Western and the Eastern blocks during the Cold War era. *Heremakhonon*'s Guinea is emerging from several decades of French colonial rule and Mwalimwana, the president, is a dictator who relies on tribalism and the Marxist Leninist discourse to consolidate his power. By constructing such an image of Guinea, Condé shows the limits of Afrocentrism, and she also rejects the Eurocentric representation of Africa as a passive continent. The adaptation of Marxism and Leninism, key political doctrines of European Modernity by Guineans, shows that Africa also played an active role during this period of post colonial history. The description of the National Institute and its curriculum captures the daily social challenges that Guinea faces, and the political and ideological manoeuvres which the government is carrying out in *Heremakhonon*:

> This National Institute to which I had the bright idea of hiring my services does not look very sharp. A few mangy lawns. Two superb flame trees, however, and lots of mango trees in the yard. Some students in boubous are watching me. No use being afraid. They know nothing about me. Besides, their looks are full of kindness. One of them is smiling. So we have nine months together, a pregnancy, to discuss Marx, Kwame Nkrumah and other African avatars of Marxist doctrine (Condé 2000, p.19).

The Guinean youth in *Heremakhonon* are being as active, revolutionary and subversive as Manthia Diawara and his friends in 'Afro-Kitsch' (1992) show. The Guinean youth even go further in that radicalism by appropriating and adapting some of the cultural and artistic values of Western Modernity represented here by African American songs. This shows that Africa is not the passive sponge which absorbs everything that European Modernity presents her with. Of course, the sceptic could argue that these Africans are merely substituting American cultural domination for European cultural domination. But one could also argue that these young people are appropriating a form of Pan African resistance by adopting African American styles or genre of music and using it to discuss African themes and issues, in order to tell African stories in much the same way as Saboro demonstrated in chapter two of this book.

One cannot fail to notice that Eurocentrism and Afrocentrism constantly impede the assertion of the Caribbean Francophone identity in *Heremakhonon*, despite the clear position of the main protagonist and her unwavering commitment to her pro African and Pan Africanist positioning and ideological alignment. Although in the novel she often stands away from the self-denial that the French education system and life style inculcated in her, she gradually focuses her self-discovery efforts on a man whom she had initially referred to as an Oroonoko, a term whose usage is not any hazard as is demonstrated later in this chapter. Veronica Mercier explains her attraction to Ibrahima Sory in these terms: 'The truth is I am attracted to him, this nigger with ancestors' (Condé 2000b, p.28). She eventually appropriates him as 'my nigger with ancestors' (Condé 2000b, p. 35).This belief and attitude expresses the motif behind the Caribbeans' flight from slavery and its auxiliary treatments meted out to slaves and their descendants. At this level, we can, therefore, read Veronica's decision to relocate to Africa as a joyous return to 'primitive life, a silent invention of freedom' as Thompson (2006) writes. This is also where she becomes a victim of Afrocentrism, a doctrine which contends among others, that the salvation of the Diasporan Black lies in Africa. Although Veronica is a cultural revolutionary who opposes Eurocentrism and Afrocentrism, her behaviour often betrays some traits of those doctrines she tries to fight against.

Veronica's search for a cure to her alienation draws her into more intimacy with Ibrahima Sory who, in her eyes, epitomizes freedom, the antithesis of slavery. She explains her attraction to him because his body does not have any mark which recalls slavery:

> This man who is about to take me does not know that I am a virgin of sorts. Of course the wrapper won't be stained with blood and the griott won't hold it up proudly to reassure the tribe. It will be another blood. Heavier and thicker. Before letting it flow, black and fast, I now realise why he fascinates me. He hasn't been branded (Condé, 2000b, p.35).

The symbolic power concentrated by Veronica's desire and invested in the African man, is a consequence of the Eurocentric construction of the hypersexual African man, and also a consequence of Afrocentric representation of Africa and Africans as the owners of the solution to the woes of the Diaspora. The Eurocentric influence on Veronica's relationship with Ibrahima Sory transpires clearly through the appellation he is given: an 'Oroonoko', which is also the name of Aphra Benh's handsome 'royal' Black slave in her work *Oroonoko; or The Royal Slave* (1866). Veronica is ironically assigning the name Oroonoko to Ibrahim Sory in order to mock her own naïve attraction to him, and to associate herself with Aphra Behn, whom according to some of her biographers, had a love affair with a man like the Oroonoko of her novel. The love affair between Veronica and Ibrahima Sory, the Oroonoko, therefore poses Veronica and Aphra Behn on a par, and Veronica surprises herself by re-producing and re-enacting some of the Eurocentric practices, that is, the attraction of the foreign woman (Veronica flew from France and Aphra Behn is British) to the body of the Black man.

Ibrahima Sory is seen by Veronica as the gree-gree or magic medicine that will cure her and grace her with a new and better past, through a rebirth: 'I came to find a cure. Ibrahima Sory, I know, will be the marabout's gree-gree. We'll exchange our childhoods and our past. Through him I shall at last be proud to be what I am. He wasn't branded. You can see that' (39). Her attitude can therefore be partly understood when one examines it in the light of Fanon's analysis of Western Modernity's construction of Africa among the Francophone Caribbeans. Fanon (1967) poses that in Western Modernity (which shapes the image of Africa and Africans in the mind of the Antillean child), the Black man or male Negro simply becomes a phallic symbol: 'one is no longer aware of the Negro but only of a penis; the Negro is eclipsed. He is turned into a penis. He is a penis (Fanon, 1967, p. 170).

In this research the issue of memory in the Francophone Caribbean context is also special because although the Francophone Caribbean has experienced the violence of plantation slavery, colonisation and decolonisation, that area also has the specific reputation of a "recolonised" area through the French departmentalisation policy of the DOM (*Departements d'Outre Mer* or French Overseas Territories). The lack of reliable history or memory also adds to the alienation of the Antillean woman. Nick Nesbitt further unearths the reasons behind the actions of Maryse Condé's heroines who tirelessly question memory and history to the point of traveling back to Africa:

> The sheer violence, first of slavery and then of colonialism and neo-colonialist globalism, remains the driving impulse behind the French Antillean questioning of memory and history. Thanks to this historical specificity, the interrogation of memory on these small islands has been so acute that it may illuminate the more general dilemmas of modernity and memory structuring recent historical experience (Nesbitt 2003, p. 4).

Veronica's firm questioning of memory and quest for a past appears in these lines, 'That's mainly why I'm here. To try and find out what was before' (Condé 2000b, p.11). Unfortunately that search is not given the right direction and it ends up in a failure and disappointment which rather complicates Veronica's misfortune. She ends up more alienated, as a sex object in the hands of the continental African man in whom she puts all her hopes. In the end, Ibrahima Sory makes Veronica come to regard herself as a whore. The long and deep intellectual and personal exchanges that she had expected from him never occurred:

> So he doesn't want to know who I am, where I come from, what I've come to do so far from home? If he's not interested, if he doesn't ask, how can I call up my *rab* so that they leave me alone? He must help me find a cure. My hatred, my contempt. My explanations must be sincere-not like those patients who continue to lie to their psychiatrist (Condé 2000b, p. 48).

Ibrahima Sory is portrayed as a 'typical' African man, who cannot understand Veronica's situation, as a Caribbean woman. He did not go through the experiences she went through growing up in the Caribbean and in Paris. Africans have not experienced slavery and racial discrimination nor are they descendants of slaves like Veronica. These fundamental differences in their personal experiences and backgrounds make it impossible for Veronica and other Caribbean women protagonists —such as Marie Hélène in Condé's other novel, *A Season in Rihata* (1988) and Juletane in Mariam Warner-Vieyra's *Juletane* (1982)— to be understood and assisted by their African lovers and husbands in such a way that their aspirations for self-discovery can be fulfilled. The individualistic romantic assumptions of Veronica, Marie Hélène and Juletane reveal a Eurocentric influence that contrasts with the communal, unidealistic reality of gender relations in Africa. The disappointment which follows Veronica's love affair in Africa proves the limits of Afrocentrism. Continental Africans and Diasporan Blacks have different experiences and backgrounds, despite their common ancestry. Veronica discovers Africa, but not the Africa that she was longing for. Her quest and experience in Africa does not affect her personality and identity in any significant way. Psychologically she remains the same alienated "invalid" (*Heremakhonon*, p.26) that she had been in France. Africa, therefore, becomes like a Europe or White America with a Black face as far as she is concerned. She eventually discovers that before her arrival in Heremakhonon (the country), a young African American girl named Shirley had travelled the same path and received a treatment which was not better than hers, as Ibrahima Sory put it: 'There was a young Black American girl here who had the same sort of problem I believe. She ended up having her hair plaited like our women and having herself renamed Salamata' (*Heremakhonon*, p.49). Veronica's reflection over Shirley's situation contributes to locate these self-searching attempts and adventures explicitly within the context of the Black Diasporan women's disappointment in their identity quest in Africa:

> What an amusing story! How it amuses him. I can imagine this poor Shirley alienated by White America and trying to cure herself. Amidst their laughter, perhaps you made love to her? Perhaps you're the specialist for neurotics from the Diaspora? We are, after all, the Diaspora! (Condé 2000b, p.48).

Maryse Condé's heroines' searches are doomed because the African men, from whom they hope to get their cure, cannot understand what the Diasporan women need, or are looking for. Ibrahima Sory's relationships with women are crude and superficial, as he reveals in a reference to Shirley when Veronica hints that he must have slept with her: 'Oh no! My weak point is pretty women. And in the name of Allah she was very ugly!'(Condé, 2000b, p.49). The African minister's treatment of the Black Diasporan as a mere prostitute is important in our study when we bear in mind that the Black female rebel or the female Maroon was considered as a 'whore' by the slave owners (Johnson Washington, 2006). The continental African and the American slave masters therefore, unfortunately, perceive the Black rebellious woman who is in search of her roots in the same way and as such they are often tagged with derogatory qualifiers. Thompson (2006) and Romero Jaramillo (1997) shed more light on the image of the Black female slave rebel by reminding the reader of the terms used to refer to both male and female Blacks who rebelled, resisted and escaped from bondage and servitude. Thompson points out that those terms focus on:

> the bad habits that they displayed, such as being drunkards, sluggards, thieves, murderers and prostitutes. Evaristo Ujueta declared that the runaway female Manuela, of Santa Marta, Colombia, was insubordinate, commonly guilty of very bad conduct, and had other despicable character traits. Jacinta, of the same province, was accused of having been a thief and a prostitute since the age of fifteen. It was further alleged that no one was interested in purchasing her because of her bad character (Thompson 2006, p.28).

The next section of this chapter looks at Francophone Pan Africanism, or the relations between continental Francophone Africa and the Francophone Diaspora. These two locations represent the areas between which Veronica Mercier, the Caribbean woman, navigates in her quest of wholeness, belonging and sanity. That relation informs the dynamics of the interaction between the Diasporan and the continental African.

Mistrust Between Continental Francophone Africans and Francophone Caribbeans

The identity crises of people like Veronica reflect the French colonial policy which portrays Africa with negative stereotypes. Seeing themselves as more closely connected to France, the Caribbean Antilleans do not want to be associated with Africa, and as a consequence a mis-trust has arisen between continental Africans and the Francophone Caribbeans. This mistrust and the rupture that it causes between continental Francophone Africans and the Francophone Caribbeans is what *Heremakhonon* strives to counteract. Nicole Simek (2008) asserts her pessimism very clearly when it comes to 'gestures' like Veronica's quest for her origins in Africa. She locates those 'dystopic' returns in general within the context of the subversion of exemplary models that are found at the heart of Maryse Condé's works.

That general mistrust is a widely recognised phenomenon between continental Africans and Caribbeans within some writings. For instance, in his memoir *La Plume raboutée* (1978), Birago Diop describes how he, as a continental African would never associate with Francophone Caribbeans when he was a student in Paris because, in his opinion, all Francophone Caribbeans were:

> des Martiniquais, des 'Macafoutes' ('je vais t'en f...'), des 'Macatjembes' (je te tiens bien, je te visse), c'est à dire , commis, gradés, administrateurs ou douaniers, des suppots du "colonialisme'. (Diop 1978, p.78) [Martinicans, or "Macafoutes" (officers of the colonial administration).

> They were clerks, bosses, administrators or custom officers. They were all allies of colonialism] (Diop, 1978, p. 78).

In *Identité Antillaise* (1979), Julie Lirus refers to the alienation at the core of the French colonial education system in the Caribbean as 'la pédagogie érronnée de la politique coloniale' (Lirus, 1979, p.24) [the erroneous pedagogy of colonial policy]. The Western modern world view is therefore inculcated in the Francophone Caribbean at an early age and as a consequence, both males and females grow up assimilating more with White French culture. As a result, the Francophone Caribbean portrays Africa with the features that Western Modernity associated with Africa: as savages and backward people who needed the benevolence of Europe to enlighten them into 'civilised ways.'

Julie Lirus further analyses the Francophone Caribbean's identity crisis by conducting a clinical study among some Francophone Caribbean students living in Paris. Some of the conclusions that Julie Lirus arrived at were the aggressivity with which Caribbeans were trying to escape 'Blackness' in general and Africa in particular. She points out that in his effort to run away from 'Blackness', the Francophone Caribbean man develops a 'negrophobia':

> En associant tout ce qui est pouvoir, richesse, puissance, à ce qui est blanc (échelle de valeur imposeé), elle l'a rendu 'négrophobe.' A force de lui montrer qu'il est important socialement d'être blanc, elle lui a appris à avoir en horreur son épiderme foncé et à apprécier un individu en fonction de sa paleur épidermique (Lirus, 1979 p.31).

> [By associating everything that is power and wealth to whiteness (the yard stick requires it), he (the Antillean) developed 'Negrophobia.' He has been taught over and over again that it is socially important to be White and that led the Antillean to see horror in his dark skin, and to judge individuals, based on the lightness of their skin].

In *Identité Antillaise*, the distance between the African and the Antillean is illustrated by the use of the term 'étranger' that the Antilleans use to refer to the Africans: 'Qualitativement, les Antillais étudiants rejettent aussi l'Africain, surtout les femmes. Ce rejet est illustré par l'usage du mot étranger (Lirus 1979, p.95) [Qualitatively, the Antillean students, especially the women also reject Africa. That rejection is illustrated by the use of the word foreigner].The author recalls a conversation with two students who categorically reject all connections with Africa: 'Nous sommes différents en tout, c'est pour moi un étranger avec lequel je ne cherche même pas à voir ce qui nous rapproche' dit l'un des deux' (Lirus, 1979, p.95) [we are different at all levels, I see them (Africans) as foreigners with whom I do not try to see what we have in common]. Negrophobia leads the Francophone Caribbean to reject himself and his compatriots in self-denial. Those with pronounced Black features are called '"nèg kongo' (*Identité Antillaise* , p.24) which means someone who is a complete Black without a drop of white blood, and that term also refers to African slaves whom they consider as the image of the servitude they were subjected to. Furthermore, Lirus provides the following statistics: eigthty six percent of the respondents openly state that they do not have any connection with Africa, sixty six percent of them state that there is a cultural difference between the Antillean and the African, thirteen percent of them stress the difference that exists between the personality of the African and that of the Antillean, and ten percent of the respondents (all women) state that they cannot get along with African men because they are too possessive and too authoritarian (*Identité Antillaise, p.* 94).

The representation of Africa as a primitive land in the works of the Caribbean Francophone writers is the consequence of the education system that the French brought to their Caribbean territories and it is also the result of the fact that the French colonial administration needed some colonial administrators whom the metropole could not provide. That led the French Government to use the service of the Francophone Caribbeans overseas for the administration of the colonial territories. As a result, the Francophone Caribbeans found themselves ruling over African populations, on behalf of the French colonial master. In René Marran's *Un homme pareil aux autres* (1947), Jean Veneuse, a Martinican, is urged to reach his administrative post in colonial Africa as soon as possible, because there is a lack of administrators, and he portrays the ship on which he travels to Africa as a 'un cercueil' (p.16) [a coffin] and its destination is 'un sale pays où l'on s'ennuie a mort'(p.33)[a dirty country where one gets bored to death] and the contrast that the book poses between life in Africa and life in Europe is as Eurocentric as Conrad's representation of Africa in *Heart of Darkness* (1902). *Un homme pareil aux autres* associates Europe with books, sport and healthy life, and associates Africa with ferocious animals and coconut trees: 'les livres et le sport --escrime et rugby-- parmi les cocotiers, le sable, les bêtes féroces, les chameaux, les fonctionnaires coloniaux et un tas de bestiaux de même farine'(p.32). [books and sport-escrime and rugby, among coconut trees, the sand, wild animals, camels, colonial civil servants, and a whole bunch of beasts of the same kind]. European education and the elevation of the Francophone Caribbean to the level of colonial administrator contributed to the negative representations of Africa in the works of Caribbean Francophone writers, and it also contributed to the mistrust between Africans and the Caribbeans. The Africans saw in the Caribbean an ally to the French coloniser.

Veronica's alienation transpires in the way in which she perceives herself, and refers to her family. She is called 'luminal protagonist *par excellence*' by some scholars and the chapter will show why such a qualifier is attributed to her. Eurocentrism had such an influence on her that subconsciously, Veronica sees her relations with her sisters as the kind of relations which Cinderella had with her sisters. She could not think of any better comparison to render her family relations than Cinderella's symbolism, one of the classic features of family tensions between girls in the Western world: 'As I've said, I and my sisters were like Cinderella and her sisters. We never liked each other' (*Heremakhonon*, p. 75). The self-hatred which is deeply rooted in Veronica emerges clearly when she recalls that the French education system made her recite that she was from a race of brutes whose nose had to be permanently kept on the grinding mill: '*Quant neg pas ka travail, I ka fe quimbois.*' When the nigger doesn't work, he casts spells' (*Heremakhonon*, p 77). Many of these Eurocentric traces slip into *Heremakhonon*, but they do not alter in any way, the Promethean quality that the novel possesses, as one of the few works concerned with the expression of a Caribbean Francophone and also Pan African identity.

Heremakhonon's Resistance to Eurocentrism and the Assertion of Caribbean Women's Resistance

While the preceding section of this chapter has presented Veronica Mercier as a woman who is entangled in the domination and inextricable chains of Western Modernity and its ancestor which is plantation slavery, this section shows that the protagonist in *Heremakhonon* ascribes to the class of the giant Caribbean women who firmly stood against 'plantocracy' and played a major role in the revolt against slavery. One can read Veronica's trip to Guinea as a brave, strong and vigorous form of maronnage: More than the male slaves who fly to freedom and create maroon communities in the Caribbean, this woman completely leaves the Americas and journeys all the way across the Atlantic Ocean to Africa where she forcefully looks for freedom, her roots and a sense of belonging. The fact that many readers fail to notice the instrumental role of Caribbean women in the anti-slavery combat is clearly captured by Johnson Washington (2006) where the general exclusion of women from the anti-slavery combat is silenced and women are even excluded from the books on Black History. She writes:

> Resistance to the institution of slavery was very widespread, persistent, and to be found in almost every aspect of slave life (Beckles, 1989: 152). All groups of slaves, regardless of sex, colour, or work had

an anti-slavery mentality when it came to obeying their masters, and women were among leaders of resistance movements. Women's leadership roles, however, have been minimised in writings about slave resistance (Beckles, 1989, p.3).

Fortunately, this unfair and unjust trend has been overturned by seminal works like Barbara Bush's *Slave Woman in Caribbean Society 1650-1838* (1990). In that work, Barbara Bush shows how slave women resisted slavery and went beyond that by maintaining and transmitting African culture. That late action can be perceived as contributing to planting the seed of pan-Africanism. Barbara Bush's work couches the forgotten role of female Caribbean women fighters as the following demonstrate:

In Bush's study, new revelations regarding the female slave in Caribbean society were uncovered, which included: the vital and significant contribution she (the slave woman) made to West Indian slave society; how she exhibited strength and independence which wasn't previously accredited; how she struggled alongside her men-folk to live, maintain her dignity, to survive, and retain her integrity and culture; and her positive role in slave resistance (Johnson Washington, 2006 p.5).

W.E.B. Dubois added his voice to this debate by criticising writers like Carter G. Woodson, the founder of the Association for the Study of Negro Life and History adding: 'he had no conception of the place of woman in creation' (Johnson 2006, p.4).

Veronica acts like Prometheus, who stole fire from Zeus in Greek mythology and gave it to mortals. She courageously travels all the way to Africa with the intention of finding the remedy to the alienation of the Caribbean Francophone woman. Her promethean side stands out clearly in the sense that she is the first one among her community to attempt such a mission. The result of her search can be viewed as a praise-worthy achievement since it contributes to neutralise or eliminate the illusions that Caribbean Francophone women had developed around Africa. In the novel, Veronica perceives Africa as the area where she can find a remedy for her alienation, or a land where her 'shattered' identity can be reconstructed. She maintains an ironic perspective in her search for African roots even as she, nonetheless, embarks upon her quest to discover authentic identity. On the one hand, she embraces the racist association of African men with dangerous hypersexuality described by Fanon in *Black Skin White Masks* (Fanon, 1967, p. 157). For Veronica, this hint of dangerous sexuality is seductive, not threatening. She seeks it in hopes of restoring an authentic African self-hood or sense of belonging. On another hand, she also seems to accept the Eurocentric stereotype of Africa as an eroticised, feminised, and submissive continent. In her relationship with Ibrahima Sory, she adopts a much more passive and submissive role than she has enacted in her previous life in the Caribbean and in Europe.

The point being made here is that superficial reading of the amorous relationship between Veronica and Sory reduces the dimension of the Caribbean woman's adventure: she is simply reduced to a sex object, in her search for her roots. But a critical reading of Veronica Mercier's life in Africa proves that she acted exactly like the Grandy Nanny, the powerful female icon in the history of slave resistance. She is the most legendary leader in slave revolts in general and in maronnage in particular. An astonishing abundant literature on her exists, due to her central role in female slave resistance and Thompson (2006) refers to her in these terms, linking her to the fight for freedom and also to Pan Africanism. The nanny is portrayed as the almost legendary female Maroon leader, Grandy (Granny) Nanny, referred to today by Jamaicans as Nanny of the Maroons, has been declared a National Heroine (Harris 1994, p.46). Edward Kamau Brathwaite (1994, p.122) and Mavis Campbell (1990, p. 51) compare her to several female warriors in Africa, particularly Nzinga, the equally legendary figure who symbolised Angolan resistance to Portuguese rule in the first half of the seventeenth century. Not least among Grandy Nanny's legendary feats was her magical display at the signing ceremony in 1739 that brought an end to warfare between the Windward Maroons and the British (Campbell, 1994, p.4).

The reduction of Veronica Mercier to a sex object tallies with Kamau Brathwaite's protrayals of the Nanny in 'Nanny, *Palmares & the Caribbean Maroon Connexion* (2004). In that article, Brathwaite meticulously walks the reader through what led to the Nanny being a Hero in the Caribbean in general and within Jamaica in particular. He points out the myth around her, and the abstruse and unclear aura that hovers around her. Kamau Brathwaite shows that the Nanny has been reduced to a being whose salient feature is her sexual nature. This establishes a similarity between Veronica Mercier and the Nanny. The latter is described in these lines by Brathwaite (2004):

> With Nanny the big thing really is her buttocks. I think that is really where the whole thing rests. Wherever you turn, you get this image of the woman with the buttocks who turns towards the enemy, catches the bullets into those buttocks and farts them out – successfully—at the enemy. I mean this is something scholars are asked to accept and the mere fact that we seem to accept it suggests that we have been trapped into this ideology of buttocks. In other words, we are in danger-no- we are losing sight of the person for the sake of a part-a distinguished part unquestionably-but still only a part. And this has been the problem of the research and everything else. Why is it that the nanny is only a part of the whole? (Agorsah 2004, p.120)

We therefore clearly see that Western Modernity and Post modernity strive to reduce the praiseworthy efforts of the Black woman freedom fighter or the courageous Caribbean female rebel into a sex object or a sexual organ. This ideology has reigned for such a long time and been strategically circulated so much by racist slave owners, that even the most devoted Pan Africanist and Caribbean woman who leaves no stone unturned in order to escape the alienating and debilitating effect of slavery and its sequels, falls once in a while into the trap that it represents. Similarly to the nanny who has been tuned into 'buttocks' by Western Modermity, Veronica Mercier is reduced to a woman whose sole role is the sexual gratification of Ibrahima Sory in *Heremakhonon*. By presenting such a picture Maryse Condé succeeds in drawing a solid similarity between her heroine Veronica and giant Grandy Nanny.

The interest that Caribbean women show towards Africa may also be influenced by the structure of the Caribbean family itself. Families in the Francophone Caribbean have been described by several researchers as 'des familles de structure essentiellement matrifocale/ families with essentially matrifocal structures (*Identité Antillaise* p.39), or families in which the mother figure dominates, and the father figure is almost absent. Julie Lirus writes that 'les pères brillent par leur absence' [fathers' main characteristic is that they are missing], and she notes that twenty percent of the students who took part in the study she conducted among the Francophone Caribbeans living in Paris had been brought up by single mothers, which is a significant percentage, considering the fact that most of those students were from relatively wealthy backgrounds where the assumed norm is to have a nuclear family structure (Lirus, p. 83). David Macey (2000) recalls that Frantz Fanon was also raised in a matrifocal family where his father Casimir Fanon was almost effaced or absent, while his mother, Eléanore was the central authority figure. Macey provides a letter that Fanon wrote to his father in 1944—while he was fighting in the Second World War, accusing him of his irresponsibility and passivity. In the same letter Fanon attributes the success of the family to his mother's strong commitment and self-sacrifice:

Papa, you really have sometimes failed to perform your duty as a father. I allow myself to judge you in this way because I am no longer of this earth. These are the reproaches of someone living in life's beyond. Sometimes Maman has been unhappy because of you. You made her unhappy enough. In future, you will try to return to her one hundredfold all she has done for the equilibrium of the family. The word now has a meaning that was previously unknown. If we, the eight children, have become something, Maman alone should take all the glory. She was the spirit. You were the arm. That is all. I can see the face you will pull when you read these lines, but it's the truth. Look at yourself. Look back at the years that have passed, lay your soul bare and have the courage to say: 'I deserted'. And then, repentant parishioner, you will be able to return to the altar (Macey, 2000, p. 57).

In the work *Two Caribbean Women Go to Africa*, Adele King states that a form of serial polyandry exists in Guadeloupe, and as a consequence a woman may never marry, but she can have children from various lovers. This means, therefore, that the Caribbean boy and the Caribbean girl most of the time grow up in an environment where the father-figure is missing, in a sort of orphaned society. The Caribbean woman who comes from a society where the father-figure is missing may subconsciously seek that father figure whom she can hope to find only in Africa, since she could not find him in her native Antilles and she cannot hope to find him in France where she is considered as a 'négresse'. Nancy Chodorow (1978) supports this view, stressing the fact that the child's early relation with a woman has subsequent effects on the object-relations in the later developmental phases of the child:

That women mother and men do not is projected back by the child *after* gender comes to count. Women's early mothering, then, creates specific conscious and unconscious attitudes or expectations in children. Girls and boys expect and assume women's unique capacities for sacrifice, caring, and mothering, and associate women with their own fears of regression and powerlessness. They fantasize more about men, and associate them with idealised virtues of growth (Chodorow, 1978, p.83).

Jonathan Ngate (1986) interprets Veronica's experience in Africa as an expression of Maryse Condé's personal attitude towards Africa. In Ngate's view, the failure of Veronica and Marie Hélène in their attempt to reconnect with Africa is a medium that Maryse Condé uses in order to show that 'her feet are firmly rooted in the Francophone Caribbean (Ngate, 1986, p. 14), or her own personal position as a diasporan Caribbean francophone, vis à vis Africa and the diasporan identity issue. In 'Maryse Condé and Africa: The Making of a Recalcitrant Daughter,' Ngate recalls Maryse Condé's main stance when it comes to the role of Africa in the identity quest of the West Indians; Condé finally believes that Africa is not needed in that quest:

La quête d'identité d'un Antillais peut très bien se resoudre sans passer, surtout physiquement, par l'Afrique, ou si l'on veut, le passage en Afrique prouve simplement qu'elle n'est pas essentielle dans l'identité antillaise (Ngate 1986, p.14).

[A West Indian's identity quest can very well be done without going through (especially physically) Africa, or to put it another way, the passage through Africa simply means that Africa is not essential in the West Indian identity].

Maryse Condé's 1984 interview in *Jeune Afrique* also contributes to shed light on her position towards Africa. She asserts that there is nothing more than professional relations between her and Africa:

> Au risque de vous decevoir, je ne lis les africains que dans le cadre de mes recherches et de mes cours.Ma bibliothèque regorge de livres relatifs aux mémoires, c'est à dire sur l'histoire, la sociologie d 'Afrique, des Antilles, d'Amérique latine. Je lis beaucoup de documents ou d'éssais politiques écrits par des Africains tels Pathé Diagne, Abdoulaye Ly....Mais uniquement dans le cadre de mon travail (*Jeune Afrique,* 1984) pp. 66-67).

> [I might disappoint you, but I only read African works for my research and my classes. My library is full of books related to the history and sociology of Africa, the West Indies, and Latin America. I read many works or political essays written by Africans like Pathé Diagne, Abdoulaye Ly....but only for my work].

In her interview with VèVè Clark (1989), Maryse Condé's final position towards Africa becomes clearer. Condé refers to a "self-distancing" that has resulted in a rejection of nostalgia in any form, rejection of historical, aesthetic, exotic or political preconceptions that tend to fetishize the past or slavery and to idealize political commitment, nature or the people; rejection of a self-pitying ideology that would reduce Guadeloupe to a marginal and oppressive land that one flees to out of necessity (Clark in *Callaloo,* 1989).

Condé even directly blames the Negritude Movement for leading them (those from the Caribbean) into a futile search for origins, at the wrong place. Condé states that in the interview I referred to, above. She puts it in these terms:

> The proponents of Negritude made a big mistake and caused a lot of suffering in the minds of the West Indian people and Black Americans as well. We were led to

> believe that Africa was the source; it is the source, but we believed that we would find home there, when it was not a home. Without Negritude we would not have experienced the degree of disillusionment that we did (Clarke, in *Callaloo*, 1989).

It is also important to avoid classifying Maryse Condé as someone who completely denies the fact that there is an ancestral connection or a 'maternal relation' between Africa and the Francophone Caribbean. She points out that Africa could stand as the '*mère adoptive*' [adoptive mother] for the West Indians, for whom the West Indies would be the '*mère naturelle*' [natural mother] (Ngate, 1986-1987, p. 15).This might be the conclusion that Veronica arrived at, after the rude awakening or disappointment she encountered in her self-searching or self-discovery attempt on the African soil. Veronica admits the error which her journey to Africa represents and she puts it in these plain terms:

> I didn't find my ancestors. Three and a half centuries have separated me from them. They didn't recognise me anymore than I recognised them. All I found was a man with ancestors who's guarding them jealously for himself and wouldn't dream of sharing them with me (Nyatetu-Waigwa , 2009, p.5).

Kemedjio (2013) recalls the Pan Africanist dimension on Veronica's trip. He even inscribes her search within a wider framework which can be traced back to Garvey and also Ngugi wa Thiongo' in some his works: Pan Africanism, in its Garveyist dimension, for example seeks to restore an historic continuity. Also, Ngugi wa Thiongo in his collection of essays *Something New and Torn: An African Renaissance* explores the possible avenues to a renaissance of communities in the black world (Kamedjio, 2013.p. 178).

Conclusion

This chapter has shown that *Heremakhonon* is a work which distinguishes itself from most other Caribbean Francophone works by the emphasis that it lays on the personal experience of the Caribbean woman who decides to break away from the general condition of Eurocentric domination and alienation which characterise the Francophone Caribbean area and also from the Afrocentric myth which emerges in some of the Francophone Caribbean writings. *Heremakhonon* attacks the foundations of Eurocentrism and tries to liberate Francophone Caribbeans from the paralysing beliefs that European colonisation and neo-colonsation inculcated in them. Veronica takes upon herself the responsibility of that existentialist project and the examination of her experience in Africa shows that Maryse Condé partly succeeds in her tasks; she craftily equates Veronica Mercier, the heroine in her novel with The Giant female black Maroon leader, Grandy Nanny. Veronica epitomises a realistic critical mind; she shows the reader that Eurocentrism and Afrocentrism are not reliable and that they simply work to establish respectively the imperialist and racist belief of Western Modernity Europeans and that of the Afrocentrists who elevate Africa to the rank of the perfect and infallible continent where the diaspora black finds salvation. She also shows the reader that those two doctrines which have smothered for centuries the expression of individual and personal Caribbean identities have such a strong hold on Caribbean collective consciousness that they somehow always find their way into the most revolutionaries of Caribbean narratives.

References

Agorsah, E. Kofi eds. (2004). *Maroon Heritage: Archaeological Ethnographic and Historical Perspectives,* The University of West Indies, Kingston, Jamaica.

Asante, Kete Molefi. (2003). *Afrocentricity: The Theory of Social Change* (Revised and Expanded). Chicago, African American Images.

Beckles, Hilary. (1989). *Natural Rebels: A Social History of Enslaved Black Women in Barbados* Rutgers University Press, New Jersey.

Behn, Aphra. (1688). *Oroonoko: or, the Royal Slave.* London, Printed for William Canning.

Brathwaite, Kamau. (1994). "Nanny, Palmares & the Caribbean Maroon Connexion" *in.*) Kofi E. Agorsah Eds *Maroon Heritage, Archaeological and Historical Perspectives,* Kingston, The University of West Indies, Canoe Press.

Bush, Barbara. (1990). *Slave women in Caribbean society 1650-1838,* Kingston, Heinemann (Caribbean).

Callaloo, Vol. 18 No 3.*Maryse Condé : Special Issue.* (Summer, 1995). pp.551-564.

Chamoiseau, Patrick. (1997). *Texaco.* Translated by Rose Myriam Rejouis and Val Vinokruno, New York, Pantheon Books.

Chodorow, Nancy. (1978). *The Reproduction of Mothering: Psychoanalysis and the Sociologyof Gender,* Berkeley and Los Angeles, University of California Press.

Condé, Maryse .(1988). *A Season in Rihata,* Oxford, Heinemann.

Condé, Maryse. (2000a). *Célanire cou-coupé.* Paris, Editions Robert Laffont.

Condé, Maryse. (2000b). *Heremakhonon,* USA, Lynne Rienners Publishers Inc.

Condé, Maryse. (1994). 'Pan-Africanism, Feminism and Culture' *in* Sidney Lemelle and Robin D.G Kelly eds. *Imagining Home: Class, Culture and Nationalism in the African Diaspora,* London, Verso.

Confiant, Raphaël. (2006). *Nègre Marron*, Paris, Ecritures.

Conrad, Joseph. (1902). *Heart of Darkness*, Great Britain, Blackwood..

Diawara, Manthia. (1992). 'Afro-Kitsch' in *Black Popular Culture: A Project*. Ed.Gina Dent and Michele Wallace Seattle, Bay Press..

Diop, Birago. (1978). *La plume raboutée*, Paris, Présence Africaine..

Fanon, Frantz. (1967). *Black Skin White Masks*, New York, Grove Press, Inc.

Fanon, Frantz. (1968). *The Wretched of the Earth*, New York, Grove Press, 1968.

Fanon, Frantz. (1955). 'Antillais et Africains' *Esprit* (Revue), Février 1955, Numéro 2.

Fanon, Frantz. (1952). *Peau noire masques blancs*. Paris: Seuil..

Fanon, Frantz. (1961). *Les damnés de la terre*. Paris : Seuil.

Harris, Joseph E. eds. (1982). *Global Dimensions of the African Diaspora*. Washington DC. Howard UP.

Jeune Afrique no. (1984). 1216, pp66-67.

Johnson, Washington Clare. (2006). 'Women and Resistance in the African Diaspora, with Special Focus on the Caribbean, Africa and USA' *PSU McNair Scholars Online Journal*. Vol.2. Issue 1.

Kemedjio, Cilas. (2013). Maryse Condé and West Indian Complexity: The Writing of Monstrosity,Postcolonial Comparativism and Cannibalistic Intertextualities. *Research in African Literatures*. Vol.44, No.3.

King, Adele. (1991). 'Two Caribbean Women Go to Africa' Maryse Condé's *Heremakhonon* and Myriam Warner-Vieyra's *Juletane"*. *College Literature*.18.3 (1991): 96-106.

Lionnet, Françoise. (1989). *Autobiographical Voices: Race, Gender, Self-Portraiture*, Ithaca, Cornell University Press.

Lionnet, Françoise. (1995). *Postcolonial Representations: Women, Literature, Identity*, Ithaca, Cornell University Press.

Lirus, Julie. (1979). *Identité antillaise: contribution à la connaissance psychologique et anthropologique des Guadeloupeens et Martiniquais*, Paris, Editions Caribéennes.

Macey, David. (2000). *Frantz Fanon: A Biography*, New York, Picador.

Maran, René. (1947). *Un homme pareil aux autres*, Paris, Editions Arc-en Ciel.

Mars, Jean-Price. (1983). *So Spoke the Uncle*.Trans. Jean Fouchard and Magdaline W. Shannon, Washington D.C, Three Continents Press.

Nesbitt, Nick. (2003). *Voicing Memory: History and Subjectivity in French Caribbean Literature*. Charlottesville, University of Virginia Press.

Ngate, Jonathan. (1986). 'Maryse Condé and Africa: The Making of a Recalcitrant Daughter' *A Current Bibliography of African Affairs*. 19.1, pp. 5-20.

Ngugi wa Thiongo. (2009). *Something New and Torn: An African Renaissance*, New York, Civitas.

Nyatetu-Waigwa. (1995). wa Wangari 'From Liminality to a Home of her Own? The Quest in Maryse Condé's Fiction' in Callaloo18.3. pp. 551-564.

Romero Jaramillo, Dolcey. (1997). *Esclavitud en la provincia de Santa Marta 1791–1851.*

Santa Marta, Colombia: Fondo de Publicaciones de Autores Magdalenenses, Instituto de Cultura y Turismo del Magdalena. (Date).

Simek,Nicole. (2008). *Eating Well, Reading Well: Maryse Condé and the Ethics of Interpretation*, New York, Rodopi.

Thompson, O. Alvin.(2006). Flight to Freedom: African Runaways and Maroons in the Americas, Jamaica, University of the West Indies Press.

Warner-Vieyra, Mariam. (1982). *Juletane*. Paris: Presence Africaine.

CHAPTER SEVEN

Pan Africanism, Anti-Eurocentrism and Slave Resistance in Raphaël Confiant's Nègre Marron

Moussa Traoré

Introduction

Raphaël Confiant's *Nègre Marron* (2006) presents some exceptional thematic and narrative features that do not appear in most of the Francophone Caribbean slave narratives. These themes include resistance against slave masters on plantations, the search for identity by slaves and at times, the return to Africa. The novel follows a trans-historical 'collective' protagonist who does not accept enslavement or assimilation, and never stops resisting; a symbolic *Nègre Marron* or Maroon Negro who resists exploitation and White hegemony in all its forms. The Nègre M*arron's* resistance begins as a reaction to the inhuman treatment and exploitation of the Caribbean plantation system, and metamorphoses into other forms of resistance like trade unionism, revolutionary socialist oppositions and the fight against corruption and racism. The novel unfolds along various terrains and situations which correspond to specific periods in the history and contemporary situation of the Francophone Caribbean and the Black Diaspora more generally. The novel also raises the social contradictions and injustices of each of those periods. This study, therefore, seeks to critically analyse how Confiant discusses Pan Africanism, resistance and maronage in his novel *Nègre Marron*.

Since the onset of the slave trade in the Caribbean region, many Martinican Negroes have been engaged in 'marooning' or trying to escape from the slave plantations, into the woods or neighbouring islands. Siméon Louis Jerome, the protagonist of the novel under study, is one such person. He lived through several experiences that Raphaël Confiant succeeds in capturing in the novel. As a transitional character, Simeon the Maroon Negro witnessed the arrival of the first group of slaves from Africa, or more specifically, Guinea in the seventeenth century, but also experiences the different aspects of European colonialism and exploitation across different time periods from the eighteenth to the twenty first centuries. The Maroon Negro in the novel symbolises the invaluable voice of the person who desires to live in dignity and freedom. In relating Simeon's story, the author, Raphaël Confiant, moves away from his usual narrative habit and ventures into a meditative, almost melancholic writing and relates thoughts, movements and sections of the Maroon Negro throughout the different centuries.

Siméon Louis Jerome the Maroon Negro and protagonist, first appears in the novel when he leaves his White master's plantation, flees to the hilly forests and begins to think of actual and practical ways in which he can kill the White master and then return to Africa. One of the key features in the story is the Maroon community that Simon and other Black male and female ex-slaves have created. As the hero moves forward in time, he emerges as a modern Black activist or freedom fighter, who reads books like the Communist Manifesto, and joins the Martinican Communist Party. Through such Pan Africanist zeal, he also ends up teaching workers how to fight for their rights. As a consequence, he is seen as a threat to the ruling elites who hunt him down in order to have him arrested by the French Security forces (Confiant, 2006, p. 15).

The Significance of Marronage in the Novel

In *Frantz Fanon: A Biography* (2000), David Macey introduces the *marronage* process itself, and shows how deeply rooted the practice of *marronage* is in Caribbean society in general and in Fanon's Martinique in particular. Macey presents two contrasting towns in Martinique, and shows that each of these towns tells a different history of the country. Fort-de France, the capital city, associates the history of Martinique with the Savanne, the area whose main attraction is the statue of Josephine, who is a source of pride to many alienated Martiniquans. She is portrayed as a White Creole born in Les Trois Ilets across the bay from Fort-de-France, and wife of Napoléon Bonaparte from 1794 to 1809, when he separated from her because she could not give him an heir. The cult of Josephine is still alive and well in Martinique (Macey, 2000, p. 10). Rivière Pilote is another town which tells a completely different history of Martinique. The dominating monument in that city defines and celebrates the practice of *marronage*:

> The streets of the little southern town of Rivière-Pilote tell a different story to those of Fort-de- France. A plaque in the rue du Marronage records the history of the runaway slaves or *Marrons* who launched armed attacks on the White plantations.
>
> It explains that in the Caribbean, some slaves fled to the hills and woods in order to rebel against slavery and to prepare for insurrection. This was *marronage*. The Marron-Blacks [*les nègres marrons*] formed communities and organised themselves into small armies under the command of one leader in order to launch attacks on the plantation of the White masters so as to liberate their brothers and their country. Their heroic leaders included: Makandal, Boukman, Palmarès, Pagamé, Moncouchi, Simao, Secho...' (Macey, 2000, p. 11).

The connection between the *Marron* as he is defined by this plaque, and Frantz Fanon was clearly expressed in 1982, when a 'Mémorial International' was organised in Fort-de-France in order to honour Fanon. Macey writes, that according to one commentator, 'the *Mémorial* marked the return to their people of the first heroes of a pantheon: *the Marron* and Frantz Fanon' (Macey, 2000, p.13). It might also help to recall here, that both Raphaël Confiant and Frantz Fanon were born in Martinique; they share a common background. *Nègre Marron* is one of the Martinican, Raphaël Confiant's numerous novels and it mainly evolves around a Caribbean strong male hero, Siméon Louis Jerome's attempt, to reconnect with his roots and literally return to Africa, which is often referred to as pays d'avant - the country before - or where we came from or Pays Guinée (Guinea in West Africa). Throughout the novel, the author attempts to undo the derogatory stereotypes that Western Modernity associates Africa with, but the work ends with an apparent defeat of the *Nègre Marron* (Maroon Negro) in his mission, since he is betrayed by the local population whom he was fighting for. One can, however, also read the hero's action as a complete victory, in that he planted a seed that the next generation can follow, and that is the seed of rebellion against slavery, colonialism, neo-colonialism perpetuated by the Western powers.

The first pages of *Nègre Marron* evoke a nostalgic longing for the African lands where the ancestors of the Nègre Marron or Maroon Negro came from: the 'Pays Guinée' or 'Pays d'Avant'. One of the most striking and anti-Eurocentric features of the novel *Nègre Marron* is the composite protagonist's burning desire to return to Africa. That feature distinguishes Confiant's novel from most of the Francophone Caribbean works, except Maryse Condé's *Heremakhonon* (2000) where the protagonist completely relocates to Africa in her search for freedom.

Just as we saw in the previous chapter, the way back to Africa is so important in Confiant's *Nègre Marron*, that it is literally shouted several times on two consecutive pages: RETROUVER LA VOIE QUI VOUS CONDUIRAIT EN AFRIQUE-GUINEE (Nègre Marron, p. 44) and RETOURNER AU PAYS D'AFRIQUE-GUINEE. Oui! (*Nègre Marron*, p. 45). [TO FIND THE WAY TO AFRICA- GUINEA, OR THE COUNTRY WHERE HE USED TO LIVE BEFORE].

One of the thrusts of this chapter, therefore, is to demonstrate that the specific features of *Nègre Marron* as a novel, place Confiant in a position between Western Eurocentrism and its related Caribbean writings at one extreme, and the Créolité movement at the other extreme. Confiant rejects Eurocentrism as he tries to undo the negative representations that Western Modernity attaches to Africa, and he also diverges from the Créolité movement in *Nègre Marron* (although he is one of the founders and main partisans of the movement); he does not solely ground his work in the Créolité context, or the Caribbean context.

It is necessary to place the study of marronage in a general context from which the novel emerges, and it is equally important to bear in mind how specific Confiant's treatment of marronage is. He engages slave rebellion and links it to Pan Africanism, which considers the Maroon Negro's burning desire to return to his roots in Africa, and also brings Feminism in the debate by focusing on the role of a woman who is the leader of the Maroon Negroes. Alvin O. Thompson, in his *Flight to Freedom* (2006), which is one of the fundamental works in the study of marrronage, describes the importance of the phenomenon in the Americas in general. He portrays it as a revolt action which is part of the fabric of the all societies where slavery existed in the Americas. He writes:

> The Maroon heritage exists almost everywhere in the Americas – especially in the large plantation societies – in extant contemporary literature, artefacts, place names, icons, and myths and legends. Richard Price (1979:105) states that the Maroon heritage is deeply intertwined in the history of the French Antilles, that

out-of-the-way rural settlements that relate to the
Maroon past are not uncommon, and that in Haiti
present-day historians glorify the Maroons' role in
the revolution that overthrew slavery and colonialism
(Thompson, 2006, pp. 2-3).

It is important to stress that resistance to exploitation is one of
the core features of the Diaspora. In 'African Diaspora: Conceptual
Framework, Problems and Methodological Approaches', Oruno
D. Lara (1982) writes:

For Blacks, to exist is to resist the capitalist stronghold
which is seeking to neutralise, to annihilate, to liquidate
them physically and culturally. In this regard, it must
be noted that the Diaspora was forged in a dynamic
framework of resistance, symbolised by a movement
extending over six centuries without interruption.
There is no existence without resistance; this will never
be emphasised enough. Those communities within
the Diaspora which have expressed their existence the
most are still the ones which have resisted with the
greatest zeal (Lara quoted in Harris, 1982, pp.59-60).

In this attempt to locate our study in the general context of
marronage, it might help to mention the astonishingly numerous
names which are associated with the marronage process. The
faces behind *marronage* were numerous. The iconography of great
leaders includes François Makandal (Macandal), Jérôme Poteau,
Polydor, Romaine la Prophetesse, Padre Jean and Boukman
Dutty in Haiti; Françisque Fabulé, Grand-Papa and Nocachy in
Guadeloupe; Pompée in French Guiana; Juan de Serras, Cudjoe
(Kojo), Grandy Nanny, Three-Fingered Jack and Leonard
Parkinson in Jamaica; Enriquillo, Diego Guzman, Juan Vaquero,
Diego de Ocampo and Lemba in the Dominican Republic; Gaspar
Yanga and Macute (Makute) in Mexico; Marcos Xiorro in Puerto
Rico; Boni, Jolicoeur and Baron in Suriname; Joseph Chatoyer in St

Vincent; Domingo Bioho, Domingo Padilla (Domingo Criollo) and Jerónimo in Colombia; Andresote (Andrés López del Rosario), José Leonardo Chirinos, Francisco Pirela, Miguel Jerónimo (Gerónimo, Guacamayo) and Guillermo Rivas (Ribas) in Venezuela; Zumbi in Brazil;and Alonso de Illescas in Ecuador (Thompson, 2006 p.19).

Various names are also given to the communities that the Maroons formed. Depending on the areas where they were located, the following names were used: palenques, quilombos, macambos, cumbes, ladeiras, or mambies (Agorsah, 1994, p. 2). Several reasons also explain the maronnage process in general. These include the unimaginable cruelty and atrocities meted out to the slaves by the enslavers. For example, there were cases of throwing people alive into ovens and suspending them over spits like barbecuing meat; burning or mutilating men's genitalia and women's genitalia and breasts; priming their anuses with gunpowder which was then set alight; burying them up to the neck alive and pouring sugar over them, to be consumed by flies or ants; making them eat their own faeces and drink their own urine; sewing their lips together with wire; raping women in front of their husbands and children; and cutting up children in front of their parents (Fouchard, 1972, pp.116-17).

The other reason behind marronage according to (García, 1996) is that the Maroons did not see marronnage as an end in itself, but rather, as the precondition for ordering their lives according to precepts that improved their self-worth as human beings and gave them an opportunity to live with a certain measure of dignity.

Several other reasons justify the maronnage phenomenon and its large scope in the Caribbean in general. In 'the true tradition of my ancestors', Colonel C.L.G. Harris (1994) a descendent of Maroons himself, delves into the genesis of marronage in the Caribbean, and enumerates the different options that the Maroons took in the context of the inhuman European slavery system. Harris proudly refers to his ancestors, and their courageous various strategies for survival and their indomitable fight for freedom:

The majority of the Maroons, as my ancestors came to be referred to, originally came from West Africa. Oral tradition claims that the majority of those who came were mainly of the Ashanti ethnic group, who were forcibly brought to Jamaica as slaves by the Spaniards who, as history has it, were later defeated by the English. Consequently, some of the slaves fled to Cuba. Others who did not flee swore never to be slaves again. They stood by their word, escaped from bondage and fought to maintain their freedom for over eighty years of bitter warfare against the British. The victory of the Maroons had far-reaching implications for world history (Agorsah, 1994, p.36).

Unlike other Caribbean writings, Confiant's portrayal of the African landscape focuses on the physical difference that exists between that landscape and that of the Caribbean. It does not celebrate the bounty of natural resources of Africa; it often rather stresses the scarcity. Confiant's protagonist prefers the hardship of African existence to the excessive and crippling richness of natural resources of the Caribbean, or 'le Pays d'ici là'. Living conditions were so challenging in the African savannah, that as a consequence, the continental African or the *Nègre Guinée* became a tough-minded, creative and ingenious person, who lived in harmony with nature in order to survive on those limited resources. However, Confiant describes the climate and living conditions of the 'Pays d'Ici-là,' as a place where nature is bountiful but also simply too hostile for survival. The Caribbean is depicted as the land of thick forests and indomitable rivers, a land enveloped in a gloomy atmosphere. This denotes the twist which Confiant administers to Eurocentric Caribbean representations of Africa, in which, as in Conrad's *Heart of Darkness* (1902), Africa is depicted as rich in natural resources available for plunder, but also darkly mysterious and dangerous. For example, René

Maran's *Un homme pareil aux autres* (1947) associates Europe with knowledge and a healthy life style, while Africa is represented by its jungle: 'les cocotiers, le sable, les bêtes féroces, les chameaux, les fonctionnaires coloniaux et un tas de bestiaux de même farine (Maran, 1947, p.32). [Coconut trees, the sand, wild animals, camels, colonial civil servants, and a whole bunch of beasts of the same kind].

Here is Confiant's contrasting view:

> Au Pays d'Avant, votre village s'etalait au mitan de la savane et sa terre rouge, ses arbustes étiques, son ciel pur. L'horizon etait à portée de regard. L'eau rare. Il fallait creuser des puits et encore des puits, les premiers se tarissant au fil du temps, et il arrivait que pendant une année entière il ne pleuve pas une seule journée malgré les prières ferventes adressées aux divinités. Ici-là, à l'inverse, tout n'est que que mornes arbustes à la végétation enchevetrée, rivières bondissantes qui déversent une onde diaphane qu'on aurait jurée infinite (Confiant, 2006, p.17).

> [In the 'Pays d'Avant' / Previous Country, your village was located in the middle of the red earth savannah, with its short trees and pure sky. The horizon was not far. Water was rare. One had to keep digging wells continuously because they would dry up as time went on and sometimes it would not rain for a whole year despite the fervent prayers addressed to the gods. Here on the other hand, everything is simply bushy intertwined vegetations, fast running rivers which project water waves which seem to be infinite].

The Nègre *Marron* can no longer enjoy those familiar living conditions that he was used to, in Africa and as a consequence, develops these feelings of nostalgia. The primitiveness of Africa is represented here as a positive ideal, where one can start a fire by rubbing two stones together, matches are not needed:

"Les premiers temps, ceux de l'échapée, furent des temps sans feu. Là-bas, au Pays d'Avant, deux pierres frottées ensemble ou une buchette habiliment tortillée dans la rainure d'un bout de bois vous suffisait pour en allumer un". Ici-là, la pluie incessante l'interdit. Tout est humide, mouillé, visqueux même. Une mousse grisâtre recouvre en permanence les troncs des rochers. Le feu vous a longtemps manqué (Confiant, 2006, p.23).

[The first times, the moment of the salvation was a time without fire. Over-there, in the previous country, two stones rubbed against each other or a stick cleverly twisted in the crack of a piece of wood was enough to make fire. Over here, incessant rains do not allow that. Everything is humid, wet, and even viscous. A grayish fungus permanently covers trunks of rocks. For a long time you missed fire].

The diasporan protagonists in *Heremakhonon* (2000) and *Nègre Marron* (2006) both consider Guinea on the West African coast as their home, as the country from which they were uprooted and shipped to the Americas. Veronica travels to Guinea with the hope of reconnecting with her roots, and the Nègre *Marron*'s main goal in his rebellion and resistance is to return to 'pays Guinee' (*Nègre Marron*, p.45). The fact that both characters view Guinea as their native land is very significant. In '*Afro-Americans and the Futa Djalon* (Harris, 1982), Boubacar Barry traces the roots of the symbolic significance of Guinea in general and the Futa Djalon mountain in particular, to the powerful personality, determination and charisma of Abdurahman, a prince from Futa Djalon in Guinea, who was sold as a slave and ended up as the property of American farmers in the South of the US. Barry writes that Abdurahman left no stone unturned in order to return to his native Guinea, and that he succeeded in combining that ambition, with hard work and dignity to such an extent, that he earned the respect and admiration of all the slaves in the South and also the White slave owners. The prince's background and the conditions of his captivity are presented in these terms:

> Abdurahman was the son of Ibrahima Sori Mawdo, the second Almami (ruler) of Futa Djalon. He studied the humanities at Timbuktu. In 1788, at the age of 26, he was taken prisoner during a battle north of Futa Djalon and was subsequently sold as a slave to a farmer named Thomas Foster in Natchez Mississippi (Harris, 1982, p.285).

The royal slave succeeded in imposing himself as an admirable and highly respected figure who makes the Black race proud in Southern United States:

> Abdurahman maintained his dignity during this long ordeal, and as a result of his unswerving faithfulness to Islam he succeeded in winning the admiration of his contemporaries. He compelled recognition in spite of many feelings of abnegation among his kin and also in the midst of the blatant brutality of the Southern slave masters. In the final analysis, he became the centerpiece of the prosperity of his master's farm (Harris, 1982, p.286).

Boubacar Barry (cited in Harris 1982) recalls that out of frustration due to the exile of his daughter who had a relationship with Foster's son, Abdurahman wrote a letter in Arabic to the Sultan of Morocco around 1826, asking him to use his influence with the president of the United States so that Thomas Foster would grant him freedom. After thirty nine years of servitude, Abdurahman was free. The American Colonisation Society lent their support to him and his family and relied on him for the propagation of Christianity in West Africa, and in 1829 he died in Liberia. According to Barry, Abdurahman's life and work ultimately became a source of hope and inspiration which was passed on to generations of Diasporan Blacks:

> The energy of this man who had lived in the unforgettable shadow of the land of his youth, was sustained by his relentless faith in the idea of a return to his native land. Like Abdurahman, thousands of Black slaves toiled in the cotton and tobacco fields of Mississippi and the South. By keeping faith in an eventual return to the ancestral land, they survived. A precious heritage passed on from father to son, this hope survived over several generations (Harris, 1982, pp.286–87).

Another connection between the Caribbean and Guinea stems from the influence of Edward Blyden (the West Indian writer who is also one of the pioneers of the organisation of the Pan African movement), who left the West Indies and settled in Sierra Leone, where he wrote extensively on the political and social organisation of the kingdom of Futa Djalon (Harris,1982, p.287). The nostalgia for Guinea in *Heremakhonon* and *Nègre Marron* therefore reflects the general influence which that part of West Africa has on the Diasporan Black. Guinea and the Futa Djalon constitute an ideal of resistance and redemption which inspires the radical and subversive position of the Nègre Marron.

Confiant tries, in *Nègre Marron*, something which is similar to what Achebe did in *Things Fall Apart* (1958) as an answer to Joseph Conrad's *Heart of Darkness*, rectifying or erasing the distorted images presented by the imperialist powers and replacing them with more accurate representations. Conrad writes that the Congo is a savage river and Africa is a land inhabited by savages and cannibals, a continent where imperialist Europe bears the weight of the 'white man's burden' through agents like Kurtz. In response to Conrad, Achebe constructs in *Things*

Fall Apart, an African society with its cultures, beliefs, practices and manners, like any other stable human society. Achebe does not present a utopian or romanticised idealist depiction of a pre-industrial African society. Nor does he allow the reader to harbor any illusion that the traditional African society will be able to withstand the pressure of Western influence without changing. But Achebe shows a pre-encounter African society that reveals a stable civilisation, and in his epilogue that consists of the notes of a myopic colonial administrator, he dramatises the disastrously presumptuous misunderstanding of traditional African societies by the Europeans. Like Achebe in *Things Fall Apart,* Raphaël Confiant presents in *Nègre Marron,* African societies with their physical and human realities, their living conditions and their interaction with other people like Arab traders. For example, *Nègre Marron* mentions the main numerous languages which were spoken by the newly arrived slaves in the Caribbeans, and the author shows that time and need led to the replacement of the African languages with Creole, the medium of communication on the Caribbean, or the 'Pays d'Ici-là'.

In the direct voice of the narrator, Confiant recalls some of the derogatory depictions of Africa created by Western Modernity, and juxtaposes those features to his representation of Africa and Africans. Some of the negative images of Africans come from local newspapers announcing the escape of some run-away slaves from the plantations, or papers broadcasting a message that the White slave owners would like to pass to the literate portion of the population.

This resonates with Edgar Robert Conrad's statement in *Children of God's Fire* (1983) when he writes that thousands of offers were promised to whoever would help to capture and return runaway slaves. Conrad adds that such announcements appeared in hundreds of newspapers over seven or eight decades. To him, that is a convincing proof that flight was a common solution to the slave's predicament.

The gross, rough and beast-like features of the African slave in this description can be contrasted with the description that Confiant's narrator provides a few pages further, of the slaves who have been bought by 'le chef blanc'[the White master] from the ship captain, when the ship reached the Caribbean. The narrator celebrates the beautiful, strong and noble stature of the slaves who survived the trip on the sea. The only female among those survivors is so pretty that the slave traders cannot resist her charm: Le chef blanc tendit une sacoche au capitaine d'un air maussade, non sans vous avoir recomptés du regard.Vous étiez douze à être marqués à la chaux. Onze jeunes Nègres à la membrature parfaite et à la taille élancée, plus une Négresse très belle que les marins avaient surnommée Oriane (Confiant, 2006, p.26). [The white master handed a small bag to the captain with an unpleasant look, and he made sure that he counted you again with his eyes. Twelve of you were branded with white paint, eleven young Negroes in perfect shape and great height, plus a very pretty female Negro whom the sailors had nicknamed Oriane].

But it is above all, the Nègre *Marron* who himself embodies all the qualities which Eurocentrism denied the Black man. The Nègre *Marron* is a brave black Caribbean man who refuses the domination of the plantation system and its slavery, and seeks refuge deep in the forest where he creates a community of *Marrons*; together, they work to undermine the domination and exploitation of the plantation system. He is the opposite of the cowardly brainless Africans who never achieves maturity and remain as children forever in Eurocentric writings. In *Le Discours antillais*, Edouard Glissant refers to the Nègre *Marron* as the courageous hero who openly opposed the mainstream policy of slave owners and plantation proprietors who, for their part, turned the image of the Nègre *Marron* into an assassin or a vulgar bandit:

Le Nègre Marron est le seul vrai héro populaire des Antilles, dont les éffroyables supplices qui marquaient sa capture donnent la mesure du courage et de la determination. Il y a là un example incontestable d'opposition systématique, de refus total. Il est significatif que peu à peu les colons et l' autorité (aidés de l'Eglise) aient pu imposer à la population l'image du Nègre Marron comme bandit vulgaire, assassin seulement soucieux de ne pas travailler, jusqu'à en faire la représentation populaire, le croquemitaine scélérat dont on menace les enfants (Edouard Glissant quoted in *Nègre marron*, p. 169).

[The *Nègre Marron* is the only real hero of the Antilles whose courage and determination can be measured through the dreadful punishment that was administered to him when he was captured. He is an incontestable example of systematic opposition and total refusal. It is important to point out that the colonial authorities (supported by the church) succeeded in imposing to the population the image of the *Nègre Marron* as an ordinary bandit, an assassin who refuses to work, and he ultimately became a popular scarecrow used to frighten children].

One of the great qualities that Confiant attributes to the *nègre marron* is his sexual attitude. Unlike the Black African men like Ibrahima Sory in *Heremakhonon* who turn women into sex objects, or unlike the Black man who is turned into a phallic symbol in Fanon's *Black Skin White Masks*, or the Black man who is tirelessly running after the virginity of the White woman as in René Maran's *Un homme pareil aux autres*, the Nègre *Marron* controls his sexual desire. He is neither passionately attracted to White women nor to Black Creole women. He has a relationship once in a while with a Creole woman who admires him and is attracted to him. The *Nègre Marron* puts his target before everything: to overthrow the

White master and if possible, to kill him and that leads the *Nègre Marron* to choose a monastic, solitary life. He stays away from the exigencies and obligation of relationships in order to devote all his time and energy to the cause he is fighting for. His relationships with women, when they exist, take place in 'le provisoire et le furtif' [in a provisory and furtive way].

Bowser (1974), Campbell (1990) and Atwood (1971) discuss the issue of the killing of the White slave master by the slaves. They confirm that the enslaved rebellious Black freedom fighter would kill his master sometimes in order to gain his freedom and they add that the White slave masters also frequently killed their slaves but the irony lies in the fact that the two killings are given different names and connotations. One was regarded as a crime, while the other was not. Thompson (2006) grasps that unjust choice of words or linguistic segregation, by pointing out that it was common for contemporary (and many modern) records to refer to the killing of Whites by insurgent Blacks, including Maroons, as 'murder', 'slaughter', 'massacre' or the like, while similar acts by Whites against Blacks, were usually referred to as 'killing', 'execution' or a less evocative term (Thompson, 2006, p. 29).

Babara Bush (1990) and Hilary McD. Hilary Beckles (1989), furthermore delve into another key feature of slave rebellion which often gets ignored in much of the literature on slave resistance, and that is, the role of women. In the same vein, by trying to redeem the image of the African in general, Raphaël Confiant grants a special place to the Black woman. One of the main characteristics of Africa in Western Europe was the 'feminised' and 'sexualised' continent and as such, both the African continent and the African woman were therefore made to deserve only one thing: to be possessed and raped by European men. Raphaël Confiant's response to such a portrayal is his representation of the strong Caribbean woman figure. Confiant's prototype of the Creole woman is a very strong, proud and authoritarian one, who teaches Creole men languages and other skills, and organises life in the Creole community while controlling everything: 'L'une des femmes pourtant était créole. Cela se remarquait à son port de tête, à la hautaineté dont était empreinte sa demarche, bien qu'elle ne se refusat point aux étreintes charnelles que sollicitait chacun des hommes' (Confiant, 2006, p.4).[One of the women was Creole, and one could notice that through her hair style and the pride in her walking style, although she never refused the sexual solicitations of each of the men]. She is the opposite of the passive dark woman who submits to White and Black men. The strength of Confiant' Caribbean woman figure lies in the control and choices that guide her sexual life. She falls in love with only the Nègre Marron, because he is courageous, and they ultimately develop a silent but infallible solidarity.

Cette solidarité muette s'étendait parfois aux femmes qui n'hésitaient pas à livrer leur corps à ces héros, au hazard d'une rencontre dans les bois, dans l'espoir d'enfanter un négrillion plein de vaillantise. Ceux qui parmi nous étaient reputés avoir pour géniteur un grand Marron étaient trés respectés. (p.122)

[That silent solidarity was often extended to women who would not hesitate to offer their body to these heroes whenever they met them in the woods, hoping to give birth to a brave Black child. Those of us who were reputed to have a great Maroon as a father were treated with a lot of respect].

Although this Creole woman is empowered with some agency and negates some of the stereotypes attached to the dark woman in Eurocentric representations, she nonetheless illustrates the eroticisation of the dark woman. This is proof that some of the features that Western modernity attributed to colonised subjects always keep creeping into the discourse emerging in the colonised, neo-colonial and postcolonial territories, regardless of the anti-Eurocentric determination of some of the writers of those areas, and Confiant is one of such writers.

There is no doubt that the Nègre *Marron* views violence as the main weapon in the anti-slavery struggle, just like Fanon assigns to violence the pivotal role in the anti-colonial struggle. This has, sadly, been a theme in this volume and was evident in chapter two by Saboro, where some of his African songs focused on violent resistance. Fanon's advocacy of violence can be explained by the main events of his life: first, his disillusion after the Second World War, when he realised that he had fought for a country (France) which claims to uphold 'égalité et fraternité' (equality and fraternity) while it invades Algeria, whose inhabitants it tortures and kills. Secondly, Fanon and all the other Martiniquans who had fought on the side of the French during the war, were still victims of racism both in France and also in Martinique, where the skin colour was still a determining factor and the 'lactification process' was the means which many dark skinned Antilleans used, in order to lighten their skin and get close to whiteness, a gesture close to what Charles refers to as 'colouring' in his chapter on 'Skin Bleaching.' Fanon's anger also stemmed from the injustice and inequality that he saw around him in the world in general. David Macey captures the sources of that anger: And yet, if there is truly a Fanonian emotion, it is anger. His anger was a response to his experience of a Black man, in a world defined as White, but not to the 'fact' of his Blackness. This formed a significant part of his a response to the systems and conditions of colonialism and inequality, which led him to address the situation of those he called the wretched of the earth (Macey, 2000, p.28).

One of the most striking moments of Fanon's advocacy and acceptance of violence in the struggle against oppression was his speech at the All African People's Congress in Accra in 1958:

> His hugely successful performance in Accra also helped to promote the image of Fanon as the apostle of violence three years before the publication of *Les Damnés de la terre*. When she met him in Rome in the summer of 1961, Simone de Beauvoir knew little about Fanon himself, though she had recently read his books, but she did know that this was the man who had been

applauded in Accra for the 'impassioned speech on the necessity for and value of violence' and for his criticisms of Nkrumah's 'pacifist these'. Fanon's reputation had also come to the notice of *L'Express*'s Jean Daniel. Daniel was not present in Accra himself, but he had, he recalled in 1961, heard many of those who were there speak of the 'poignant speech' in which Fanon justified the use of violence 'with accents that reduced him to tears and made his audience feel a sort of communion' (Macey, 2000, p. 371).

Fanon's emphasis on the legitimacy of violence within the context of the liberation struggle can be better understood if we examine it this way. He first made it clear that the colonial process or the colonising enterprise itself was founded on violence, and the only way in which the colonised could get their freedom from the coloniser was also through a violent liberation struggle. Then, he extrapolated his discussion to the personal or individual virtue of violence, or the way in which the colonised people can 'expunge' themselves of the poisoning and incapacitating effect of colonisation, and he adds that this stage also prepares the individuals when it comes to protecting their newly found liberty and independence:

> At the level of individuals, violence is a cleansing force. It frees the native from the inferiority complex and from his despair and inaction; it makes him fearless and restores his self-respect. Even if the armed struggle has been symbolic and the nation is demobilised through a rapid movement of decolonisation, the people have the time to see that the liberation has been the business of each and all and that leader has no special merit (Fanon, 1968, pp. 73-74).

Fanon's emphasis on the cathartic effect of violence is what critics like Irene L. Gendzier (1973) find to be less convincing.

For example, they claim that Fanon's thesis, as expressed in his notion of the cathartic effect of violence, was that decolonisation could only occur successfully where the colonised not only seized their freedom through a liberation struggle, but participated in violent actions to individually expunge themselves of the colonial heritage of inferiority and submission. It is this aspect of violence which, so graphically expressive in words, is considerably less convincing as a policy (Gendzier, 1973, p.198).

The violence in the *Nègre Marron* resonates with Fanon's idea of the 'cathartic effect of violence', which means that in order to regain her or his sanity, the dominated or colonised person on whom violence has been inflicted needs to react by inflicting violence onto her/aggressor. In the novel under study, Siméon Louis Jerome's ultimate aim is to kill his white master, leave the plantation and return to Africa. Coincidentally, Fuentes (1979) examines marronage as an act which brings healing after one is hurt; he also associates marronage to a catharsis, the term used by Fanon in the fight for freedom. Fuentes goes back to the connection between that term and Greek Drama. According to him the Maroons fought for the ideal of freedom as a right, not a legal prescription. It was all these factors that made *marronage* (and other forms of armed uprising) such a titanic struggle, in some ways comparable to a Greek tragedy – or a series of 'great tragic dramas' and 'collective explosions of redemption' with all its catharsis and *dénouement*. But *marronage* on the whole did not end in tragedy. It ended in triumph for the former enslaved persons (Fuentes,1979, p.13).

Fanon's emphasis on violence was also often interpreted as a call for terrorism, a revival of extreme nationalism. Critics who were enraged at Fanon's advocacy of violence, condemn both Fanon and Sartre, who was Fanon's ideological mentor. Macey brands such interpretations of Fanon as negative readings. He argued that when he is read, the readings are negative. In an essay which turns the 'White man's burden' *(le fardeau de l'homme blanc)* into the

White man's sob (*le sanglot de l'homme blanc*) and argues that there is no viable alternative to white European civilisation. Bruckner (1983) claims that Sartre's support for Fanon was no more than masochism, and argues that Fanon's writings are based upon an analogy between the thesis that maturity is a form of decadence that has not lived up to its promise, and the adulation of the south, seen as the north's only future. In 1982, former Maoist, turned New Philosopher and anti-Marxist, Andre Glucksmann, could claim that Fanon was responsible for celebrating the 'second wave' of 'planetary terrorism' that came to Paris when a bomb exploded in the rue Mabeuf (Macey, 2000, p. 21).

Fanon's advocacy of violence is also the main element which transpires in the US when his works are criticised. *The Wretched of the Earth* is considered by most American critics of Fanon as a work which spreads violence among the youth in the Black slums. The Grove Press advertised *The Wretched of the Earth* as 'a handbook for a Negro Revolution.' Here, at last, is Frantz Fanon's fiery manifesto-- which in its original French edition served as a revolutionary bible for dozens of emerging African and Asian nations. Its startling advocacy of violence, as an instrument for historical change, has influenced events everywhere from Angola to Algeria, from the Congo to Vietnam, and is finding a growing audience among America's civil rights workers (Macey, 2000, p. 23).

American pacifists are also strongly advised to read *The Wretched of the Earth* because of the danger that it represents. In *The New Yorker* of January 15, 1966, Nat Hentoff issued one of those warnings:

> His arguments for violence are the most acute in current revolutionary theory... they spread amongst the young Negroes in American slums and on American lecture platforms. Those who are engaged in rebutting these precepts of violence (which includes arming for self-defense) ought to find his book a fundamental

challenge, and for this reason, if for no other, Fanon should be read by the non-violent activists, and by people who are simply opposed to violence (Hentoff, 1966, p. 115).

In *On Violence*, Hannah Arendt contends that Fanon had an influence on the violence that affected American university campuses in the 1960s. Another dominant image of Fanon stems from the 'Americanisation' of Fanon in Charles Lam Markmann's translation of *Peau noire masques blancs* (1952) David Macey refers to that translation as a 'seriously flawed one' because it eradicates the specifically French and Martiniquan dimensions of Fanon's colonial experience. Fanon refers at three points to an image of a grinning *Tirailleur sénégalais* (a black colonial infantry man) who is eating something from a billy can. He is saying '*Y a bon banania*', which is an advertising copy-writer's idea of how an African says '*C'est bon, Banania*'. In the English translation, this becomes 'Sho good eating'. The *tirailleur* has become the caricatured Black of the Deep South, and he is supposedly eating 'some chocolate confection'. In the original, he is eating something very specific, and with specific connotations. Banania is a 'breakfast food' made from banana flour, cocoa and sugar. Posters of the *tirailleur* and his dish of Babania were still a familiar sight in the France of the 1940s and the 1950s; the Senegalese poet and politician Léopold Sédar Senghor wanted to rip them down from all the walls of France (Macey, 2000, p. 29).

One can understand David Macey's indignation at the changes that Markmann made in the translation of *Peau noire*. Macey's position is marked by the need to remain as faithful as possible to the original text, but it can also be perceived as reasons behind the Americanisation of *Peau noire* in this translation process. The battle African Americans were waging in the 1960s shared some similarities with the Algerians' fight for independence. Both combats aimed at achieving freedom and human rights from an oppressing force, although the French occupation of Algeria was certainly more cruel and atrocious, as Fanon's portrayal of the torture and trauma that French soldiers and police officers caused in pre-independent Algeria in *The Wretched of the Earth* (1968) shows. Markmann's translation of *Peau noire masques blancs* is an attempt to create a motivating solidarity between the Civil Rights Movement and the Algerian liberation war. Markmann's translation of Fanon's works into English inspired African Americans. Fanon became one of Stokely Carmichael's 'patron saints' and 'every brother on a roof top' could quote Fanon (Macey, 2000, 24).

The *Nègre Marron* is endowed with an exaggerated masculinity which seems to be a reaction against the feminised or emasculated Eurocentric image of Africa. He is an indefatigable militant or combatant whose struggle begins historically with mere *marronnage* and gradually extrapolates to trade unionism and leftist radical political commitment. The *Nègre Marron* is therefore a symbolic figure whose personality constantly changes in the novel. From the run-away slave who refuses the submission of the plantation system and seeks refuge in the forest, he becomes the one who organises the workers and eloquently teaches them how to discuss and argue for better salaries and working conditions when slavery ends and Blacks become workers on the fields of the rich land owners. Confiant adapts the resistance of the *Nègre Marron* to the evolution which affects the world in general and the Caribbean in particular. The leadership of the *Nègre Marron* begins at a period which corresponds to the Cold War era of tensions between the West and the Soviet bloc. At this time the French Government feared the rise of Soviet influence, which prompted the beginning of the 'departmentalisation' of some of the French Caribbean islands. The *Nègre Marron* character switches into a labour activist whose companion in the workers' struggle is Leon, a name which is reminiscent of Leon Trotsky, one of the main ideologists of the Soviet revolution. Léon était, en effet, le bras droit de Simeon lors des grèves marchantes. Il devenait soudain loquace quand tous deux se rendaient de plantation en plantation pour convaincre les travailleurs de baisser leur coutelas. Il savait trouver le mot juste, l'argument qui faisait mouche, si bien qu'à chaque début de recolte, les Békés de la côte caraibe essuyaient des débrayages implacables qui les contraigaient à faire appel à la gendarmerie (Confiant, 2006, p.148). [Leon was indeed Simeon's right hand man during protest marches. He would suddenly become loquacious when the two of them would go from one plantation to another in order to convince the workers to put their cutlasses down and stop work. He would always find the right word, the argument which would fit the context and as a consequence at the beginning of every harvest season, the white farm owners of the Caribbean coast would face severe clashes and call for the rescue of the gendarmerie].

The Nègre *Marron*'s radicalism transpires in the fact that he reads *The Manifesto of the Communist Party*, and openly asserts his allegiance to the 'défenseurs de la classe ouvrière (p.15) [defenders of the working class], a group who regularly distribute tracts or leaflets issued by 'le Mouvement Communiste Martiniquais (p.166).[Martinican Communist Movement]. Confiant associates him with the most radical and revolutionary movements which existed in the twentieth century, the Communist Party of the Soviet Union, and the Black Panthers Movement of the USA. The Nègre *Marron* is referred to as 'la panthère noire' in the last section of the novel, where he becomes an armed 'bandit' who attacks wealthy traders and corrupt public civil servants, aided by the local populations who protect him and support him. At the highest level of those activities, his name becomes Siméon Louis Jerome, and the first component of the name is said to be that of a famous African King, perhaps Samory Touré, one of the most famous kings in African History. Samory Touré who was also known as 'The Black Napoleon of the Sudan' repeatedly defeated the French colonial troops for 18 years in West Africa until he was betrayed by one of his generals, captured and deported to Gabon where he died in 1900. Siméon Louis Jerome seems to combine 'Samory' and 'Louis Jerome' or African and French components, two features which are also present in 'Samory the Napoleon of the Sudan.' By naming the Nègre *Marron* 'Siméon Louis Jerome,' Confiant makes his position very clear. He is actually glorifying the African past and the African famous kings and he shows admiration and devotion to the Nègre *Marron*, the one who challenges Western suppression and domination and follows the same path which the famous African kings followed. These names also ground the mission of the Nègre *Marron* into the Martiniquan soil: the plaque in the southern town of Rivière Pilote in Martinique, which was referred to at the beginning of this chapter, mentions 'Simao' as one of the leaders of the Nègres *Marrons*. Finally the names of those Marniquan Maroon leaders could have been African in origin as was initially said, if one juxtaposes samory and 'Simao'.

In the novel, Confiant criticises the internal divisions which weaken leftist political struggles. The Nègre *Marron*, who had suffered imprisonment, hunger and insecurity because he was wanted by the forces of the repressive French authorities who were governing the island is finally betrayed by his comrades. This betrayal emphasises that political ideologies (the revolutionary leftist or communist ones which claim to defend the cause of the grassroots or the downtrodden included) often remain only theoretical and leave the needy ones to die. On the last pages on the novel, before his defeat, the Nègre *Marron* remembers his mother warning him against the unreliability of Blacks, whom she paints as a doomed race of people with betrayal in the blood. The Nègre *Marron* realises that he has been abandoned by his race, the Black race, and his mother's statement provides a very strong illustration of Eurocentrism and Afro pessimism finding their way into the Nègre *Marron*'s discourse. The old Black lady reiterates that Blacks are the last race, a race which is not far from animals. Pourtant ma vielle mère m'avait prévenu: complot de Nègres, ça ne tient jamais; le Nègre est en deveine depuis l'arche de Noé; aide un Nègre et aussitôt il voudra te défier à la course; le nègre est la dernière des races après les crapauds ladres et patati et patata. Elle avait eu bien raison! (p.205) [I had however been warned by my old mother: Negroes' plots never succeed. The Negro has been cursed since Noah's Ark; help a Negro and he will soon try to beat you in the race. The Negro is the last race after toads, and so on and so forth. She was right!]

The betrayal of Simao the Nègre *Marron* by his people discourages all other similar existentialist adventures. One is almost sure that nobody else will be interested in a battle or a quest of the type that the *nègre marron* led, as the last sentence the novel shows: 'Je suis, je serai le dernier Nègre Marron d'ici-là… (Confiant, 2006, p.211) [I am and I will be the last *Nègre Maron* of this place….]. The betrayal of Maroons was a common phenomenon and in order to avoid it, the "solitary Maroon" became a common practice. Thompson (2006) sums up that betrayal among Marrons in the following expression: 'Runaway with runaway sells runaway' (Thompson, p.60) and the renown Cuban Maroon Esteban Montejo reinforces the views and attitude of the solitary Maroon through his life style. Barnet (1996) puts that in these words: 'Montejo lived alone, and a lonely life it was. He declared that he had trusted no one' (Barnet, 1996, p. 37).

The actions of the Nègre *Marron* represent an assertion of the existence of the Francophone Caribbean, a diasporan existence which cannot be expressed through any other medium except the power of the resistance of marronage. In that respect, the Afro-Brazilian counter-part of the Nègre *Marron*, the *kilombo* asserts the existence of the Afro-Brazilian community by 'setting on fire and painting red the colonial [slave master's] society' (Harris, 1982, p. 60).

Conclusion

Raphaël Confiant's *Nègre Marron* tries to undo the Eurocentric influence that Western Modernity had on the representations of Africa in Western writings and in Caribbean Francophone writings. Through the character of the Nègre *Marron*, Raphaël Confiant shows that Blacks can resist the enslavement and inhuman exploitation of the plantation system and fight for their rights, and for better conditions. Confiant's Nègre *Marron* is not a Black man who is in a constant pursuit of the White woman's body. His priority in life is his combat against White injustice and only Black beautiful and politically conscious women have the chance to get close to him, with the hope of giving birth to heroes like the Nègre *Marron*. Unlike the mentally enslaved black Caribbean who associates Africa with savagery, the Nègre *Marron* is proud of his African origins, and draws inspiration from them in time of serious combats and that emphasis on African culture places Confiant between Eurocentrism which his work refutes, and the Créolité movement which advocates the predominance of the Creole culture in Caribbean writings. The Nègre *Marron*'s political commitment makes him stand against European domination in the Caribbean, and it also makes him espouse the ideology of the working class and the victims of exploitation and segregation all over the world. It is clear from this chapter that many Black people sought to find places of escape where they could live with some degree of independence. Others were not so fortunate, and had to remain in the Black Diaspora and find ways to cope with discrimination and oppression. One method used to deal with this, by a few people, was to skin bleach their dark skin so that they could derive greater benefits from an otherwise unequal society. This issue forms the basis of the next chapter.

References

Achebe, Chinua. (1958). *Things Fall Apart,* London, Heinemann.

Atwood, Thomas. (1971). *The History of the Island of Dominica,* London, Frank Cass.

Barnet, Miguel. (1996). *Biografía de un Cimarrón,* La Habana, Editorial Academia.

Bowser, Frederick P. (1974). *The African Slave in Colonial Peru 1524–1650,* Stanford, Stanford University Press.

Bruckner, P. (1983). *The Tears of the White Man,* Translated by William R. Beer, France, Éditions du Seuil.

Bush, Barbara. (1990). *Slave Women in Caribbean Society 1650-1838, Kingstion, Jamaica,* Heinemann Publishers, Indiana University Press, James Currey Publishers, London.

C.L.G. Harris. (1994). 'The True Traditions of my Ancestors' in in Kofi E. Agorsah eds. *Maroon Heritage,* Kingston, The University of West Indies, Canoe Press.

Campbell, Mavis. (1990). *The Maroons of Jamaica 1655–1796 A History of Resistance, Collaboration and Betrayal,* Trenton, NJ Africa World Press.

Condé, Maryse. (2000). *Heremakhonon* Trans. Richard Philcox. USA, Lynne Rienners Publishers Inc.

Confiant, Raphaël. (2006). *Nègre marron,* Paris, Ecritures.

Conrad, Joseph. (1902). *Heart of Darkness,* Great Britain, Blackwood.

Conrad, Robert Edgar. (1983). *Children of God's Fire: A Documentary History of Black Slavery in Brazil,* New Jersey, Princeton University Press.

Fanon, Frantz. (1952). *Peau Noire Masques Blancs,* Paris, Seuil..

Fanon, Franntz. (1968). *The Wretched of the Earth,* New York, Grove Press.

Fouchard, Jean. (1972). *Les marrons de la liberté.* Paris, Editions de l'École.

Fuentes, J. (1979). *El Cimarrón, 1845.* San Juan de Puerto Rico, Instituto de Cultura Puertoriqueña.

Garcia, Jesus. (1996). *Africanas, esclavas y cimarronas,* Caracas, Fundación Afroamérica.

Gendzier, Irene L .(1973). *Frantz Fanon: A Critical Study,* New York, Pantheon Books.

Glissant, Edouard. (1989). *Caribbean Discourse: Selected Essays,* Charlottesville, UP of Virginia.

Harris, Joseph eds. (1982). *Global Dimensions of the African Diaspora,* Washington DC, Howard UP.

Macey, David. (2000). *Frantz Fanon: A Biography,* New York, Picador.

Maran, René. (1947). *Un homme pareil aux autres,* Paris, Editions Arc-en Ciel, *The New Yorker* of January 15, 1966.

McD. Beckles, Hilary. (1989). *Natural Rebels: A Social History of Enslaved Black Women in Barbados,* London, Zed Books.

CHAPTER EIGHT

Skin Bleaching, Oppression and Black Resistance

Christopher A.D. Charles

Introduction

The popular explanation for skin bleaching among Blacks is the self-hate thesis, which is a legacy of slavery. This chapter rejects the self-hate or internalised oppression thesis as the reason for skin bleaching in Jamaica with empirical evidence, and posits the alternative explanations of colourism and miseducation which are the legacies of White domination. The self-hate thesis is a one-size-fits-all explanation that ignores the variegated history and culture of Blacks as a racial group and their resistance and resilience in the face of oppression. Some skin bleachers do in fact suffer from self-hate, but the large majority do not hate themselves, so it is important to interrogate the culture and their engagement of oppression that influences them to alter their Black physicality. This interrogation requires a study which measures the self-esteem of Jamaicans who bleach their skin and also those who do not, and compare the mean self-esteem scores of the two groups. This divergence reveals the nuances, complexities, continuities and discontinuities of Black resistance. The study participants who lighten their complexion are referred to as skin bleachers (also known as rubbers) in this chapter because this is what they call themselves in Jamaica. The objective of this chapter is to get a better understanding of the relationship between self-hate and skin bleaching among Blacks in Jamaica within the context of oppression and Black resistance. The study looks at how skin bleachers in particular respond to oppression and Blacks in general resist this oppression. The chapter begins with an illustrative review of the literature on colourism and miseducation, skin bleaching, and internalised oppression. Following the literature review, the method, results, discussion and conclusion sections of the chapter are presented.

Colourism and Miseducation

The ideology of racism is used in this chapter to refer to the justifications offered or used by Whites to deny non-Whites their rights and opportunities because of their race and ethnicity. Colourism, which is the corollary of racism, is the ideology, which assigns light-skinned people in society privileges and benefits unlike their dark skinned counterparts. Racism discriminates based on race, and colourism discriminates based on complexion. Colourism is a legacy of the racist ideology, which justified European colonisation and African captivity in the Americas (Charles, 2012, 2014).

In the contemporary United States, it was found that Black children had a preference for lighter shades of brown skin compared to dark brown skin, and this was evident in the school and classroom contexts (Davis, 1998). Black adults compared to White adults, had a skin colour schematic that indicated light, medium and dark complexions (Jenkins, 1993). Therefore, the Black community is socially stratified based on skin colour (Keith & Herring, 1991), which determines life chances because light skinned Blacks tend to have higher social and economic status than dark skinned Blacks (Hughes & Hertel, 1990). Having a light complexion is a more favourable asset for Blacks seeking employment than their job experience and level of education (Harrison &Thomas, 2009). The discrimination experienced by dark skinned Blacks leads some of them to marry an interracial partner not only because of love, but also because they prefer a light skinned partner (Craig-Henderson, 2014).

In colonial Jamaica, Black customers preferred to be served by fair-skinned girls (although these girls treated Blacks disrespectfully), so businesses in Kingston readily employed these girls (Henriques, 1951). Colourism continued after Britain granted political independence to Jamaica in 1962. For example, a young Black woman in the early post-independence years destroyed her photograph because she looked too dark in it (Charles, 2011a; Brown, 1979). One study found that adolescents judged each other using the benchmark of White physicality, so the preferred complexion was clear or fair (Miller, 1962). White adolescents saw themselves as higher and more worthy than Brown adolescents, who saw themselves as higher and more worthy than Chinese and Black adolescents (Miller, 1973). Jamaica is a plural society with three unique cultural sections based on race or ethnic and cultural ancestry, Whites, Brown and Black. The Brown cultural section reveals that colourism also influences social stratification (Smith, 1990). A review of 1000 newspaper ads for household workers from 1920-1970 revealed that employers had a preference for light-skin workers and these workers revealed their skin tone in the ads they placed (Johnson, 1996). Some Black Jamaican men prefer to have a lighter skinned parner ('browning partner') which is the contemporary manifestation of the desired Mulatto woman of the colonial period (Mohammed, 2000).

Colourism influences the behaviour of some Blacks because they are miseducated to believe that the standard for beauty, status, intelligence, moral integrity, progress, enlightenment and so on, are determined by Whites and their culture. This miseducation occurred because these Blacks were indoctrinated in schools about European heroes, culture, history and achievements. At the same time, Black heroes, culture, history, achievements and Africana philosophy were excluded or downplayed because they were deemed inferior, hence irrelevant. The resultant Eurocentric thinking via White educational management influences the minds of some Blacks, both teachers and students (Carruthers, 1977; Cozart, 2010; King, 2006; Lewis, 2008; Woodson, 2010). Therefore, these Blacks used White physicality as the standard and graded the shades of brown skin as being superior to Black skin. This Eurocentric or miseducated worldview of Blackness influences some Blacks to bleach their skin to reap the social benefits and privileges of light skin in society (Charles, 2003; Charles, 2009a). Colourism and miseducation are the legacies of White domination and they influence the skin bleachers to modify their complexion.

Skin Bleaching

With regard to the issue of skin bleaching itself, this popular and controversial practice, also called skin lightening, skin toning, and skin whitening, is the process of using homemade concoctions, dermatological or cosmetic products to remove melanin from the skin (Charles, 2014). The process is done formally by some dermatologists and informally by non-doctors. This chapter focuses on informal skin bleaching. Skin bleaching may be done for a few weeks to upwards of twenty years because for some individuals, it is an everyday practice and for others, it is done for specific celebratory occasions. Some people bleach their entire bodies, and others only bleach their faces. Skin bleaching is an old practice because it existed in ancient Egypt, medieval Europe, colonial North America, the colonial Caribbean and colonial Africa. Skin bleaching is not only popular and controversial in the contemporary era, it is also global. The practice occurs in the Caribbean, Asia and the Pacific region, Europe, Africa, North America, Central America and South America. People from all backgrounds regardless of race or ethnicity, levels of education and income, engage in the practice (Charles, 2003; Blay, 2007; de Souza, 2008; Dorman, 2011; Gooden, 2011; Saraswati, 2010; Winders, Jones III and Higgins, 2005).

Skin bleaching products are manufactured, marketed and distributed globally by multinational corporations (MNCs) that are influenced by the racial and complexion memes that are the legacies of colonisation. The MNCs sell popular brands of skin bleaching products that can be found globally. Some of the more popular brands are African Queen Beauty Cream, Madre Pearle, Clear Fast, Sure White, Maxi White, Body Clear, Immediate Clear, Topiclear, Nadinola Skin Fade Cream, Symba Cream, and Neoprozone Gel. Some of these products are also marketed for specific parts of the body. There is the Facial Fade Lightening Cream, Leg Fade Cream, Hand and Body Lightening Cream, and the Knee and Elbow Lightening Stick (Charles, 2010a, 2010b).

Skin bleaching products are dangerous because they contain chemicals such as hydroquinone, corticosteroid, or mercury, which have led to Cushing's syndrome, vulval warts, pitch black pigmentation, fragile skin, colloid milium ochronosis and scabies among other illnesses (Charles, 2010a). The use of skin bleaching products has also exacerbated illnesses such as adrenal insufficiency, diabetes, hypertension, renal damage, insomnia, memory loss, glaucoma, and cataracts (Charles, 2010a). It was documented in one case report that the diagnosis of leprosy was not made earlier because the patient was bleaching her skin. Lactating mothers who are bleaching their skin also pass mercury to their babies. Critics of skin bleachers argue that they would not engage in a practice that is dangerous to their health if they did not hate themselves (Charles, 2010a, Dadzie & Petit, 2009; Kpanake, Munos Sastre &Mullet, 2010; Mahe, Ly & Perret, 2005.

The literature on skin bleaching cites various, sometimes conflicting reasons for the practice. Some of the reasons cited are purely aesthetic. Charles found that skin bleaching is popular and fashionable, the skin is too dark, the practice is done to tone the skin, remove facial pimples and to look cool, to appear beautiful and attract a potential partner (Charles, 2003a, 2003b, 2006, 2009a, 2010a, 2011b). In contrast, Dorman (2011) argues that people bleach their skin because of racial formation; for Blay (2007) it is the colonial mentality; for Hunter (2011) it is racial capital; and according to Mahe, Ly, and Guonongbe (2004) people bleach because it is a modern phenomenon.

Skin Bleaching in Jamaica

Skin bleaching has a long history in Jamaica. Captive Africans bleached on commercial plantations in the eighteenth and nineteenth centuries by using cashew oil to flay the skin in response to the colonial racial-skin colour hierarchy (Charles, 2010a). Skin bleaching newspaper ads were popular in the colonial period and they extolled the 'beauty' and 'virtues' of light skin (Charles, 2010a). Today, skin bleaching is viewed as the expression of mental slavery (Shepherd, 2000) and the desire to attain whiteness (Hickling & Hutchinson, 2000). The critics of skin bleaching frame it as pathology because the skin bleachers reject Afrocentricity (Brown-Glaude, 2007). However, several small self-esteem and skin bleaching studies found that the skin bleachers did not suffer from low self-esteem (Charles, 2003a, 2003b, 2006). The skin bleachers were influenced by colourism, so they saw light skin as sexy and created a browning identity because they were miseducated to represent or accept light skin as superior and dark skin as inferior. This miseducation has been mistakenly conflated with internalised inferiority or self-hate, which is taken as the mark of oppression not just for skin bleachers but Blacks in general (Charles, 2003a, 2003b, 2006, 2009a, 2010a, 2011a, 2011b).

Internalised Oppression

The notion of internalised oppression states that over time, the members of an oppressed minority group internalise the virulent racism they experience, which is perpetuated by the members of the oppressive dominant group. Internalised oppression is self-hate, and low self-esteem is a form of self-hate (Clarke & Clarke, 1950). Self-esteem is the regard people have for the self. People with high self-esteem have a high regard for the self, unlike those with low self-esteem who have low regard or contempt for the self (Rosenberg & Simmons, 1971; Rosenberg, 1989). Individuals who have high self-esteem look for feedback that verifies the self, even when the feedback is negative. However, individuals who have low self-esteem are concerned with protecting the self so they look for positive feedback, even if this feedback does not verify the self. The interactions between global self-esteem which is the general value a person places on the self, and views that are -specific to the self, influence people's responses to feedback (Bernichon, Cook & Brown, 2003).

The psychological scars of African captivity or the self-hate thesis among Blacks arising from captivity, and racial discrimination have a long history in the United States. Clark and Clark (1950) conducted the famous first doll study among Black and White children, who were given a black doll and a white doll and asked to choose the nice doll. Some eighteen percent of Black children from the South and nine perecent from the North gave anti-Black statements. Only fourteen percent of the children in the total sample made anti-Black statements. These results were interpreted to mean that Black adults hated themselves because they internalised their oppression (Cross, 1991). The doll study has been replicated relatively recently in the United States in the film *A Girl Like Me* (Media That Matters n. d.), and also in Jamaica, (Cramer & Anderson, 2003; Goupal-McNicol, 1995) with the findings that the Black school children hate themselves because the majority selected the white doll.

The following year, Kardiner and Ovesey (1951) conducted a psychoanalytic study of 25 Blacks of various classes in New York City. They argued that the personality of Blacks was an adaptive response to the oppressive environment they were living in. The adaptation of Blacks to this environment created psychological scars that were the marks of oppression. DeGruy Leary (2005) argues that Blacks' experience of slavery produced centuries of spiritual, physical and psychological damage exacerbated by post-slavery racial oppression that have created destructive behaviours dubbed the post-traumatic slave syndrome.

The best way to determine if Blacks as a group suffer from self-hate, the purported legacy of the psychological damage of slavery and post-slavery racism, is to measure their self-esteem because self-esteem is a form of self-hate. Caldwell (1998) found that the personal self-esteem of Black children were less likely to be affected by peoples' perception of their racial group, compared to the personal self-esteem of European children. The foregoing findings support the earlier findings of Rosenberg and Simmons (1971) that Blacks have higher self-esteem than whites. Pierre and Mahalik (2005) found that Black men who buttressed themselves against racial hassles had high self-esteem and experienced less psychological distress. The foregoing occurs, according to Neblett, Shelton and Sellers (2004) because Blacks in general use their racial identity to manage daily racial hassles and resist their oppression, thereby protecting the self from psychological damage. This further supports the view that Black people, in the face of oppression, have learned to find ways to challenge and resist European systems of domination. The problems with doll studies in particular, and the self-hate argument in general, is that they both ignore the significance of Black resistance. The self-hate argument within the context of Black resistance will be addressed in the discussion section of the chapter as well as the issues of colourism and miseducation and their influence on skin bleachers.

The objective of this chapter is to get a better understanding of the relationship between self-hate and skin bleaching among Blacks in Jamaica within the context of oppression and Black resistance. The study looks at how skin bleachers in particular respond to oppression and Blacks in general resist such oppression.

The popular explanation given for Blacks who bleach their skin is self-hate, which, it is believed, is also common among Blacks in general. It is important to determine whether this is true.

The earlier skin bleaching and self-esteem studies conducted in Jamaica (Charles, 2003a, 2003b, 2006) used very small samples; thus, it is imperative to use a much larger sample in the current study to see if there is still a negative relationship between skin bleaching and self-hate, which is operationalised as low self-esteem. The hypothesis of the current study states that there is a negative relationship between self-esteem and skin bleaching.

A convenience sample of 326 persons (who were bleaching their skin and those who were not) were selected for the study from the streets of Kingston, Jamaica. The division of the sample created a bleaching group (n=160) and a non-bleaching group (n=166). The city of Kingston was chosen because skin bleaching is prevalent in this capital city, and the people in this metropolis were more likely than elsewhere in the country to speak candidly about skin bleaching (Charles, 2010a).

Procedure

The data was collected by a research assistant (RA) who was trained to administer the instrument. The RA approached people on the streets who were bleaching and those who were not and explained the study to them and asked them if they wanted to participate. Persons were selected as a potential bleacher to be interviewed if their faces had a lighter complexion than their necks, hands, legs, and so on. The participants who agreed to participate in the study were asked to sign a consent form. The instrument had demographic questions, the Rosenberg Self-Esteem Scale, questions asking the participants if they bleached their skin, the reasons for bleaching, and questions regarding the products they used to bleach their skin. The Rosenberg Self-Esteem Scale is a 10-item scale, which measures the regard a person has for the self. An exemplar item states, 'I feel I do not have much to be proud of, with the responses strongly agree, agree, disagree, and strongly disagree. Higher scores indicate higher self-esteem.

The reasons reported for skin bleaching were grouped together based on similarity. For example, responses such as, 'the man them like it' and 'the girl them like it' were coded as 'to attract a partner.' Reasons such as, 'to remove scars,' 'get rid of bumps,' and 'fade out spots' were coded as 'to remove skin blemishes.' Two independent coders were used with an inter-coder agreement of .81 and .86.

Results

For skin bleaching M= 1.51, and M= 22.36 for self-esteem, SD=.501 for skin bleaching and for self-esteem SD= 4.556. Female accounts for 61.3% of the sample and males 38.7%. The 18-22 age cohort accounts for 31% of the sample, 23-27 is 25.5%, 28-32 is 16.6%, 33-37 is 9.8%, 38-42 is 8%, 43-47 is 3.1%, 48-52 is 3.4%, 53-57 is 0.6%, 58-65 is 1.2% and the over 65 is 0.9%. With regard to level of education, 12.9% attended junior high schools, 61% high schools, 25.2% college or university and 0.9% attended graduate school. The average income per month is JA$57,944.44 (US$579.44).

A Man Whitney Test was performed to determine if the difference in the mean self-esteem score of the skin bleaching group and the mean self-esteem score of the non-bleaching comparison group was statistically significant. The results reveal that there is no statistical difference in the level of self-esteem based on whether or not an individual practices skin bleaching ($U = 27022.000$, $p=.888$). The study participants who bleach their skin do not have low self-esteem, so they do not suffer from self-hate.

Discussion

This chapter examined the relationship between skin bleaching and self-esteem in Jamaica within the context of White domination and Black resistance. The results of the study suggest that there is no statistical difference between the bleaching group and the comparison non-bleaching group in terms of self-esteem.

Therefore, the study participants who bleached their skin do not have low self-esteem. This finding supports the small skin bleaching and self-esteem studies conducted earlier in Jamaica (Charles, 2003a, 2003b, 2006) that also found that the skin bleachers do not hate themselves. The fact that the skin bleachers do not suffer from self-hate refutes the psychological scars of slavery thesis. This thesis posits that there is self-hate or low self-esteem not only among Black skin bleachers but also among Blacks as a racial group, and this self-hate is the legacy of plantation slavery and European colonialism.

The participants in this study reported six categories of reasons for bleaching their skin. They stated that they bleached their skin 'to remove blemishes,' 'light skin is pretty,' to attract a partner,' 'to get light complexion,' the altered complexion is 'style and fashion,' the practice is popular because our friends and other people are doing it.'

The self-hate thesis as an explanatory factor for skin bleaching is problematic even without the empirical refutation provided by the present study. There is no scientific evidence in the psychological and historical literature that there is the intergenerational transmission of the psychopathology of self-hate, which the critics of the skin bleachers argue originated in slavery and colonialism. The captive Africans, the ancestors of the skin bleachers who worked on commercial cotton and sugar plantations in the Americas and the Africans at home in Africa, were not self-haters because they vehemently rejected their oppression and sought to change the status quo. There are misunderstandings regarding the effects of African captivity. African bondage in the Americas did not cause the Africans to hate themselves because the majority of Africans consistently engaged in violent and non-violent forms of resistance against their oppressors. It is psychologically impossible for people to hate themselves and fight for their liberation at the same time. The captive Africans in the Americas expressed agency daily in support of freedom because they saw themselves as free people (Dunkley, 2013). The same is true for the Africans on the continent because the European colonisers also faced constant resistance in Africa, as was discussed by Talburt in the first chapter of this volume, as well as the chapter by Beckford and Charles.

The descendants of the captive Africans after their captivity have consistently fought institutional racism to become full citizens in their respective societies in the Americas. If Blacks as a racial group were self-haters, they would not have displayed Black motivation and achievement in the Americas and Africa. Even if the skin bleachers in this study were found to be self-haters, it does not mean that, because two variables occur together (in this hypothetical case skin bleaching and low self-esteem or self-hate), one causes the other. There are also many factors in the post-slavery and post-colonial environments that could explain this self-hate that have nothing to do with plantation slavery and colonialism. Some of these factors are severe child abuse and neglect, long-term unemployment, repeated failures over many years, a traumatic intimate-partner relationship and/or divorce, and a protracted civil war. Moreover, the proponents of the self-hate thesis place this alleged legacy of enslavement and colonisation solely on the Africans in the plantation societies of the Americas and their descendants, as well as those in Africa when slavery and colonialism existed in nearly all societies at various times from the start of human history (Patterson, 1985).

Doll studies using preschoolers that support the self-hate thesis are problematic because dolls are not psychometric tests, and preschoolers do not understand the social and biological meanings of race, nor have they developed global self-esteem (Rosenberg, 1989). Moreover, the White children in the sample who selected Black dolls in the original doll study (Clark & Clark, 1950) were not viewed as self-haters but the Black children who selected white dolls were viewed as self-haters. The doll study recorded in the film *A Girl Like Me* did not use a comparison group of children, so the findings are flawed. Supporters of the self-hate thesis ignore the fact that the Black children in the dolls studies in the United States might have been socialised by their parents to be nice to Whites and say nice things about them as a means of surviving in a White racist society, so the children said the white dolls were nice as camouflaged resistance. The interpretation of self-hate from dolls studies is erroneous at best and unscientific at the worst because the choices of dolls by Black pre-school children were used to measure and interpret the interior psychology of Black adults. Racial oppression negatively impacts Blacks in terms of discrimination in trade, aid and grants, housing, employment, education, health and criminal justice and a tendency to racialize all sites of oppression, but not in terms of self-esteem (Alexander, 2012; Beatty, 2007; Gordon, 1997; Jones, 2006; Schaefer, 2012; Schulman et al, 1999).

The skin bleachers reported that they bleached their skin to 'remove skin blemishes,' and because 'light skin is pretty,' and 'to get a light complexion.' These reasons point to the correction of some physical defect on the skin such as spots, pimples and scars buttressed by the belief that light complexion is beautiful. These reasons suggest that skin bleaching, which produces a light aesthetic physicality, elevates the skin bleachers in the society because they no longer have dark skin. These reasons also point to the influence of colourism on the practice of skin bleaching because the skin bleachers hold the Eurocentric worldview, that light skin is prettier than dark skin. This mistaken belief that dark skin is inferior to beautiful light skin in the Jamaican society, can be traced to the ideologies of racism and colourism developed during British colonialism to justify the exploitation of Blacks as part of its civilising missions.

The belief in the superiority of light skin in Jamaica (as in other post-colonial societies) has been transmitted from the colonial period to the present via the school system and has created a colonial mentality among some Jamaicans (Blay, 2007). The miseducation of some Jamaicans in schools occurs through the promotion of the Eurocentric worldview over the Afrocentric worldview in the curriculum (King, 2006; Woodson, 2010). An examination of the high school curriculum suggests that for a large part of Jamaica's history as an independent country, it was British until the late 1970s to the early 1980s when the school leaving British General Certificate of Education (G.C.E) was replaced by the Caribbean Examination Council (C.X.C.) certification in the high schools. The replacement of the Eurocentric GCE curricula were resisted by some Jamaicans, with the colonial mentality who argued that that G.C.E was superior to C.X.C., but the government backed by the Afrocentric Jamaicans successfully resisted the Eurocentric curriculum. This resistance against miseducation was very important because before the advent of C.X.C, all school textbooks were imported from England and the United States (Charles, 2009a, 2010a).

Even today, Jamaicans who received their university education in North America, Europe, Australia and New Zealand are deemed to be better educated than those who received their tertiary education at home because of the perceived superiority of the White world and things associated with it in the society despite centuries of Black resistance. The same is true in all Black societies. Despite the fact that C.X.C. exists today, some Jamaican high school teachers refuse to teach about National Hero Marcus Mosiah Garvey, although the Garvey curriculum has been approved by the government for use in high schools. These teachers stubbornly refuse to educate the children about Black heroes, history, culture, achievements and African philosophy (Carruthers, 1977; Cozart, 2010; Blay, 2007; Lewis & Bryan, 1988; Gordon, 2008; Woodson, 2010). Skin bleaching is rampant in some Jamaican high schools because the children are not receiving the education in high schools and the society that would discourage them from bleaching their skin. Skin bleaching is also reinforced in some high schools by the fact that some teachers treat the light-skinned students better than they treat the dark-skinned students (Charles, 2009a, 2010a).

The skin bleachers who create a 'browning identity' (Mohammed, 2000) are supported by social institutions that promote colourism. A light skin partner is a premium in some intimate-partner relationships in Jamaica. Some of the skin bleachers stated that they bleached 'to get a partner.' Social relationships also support the practice of skin bleaching. Some skin bleachers reported that the practice 'is popular' and 'our friends and other people are doing it.' The importance of light skin in intimate-partner relationships and broader social relationships and the popularity of skin bleaching in the society suggest that light complexion increases social acceptance and validation in the colourised society. Moreover, the altered dark complexion is viewed as 'style and fashion' by some skin bleachers because light complexion is an important part of their adornment aesthetic style in the fashion domain. The reasons given for skin bleaching in the present study also corroborates the reasons reported in earlier studies (Charles, 2003a, 2003b, 2006, 2009a, 2010a, 2011b). The skin bleachers engage their oppression by altering their Black physicality to receive the societal benefits accorded to light skin Jamaicans in order to survive. In other word, this is just one way how a small group of Black people in Jamaica have chosen to deal with or confront the positions of powerlessness they find themselves in. Skin bleaching reveals that some Blacks have altered their Black physicality in response to racial oppression via racism, colourism and miseducation. However, the majority of Blacks do not bleach their skin, so the behaviour of the skin bleachers should not be used to understand how Blacks in general resist their oppression.

The reported reasons for skin bleaching reflect the level of miseducation and colourism that are the contemporary legacies of White domination. Skin bleaching is an accommodation of domination among the Blacks who bleach but not among the majority of Blacks. The non-bleachers unlike the skin bleachers have grounded their education of the self in Afrocentricity to varying degrees so the behaviour of the skin bleachers should not be generalised to all Blacks.

The Jamaican society should be seen as an organic whole where sites of oppression like colourism and miseducation that influences some Jamaicans to bleach their skin intersects with domains of Black resistance. These domains of resistance are evident in the historical memory of the rebellions of the Captive Africans against their enslavement and can be seen from the long list of examples. The major ones include: the Maroon wars against the British colonial government, the powerful Pan African philosophy of Marcus Garvey, the Black Power Movement in the 1960s and 1970s and the ideas of Walter Rodney, the manifestation of Rastafari, the indigenisation of the high school curriculum, the contemporary fight for reparations from the British Government and the use of popular songs that lyrically challenge White supremacy. These have all created a resilient Black worldview that continues to challenge White domination. The skin bleachers who carry the marks of oppression, such as colourism and miseducation interact in the society with other Blacks who resist White domination and oppression (See Beckford and Charles in this volume). Although the skin bleachers yearn for a lighter shade of Black, they have consistently argued that they do not want to become white because they are Black (as a result of the intersectional influences of Black Resistance in Jamaica) though not in the hardcore Afrocentric sense (Charles, 2006). Many skin bleachers, therefore, form part of the society of Black people who are not denying their Blackness, but rather, seek an alternative strategy to deal with the discrimination they face. The skin bleachers should be re-educated. Afrocentric Jamaicans promote the content of the reeducation of the skin bleachers that beauty and intelligence exists among all peoples and cultures, that Blacks are a great people with a glorious history despite the rupture of

African captivity. This re-education comes from the Rastafarian worldview of Black liberation and redemption, African retentions, the Black Power ideology in the Americas, and in the traditional cultures and indigenous knowledge systems of Africa. Therefore, the content of re-education is anchored in the black radical tradition.

Conclusion

This chapter has contributed to the literature on skin bleaching by empirically testing the self-hate hypothesis and discussing the findings within the Black radical tradition. The skin bleachers as a group do not suffer from self-hate. The interrogation of the reasons the skin bleachers gave for altering their black physicality all points to colourised miseducation. The skin bleachers use this colourised miseducation to define themselves and make sense of the colour conscious social world in order to survive. The skin bleachers have altered their Black physicality to accommodate White domination. They are linked to British colonialism and plantation slavery through colourism and miseducation rather than self-hate. The captive Africans and the majority of their descendants as well as the Africans at home have consistently resisted White oppression.

Finally, it is a very dangerous practice to blame skin bleaching on the evaluative trait of the personalities (self-esteem) of skin bleachers. This practice of blaming the oppressed hides the colourised and racial discrimination that Blacks experience, which influences some of them to bleach their skin. The take home message is that people who blame the victims of racial oppression have missed how the oppressed deals with the intersectionality of history, culture, institutions, social structures and values in order to survive. Moreover, the purveyors of the self-hate argument ignore the ongoing Black resistance from the beginning of the European presence and erroneously conflate the actions of skin bleachers with the interior psychology of all Blacks, the majority of whom have consistently resisted White supremacy.

References

Alexander, Michelle. (2012). *The new Jim Crow: Mass incarceration in the age of colorblindness*, NewYork, New Press.

Beatty, Danielle, L. (2007). *The dynamic role of ethnic identity in the link between interpersonal racism and ambulatory blood pressure*, Ph.D. diss, City University of New York.

Bernichon, Tiffiny, Cook, Kathleen E and Brown, Jonathon D. (2003). Seeking self-evaluative feedback: The interactive role of global self-esteem and specific self-views, *Journal of Personality and Social Psychology*, 84(1): 194-204.

Blay, Yaba, A. (2007). *Yellow fever: Skin Bleaching and the Politics of Skin ColoUr in Ghana*, Ph.D. diss, Temple University, United States.

Brown, Aggrey. (1979). *Colour, Class and Politics in Jamaica*, New Brunswick, Transaction Books.

Brown-Glaude, Winnifred. (2007). The fact of Blackness? The Bleached Body in Contemporary Jamaica, Small Axe, 11(3): 3-51.

Caldwell, Melissa B. (1998). *Individual and Collective Self-Esteem, School Climate, and Achievement in African-American, White and Latino Children*. Ph.D. diss., Yale University, United States of America.

Carruthers, Iva, E. (1977). 'Centennials' of Black miseducation: A study of White educational 'management', *Journal of Negro Education*, 46(3): 291-304.

Charles, Christopher, A. D. (2003a). 'Skin Bleaching, Self-Hate and Black Identity in Jamaica', *Journal of Black Studies*, 33(6): 711-728.

Charles, Christopher, A. D. (2003b). 'Skin Bleaching and the Deconstruction of Blackness', *Ideaz*, 2(1): 42-54.

Charles, Christopher, A. D. (2006). *The Crowning of the Browning: Skin Bleaching and the Representation of Black Identity in the Context of Dancehall Music*. MA thesis, Hunter College of the City University of New York, United States of America.

Charles, Christopher, A. D. (2009a). 'Skin Bleachers' Representations of Skin Colour in Jamaica', *Journal of Black Studies*, 40(2):153-170.

Charles, Christopher, A. D. (2009b). 'Liberating Skin Bleachers: From Mental Pathology to Complex Personhood, Jenda', *A Journal of Culture and African Women Studies*, 14, 86-100.

Charles, Christopher, A. D. (2010a). *'Representations of colourism in the Jamaican culture and the practice of skin bleaching'*, Ph.D. diss. City University of New York, United States of America.

Charles, Christopher, A. D. (2010b). *Skin bleaching in Jamaica: Self-esteem, racial self-esteem and black identity transactions*, Caribbean Journal of Psychology, 3(1): 25-39. Springer Iternational Publisher.

Charles, Christopher, A. D. (2011a). 'The derogatory representations of the skin bleaching products sold in Harlem', *Journal of Pan African Studies*, 4(4): 117-141.

Charles, Christopher A. D. (2011b). 'Skin Bleaching and the Prestige Complexion of Sexual Attraction' in *Sexuality and Culture*, 15(4): 375-390.

Charles, Christopher , A .D. (2012). 'Skin Bleaching: The Complexion of Identity, Beauty, and Fashion' in *Meanings of Dress*, Miller-Spillman, Kimberly, Reilly, Andrew H, Hunt-Hurst, Patricia and Damhorst Mary L eds, 3rd edition, New York, Fairchild Books, 254-161.

Charles, Christopher, A. D. (2014). 'Skin Bleaching, *Encyclopedia of Critical Psychology*', New York, Springer Iternational.

Clark, Kenneth, B. and Clark, Mamie, P. (1950). 'Emotional Factors in Racial Identification and Preference in Negro children' *Journal of Negro Education*, 19(3): 341-350.

Cozart, Sheryl, C. (2010). 'Becoming whole: A letter to a Young, Miseducated Black Teacher' *The Urban Review*, 42(1): 22-38.

Craig-Henderson, Kellina, M. (2014). 'Colourism and Interracial Intimacy: How Skin colour Matters in Norwood', Kimberly J ed, New York, Routledge/Taylor & Francis Group,119-138.

Cramer, Phebe, and Anderson, Gail. (2003). Ethnic/racial attitudes and self identification of Black Jamaican and White New England children, *Journal of Cross Cultural Psychology*,34 (4):395-416.

Cross Jr., William E. (1991). *Shades of black: Diversity in African-American identity*, Philadelphia, Temple University Press.

Dadzie, O. E. and Petit, A. A. (2009). 'Skin Bleaching: Highlighting the Misuse of Cutaneous Depigmenting Agents' *Journal of The European Academy of Dermatology and Venereology*, 23(7) 741-750.

Davies, Marquita, F. (1998). *Understanding the Skin colour Perspectives of African American Kindergarten Students in an Urban School*. Ph.D. diss., University of Alabama.

DeGruy Leary, Joy. (2005). *Post Traumatic Slave Syndrome: America's Legacy of Enduring Injury and Healing*, Portland, Oregon, Uptone Press.

de Souza, Melanie, M. (2008). 'The Concept of Skin Bleaching in Africa and its Devastating Health Implications', *Clinics in Dermatology*, 26 (1): 27-29.

Dorman, Jacob, S. (2011). 'Skin Bleach and Civilisation: The Racial Formation of Blackness in 1920s Harlem', *Journal of Pan African Studies*, 4(4): 47-80.

Dunkley, Daive, A. (2013). *Agency of the Enslaved: Jamaica and the Culture of Freedom in the Atlantic world*, New York, Lexington Books.

Gooden, Amoa, ba. (2011). 'Visual representations of feminine beauty in the Black Press: 1915-1950', *Journal of Pan African Studies*, 4(4), 81-96.

Gordon, Lewis, R. (1997). 'Her *Majesty's Other Children'*, New York, Rowman and Littlefield.

Gordon, Lewis, R. (2008). *An introduction to Africana Philosophy*, Cambridge University Press.

Goupal-McNicol, Sharon-Ann. (1995). 'A Cross- Cultural Examination of Racial Identity and Racial Preference of Preschool Children in the West Indies', *Journal of Cross Cultural Psychology*, 26(2):141-152.

Harrison, Mathew, S. and Thomas, Kecia, M. (2009). 'The Hidden Prejudice in selection: A Research Investigation on skin colour Bias' *Journal of Applied Social Psychology, 39,*134-168.

Henriques, Fernando. (1951). 'Colour Values in Jamaican society', *British Journal of Sociology, 2,* 115-121.

Hickling, Frederick, W. and Hutchinson, Gerrard. (2000). 'Post-colonialism and Mental Health: Understanding the Roast Breadfruit' *Psychiatric Bulletin, 24,* 94-95.

Hughes, Michael, and Hertel, Bradley, R. (1990). 'The Significance of Colour Remains: A Study of Life Chances, Mate Selection, and Ethnic Consciousness Among Black Americans' *Social Forces,* 68(4): 1105-1120.

Hunter, Margaret, L. (2011). 'Buying Racial Capital: Skin Bleaching and Cosmetic Surgery in a Globaliszed World' *Journal of Pan African Studies* 4 (4), 142-164.

Jenkins, Susan, M. (1993). *The Socially Constructed Meaning of Skin Color Among African-American Adults*, Ph.D. diss., University of Michigan, United States.

Johnson, Michelle, A. (1996). 'Decent and fair: Aspects of Domestic Service in Jamaica, 1920-1970' *Journal of Caribbean History*, 30.1, 83-106.

Jones, Hollie, L. (2006). 'Experiencing, Appraising and Coping with Race Related Stress: Black Women Living in New York City', Ph.D. diss. City University of New York, United States..

Kardiner, Abram, and Ovesey, Lionel. (1951). *The Mark of Oppression: A Psychosocial Study of the American Negro*, New York, Norton.

Keith, Verna, M. and Herring, Cedric. (1991). 'Skin Tone and Stratification in the Black Communit' *American Journal of Sociology*, 97(3): 760-778.

King, Joyce, E. (2006). 'Dysconscious Racism: Ideology, identity, and the Miseducation of Teachers' *Journal of Negro Education*, 60 (2), 133-146.

Knapake, Lonzozou., Munos Sastre, T.M. and Mullet, Etienne. (2010). 'Skin Bleaching Among Togolese: An Inventory of Motives' *Journal of Black Psychology*, 36(3):350-368.

Lewis, Rupert, and Bryan, Patrick. (1988). *Garvey: His Work and Impact*, Jamaica, Institute of Social and Economic Research.

Lindsey, Treva, B. (2011). 'Skin Bleaching and the Emergence of new Negro Womanhood Beauty Culture' *Journal of Pan African Studies*, 4(4): 97-116.

Mahe, Antoine ., Ly, Fatimata and Guonongbe, Ari .(2004). 'The Cosmetic Use of Bleaching Products in Dakar, Senegal: Socio-Factors and Claimed Motivations' *Sciences Sociales et Sante*, 22(2): 5-33.

Mahe, Antoine, Ly, Fatimata and Perret, Jean-Luc.(2005). 'Systematic Complications of the Use of Skin Bleaching Products' *International Journal of Dermatology*, 44(1): 37-38.

Media That Matters. (n.d.) *A Girl like Me*. http://www.youtube.com/watch?v=YWyI77Yh1Gg.

Miller, Errol. (1969). 'Body Image Physical Beauty and Colour Among Jamaican Adolescents' *Social and Economic Studies,* 18(1): 72-89.

Miller, Errol. (1973). 'Self-evaluation Among Jamaican High School Girls' *Social and Economic Studies,* 22(4), 407-426.

Mohammed, Patricia. (2000). 'But Most of all Mi love Mi Browning: The Emergence in the Eighteenth and Nineteenth Century Jamaica of the Mulatto Woman as the desired' *Feminist Review,* 65, 22-48.

Neblett, Jr., Enrique,W., Shelton, J. Nicole and Sellers, Robert M. (2004). 'The Role of Racial Identity in Managing Daily Racial Hassles' in *Racial Identity in Context: The legacy ofKenneth B. Clark* Gina Philogène ed, Washington, DC, American Psychological Association, 77-90.

Patterson, Orlando. (1985). *Slavery and Social Death: A Comparative Study,* Cambridge and Harvard University Press.

Pierre, Martin, R. and Mahalik, James, R. (2005). 'Examining African Self-Consciousness and Black Racial Identity as Predictors of Men's Psychological Well-being' *Cultural Diversity and Ethnic Minority Psychology,* 11(1), 28-40.

Rosenberg, Morris and Simmons, Roberta ,G. (1971). *Black and White Self-esteem: The Urban School Child,* Washington, American Sociological Association.

Rosenberg, Morris. (1989). 'Old Myths Die Hard: The Case of Black Self-Ssteem' *Revue Internationale de Psychologie Sociale,* 2(3),355-365.

Schaefer, Richard, T. (2012). *Race and ethnicity in the United States,* New York, Pearson.

Shulman, Kevin A et al. (1999). 'The Eeffect of Race and Sex on Physicians' Recommendations for Cardiac catheterizatio' *The New England Journal of Medicine,* 340, 618-626.

Shepherd, Verene. (2000). 'Image, Representation and the Project of Emancipation: History and Identity' *in the Commonwealth Caribbean in Contending with Destiny' The Caribbean in the 21st*

Century, Kenneth Hall and Dennis Benn eds, Kingston, Ian Randle Publishers, 53-79.

Smith, Michael, G. (1990). *Culture, Race and Class in the Commonwealth Caribbean*, Jamaica, University of the West Indies Press.

Winders, Jamie., Jones III, John P. and Higgins, Michael, J. (2005). 'Making Gueras: Selling White Identities on Late-night Mexican Television' *Gender, Place and Culture*, 12(1), 71-93.

Woodson, Carter, G. (2010). *The miseducation of the Negro*, New York, Create Space Independent Publishing Platform.

CHAPTER NINE

Realigning and Reframing Pan African Resistance

Tony Talburt

Introduction

The broad-based Pan African ideology and movement can be considered as one of the most universally organised and sustained forms of Black resistance that was established to counteract the European control, dominance and exploitation of Black people in the modern era. These were more than Black resistance campaigns. At the heart of many of these initiatives, was a strong desire to assert, reinforce and retain aspects of Black identity and independence in the face of the prevailing Eurocentric systems. In much of the literature on Pan Africanism, however, the focus is very often centred on the twentieth century initiatives, campaigns and ideologies propounded by such leading personalities as: Henry Sylvester Williams, Marcus Garvey, William Dubois or Kwame Nkrumah. As a consequence, many aspects of Pan Africanism, as well as the individuals involved in such initiatives during the eighteenth and nineteenth centuries, throughout the African Diaspora, have been largely ignored. The purpose of this chapter, therefore, is to examine two major features within the Pan African tradition which were clearly present prior to the twentieth century, and which most people today would regard as distinctly Pan Africanist. The first of these features is the back to Africa ideologies and campaigns, while the second issue is the use of religion as vehicles through which to engage in Black resistance. This chapter considers whether discussions about these movements and initiatives should be much more explicit in acknowledging this early period in their contextualisation of this important Black resistance ideology.

In order to fully understand and appreciate the very idea of Pan Africanism prior to the twentieth century, it is important to be clear, in the first place, of its various shades of meaning and interpretations. What becomes clear from this is that whilst there is more of a general agreement regarding what constitutes Pan Africanism, the main point of departure centres upon arriving at a consensus as to when it was started. Ali Mazrui regarded Pan Africanism as the ideas to liberate Africa from European political, economic and socio-cultural control and to provide a movement to demonstrate the ability of Africans to govern themselves and contribute to world civilisation which he said had emerged within the African Diaspora (Mazrui, 1999, p. 706). Pan Africanism was, therefore, the idea of redemption of Africa to provide freedom for Black people and led to the development of a number of international Black movements for freedom. This movement, he asserts, reached its peak during the period 1900 to 1935 with such influential leaders as Marcus Garvey and W.E.B. Dubois and others in Europe and the United States (Mazrui, 1999, p. 706). Therefore, Mazuri, in common with a number of other writers (discussed below), considered Pan Africanism within the context of the twentieth century. He pointed out that from the 1930s until the 1960s the single most important factor which drove or motivated the Pan African ideology was the notion of an anti colonial struggle. This drive was facilitated by the large number of Africans who were demanding political and economic independence and who had gone to live, work or study in Europe and the USA. This was especially true for the French North African colonies and the Belgian colonies. For example during the

Algerian War of Independence, there were some four hundred and fifty thousand Algerians living in France.

Another major writer on Pan-Africanism, Vernon McKay (1963) divided the Pan African movement into four phases; 1900-1945 when it was dominated by African Americans and Caribbean people; 1945-1958 when it was dominated by African nationalists who were still under colonial rule whose aim was political sovereignty; 1958-1959 when President Nkrumah emerged as the ideological leader for a united states of Africa and finally the period after 1960 when many different African leaders were emerging which ended Nkrumah's dominance and led to the creation of rival Pan African initiatives (McKay, 1963, p. 94). The idea was to bring people of African descent much closer together (McKay, 1963, p. 98). Therefore, as far as Mckay was concerned, these campaigns of Black resistance were very definitely twentieth century movements seeking to improve the general civil liberties and human rights of Black people.

Apter and Coleman (1962) in their study on the evolution of political Pan Africanism, identified three phases in the evolution of the movement. The first phase centred on the campaigns of the 'exiled Africans' who found themselves in America and Europe. They organised ad hoc meetings and conferences, student groups, cultural associations, and also called for the independence of Africa itself. The second phase was the establishment of nationalist movements in the different territories of Africa in the Post-War period. The third phase was concerned with the attempts to create a wider African unity following the achievement of political independence (Apter and Coleman, 1962, p. 84). By making reference to the exiled Africans, the authors implicitly suggest that the first phase must have occurred before the twentieth century when Africans were forcibly transported to settle in the Americas. They, however, focused their attention on the campaigns in the twentieth century.

John Davis explained that the interest of the American Negro in Pan Africanism was not only long-standing, but went back to the year 1900 when Dubois got involved in the first Congress (Davis, 1962, p. 31). In the introduction to the book *Pan Africanism Reconsidered* (1962), the concept was described as the rallying slogan, the springboard, the ideological vehicle for the common efforts of exiled Africans, West Indians, and African Americans to advance the cause of Africa and Africans. Furthermore, it was pointed out that in its initiation, Pan Africanists were primarily interested in improving the conditions under which most Africans lived, but later, influenced in part by Dubois, the emphasis changed to a more militant programme of nationalism and African independence (American Society of African Culture, 1962, p. 5).

According to Thompson, the Pan Africanist movement was dominated by intellectuals or, at the very least, 'budding intellectuals' who spent a great deal of their time researching or sharing their experiences of the African experience in relation to European exploitation. These people could be found in the USA, the Caribbean, Britain and France (Thompson, 1969, p. 23). The list of personalities that Thompson then mentions consisted of such Pan-African heavy weights as the French-speaking Leopold Senghor, Cheikh Anta Diop and Aimé Césaire. The Anglophone Caribbean figures such as Garvey, as well as African thinkers such as Kwame Nkrumah. Whilst very few would argue against the names included in this list, the issue is that they were all personalities of the twentieth century.

Even in the current period, these general definitions of Pan-Africanism have not undergone any significant alteration. According to the Directorate of Information and Communication of the African Union (AU) in their 20th special edition of the *AU Echo* (2013), Pan Africanism was defined as an ideology and movement that encourages the solidarity of Africans world wide. It is based on the belief that unity is vital to economic, social and political progress and aims to 'unify and uplift' people of African descent.

The ideology asserts that the fates of all African peoples and countries are intertwined. At its core Pan Africanism is a belief that African peoples, both on the continent and in the Diaspora, share not merely a common history, but a common destiny. Although some of these writers did not make it explicit, it is clear that there was some recognition of active Black communities in America, the Caribbean and Europe which had organised some level of resistance against the various forms of discrimination they were experiencing prior to the year 1900. It is in this sense, therefore that Horace Campbell's definition of Pan Africanism regards it as an exercise in consciousness and resistance that reflects the self-expression and self-organisation of the African peoples and expresses their resistance to Eurocentrism (Campbell, 1994, p. 285).

Although not focusing on the period before the year 1900, Campbell made a very important point in declaring that Pan Africanism has 'always existed at different levels and manifested itself in village communities and has been disseminated through oral history, songs, stories, dances and other cultural media' (Campbell, 1994, p. 288). Furthermore, Apter and Coleman added, that the colonial governments in Africa made it very difficult for Black people to engage in any meaningful Pan African resistance campaigns in Africa itself. As a consequence, it was Africans abroad who first developed Pan Africanism. They claimed that most of the early Black organisations did not 'espouse nationalism or racial agitation' but rather focused on ameliorating the lives of Black people living abroad through 'persuasion and petition' (Apter and Coleman, 1962, p. 85). Similarly, Dubois was quoted as saying: the idea of one Africa to unite the thoughts and ideals of all native peoples of the Dark Continent belongs to the twentieth century and stems naturally from the West Indies and the United States (Thompson, 1969, p. 23). He might certainly have a point about the American and Caribbean involvement, but the movement had its roots in the eighteenth and nineteenth centuries.

Very importantly, it should be stressed at this juncture that, not every Black struggle against European domination or control should be subsumed under the heading Pan Africanism. A central feature of Pan Africanism is the fact that they are organised and sustained campaigns of resistance with the main objective being to fight not only for individual freedom but, symbolically at least, the freedom of a people. From the preceding discussion, therefore, it becomes clear that there are certain common factors which help to define or influence the main objectives or aims of Pan African resistance.

There are at least three key features which lie at the heart of most Pan African campaigns. First, there is a rejection of the European systems of colonialism, slavery and other forms of European political, economic and cultural discrimination and oppression. Secondly, there is an organised and sustained campaign of resistance or rebellion against the main institutions and systems of colonial governments often resulting in the establishment of alternative Black-based ideologies and organisations. These Pan African struggles, though often championed by a particular individual, have as their core value and purpose, a collective struggle rather than an individually focused engagement, thereby placing the emphasis on fighting for the freedom of the African or Black community. Thirdly, there is a desire to reconnect with Africa whether in the physical sense or spiritually. This is often based on the need of Black people in the Diaspora to not only relink with Africa, but also to re-assert pride in their own Blackness and identity and, therefore, posit a more African-centred world view by forming Black ideologies organisations specifically dedicated to raising their profile and struggles.

In effect, therefore, Black communities will invariably seek to establish alternative organisations to counteract the more exclusive and mainstream European models. A Pan African struggle should, at the very least, accept the idea of the African brotherhood of nations and common identity with its peoples whether they are on the African continent or within the Diaspora. Furthermore, those not directly involved in the same struggle, should be able to draw inspiration from such Black struggles. From the foregoing, we can claim, that Pan Africanism, in its broadest sense, refers to the establishment of Black organisations, campaigns or ideologies which seek to challenge particular aspects of European dominance or exploitative influence over Africa and Africans whether on the continent or in the African Diaspora. It thereby not only challenges, but seeks to assert the significance of Black pride and identity through the establishment of alternative ideologies and organisations.

In this sense, therefore, Pan-African resistance is closely associated with, or organised through, the use of pressure groups. Wherever they exist, pressure groups or interests groups seek to do two things. They either attempt to raise public awareness of a particular issue, or they seek to put pressure on the authorities to change some aspect of society with which they are not satisfied. In many instances, members of the Black community formed their own organisations or pressure groups specifically dedicated to a particular aspect or feature of Pan Africanism highlighted above. Some of the leading Pan Africanists such as Williams, Garvey or Dubois were all associated with particular pressure groups; Pan-African Association, Universal Negro Improvement Association (UNIA) and Niagara Movement respectively. In each case, these Black organisations were established to raise public awareness as well as challenge the prevailing colonial attitudes and systems of governments so as to implement change.

Pan African Resistance and Repatriation Prior to the Twentieth Century

According to Olisanwuche (1982) the Chicago Congress on Africa which was held in August 1893 was the beginning of Pan-Africanism as a movement. This congress lasted for a whole week. A few years later, partly as a stance against colonialism, Henry

Sylvester Williams, A Trinidad and Tobago lawyer, was influential in establishing an organisation called the African Association in London on September 24 1897. The organisation aimed to encourage a feeling of unity, to facilitate friendly intercourse among Africans in general, and to promote and protect the interest of Africans in the Diaspora. By June 1900 a Pan African Conference Committee had been established and a Pan African meeting actually took place in on 23-25 July, 1900 in Westminster Town Hall. There were thirty two delegates. These two events were seen as the formal starting point of what would later become known as the Pan African movement. In fact, Henry Sylvester Williams is often regarded as the originator of the term Pan African which he used from at least 1897. Although this Pan African meeting in 1900 had great symbolic significance, its achievements were short lived. Its main achievement was the publication called *The Pan African* journal which was launched in 1901 with the motto 'light and liberty'. It was edited by Henry Sylvester Williams and was supposed to be a monthly publication but never survived a year. By 1902 this Pan African Association had lapsed into obscurity (Olisanwuche, 1989, pp. 46-57). From this standpoint, therefore, it becomes easy to understand why discussions pertaining to Pan Africanism, would have as its starting point, the very late nineteenth century, with a strong focus on the developments in the twentieth.

Whereas the studies outlined above typically describe Pan African resistance as a twentieth century phenomenon, a few studies have offered an alternative position. Imanuel Geiss (1960) pointed out that the concept itself is one of the least known as well as very vague, due in part, to the reliance on a few short accounts by Dubois and the more detailed works of Padmore. Geiss acknowledged that whilst Pan Africanism may have burst on the global stage in the second half of the twentieth century, its roots could be traced to the late eighteenth century (Geiss, 1969).

At the very period when slavery and colonialism were rampant from the seventeenth to the nineteenth centuries, organised Black resistance initiatives were also being established by different groups largely independent of each other but nevertheless working towards the same general set of objectives. In effect, the slaves and ex-slaves in the African Diaspora as well as their immediate descendants established the roots of what would later come to be known as Pan Africanism. It was, as Geiss said, these Black activists in the Americas, Britain and later Africa who were able to articulate the concept of Pan-Africanism and translate it 'into political agitation and action in the twentieth century' (Geiss, 1969, p. 188). Starting from the eighteenth century Geiss listed the major fore-runners in this evolution of Pan-African ideology and agitation such as Cugoano and Equiano, through to nineteenth century writers like Horton, and Delaney and twentieth century champions such as Williams, Dubois and Padmore.

In his later work on Pan Africanism (1974) Geiss defined the Pan-African concept as the intellectual and political movements among Africans and African Americans who regard all peoples of African descent as homogeneous and view Africa as their real homeland. It also involved attempts to bring about political independence of, and cultural unity with, Africa and Africans (Geiss, 1974, pp. 3, 4). He also suggested that this was a movement of all 'coloured and colonial peoples' which at least embraces the idea of the movement's universal appeal. In this sense, he saw Pan Africanism as forms of resistance which stood for the economic, technological, social and political modernisation of a whole continent and its calls for equal rights for Africans and people of African descent (Geiss, 1974, p. 5). As far as Geiss was concerned, Pan Africanism was essentially a movement brought about by Black people in the Diaspora who had either been successfully educated or brought up in the Western world and were seeking to emancipate their fellow Black people from the clutches of White supremacy. In this sense, therefore, Pan Africanism was both a liberation movement as well as a means to help assert Black pride and identity.

Geiss referred to the early phase of Pan Africanism prior to the twentieth century as one of 'proto-Pan Africanism' (Geiss, 1974, p. 8). He acknowledged that the development of Pan Africanism did not wait until the twentieth century to present itself. In fact, he said that Pan Africanism, as a protest movement of Black people against White domination, cannot be understood without looking at the historical background of the slave trade, slavery and the abolitionist movements.

He regarded the year 1787 as an important point in terms of the roots of Pan-Africanism or what he called the 'proto-Pan African' movement for at least four reasons. Firstly, it was because in that year Richard Allen and a number of other religious leaders founded the free African society in a Methodist church in Philadelphia. By 1816 the African Methodist Episcopal (AME) was formed in America which was the first independent Afro American denomination. Secondly, 1787 was also the year when Prince Hall originally from Barbados, was probably the first advocate of equal rights in education. Furthermore he had led a petition on 17 October 1787 to the Parliament of Massachusetts asking for Black children to be given educational facilities especially because they had been loyally paying their taxes. He was also an advocate of African repatriation and the back to Africa movement. The third reason why 1787 was also considered important was because this was the year when the Society for the abolition of the slave trade, led by William Wilberforce, Granville Sharpe and Thomas Clarkson, was established. This movement, which also included Black activists such as Equiano and Cugoano, was very active in their campaigns against the slave trade. The last reason for the significance of the year 1787 stemmed from the fact that this was when we witnessed the first landing in Serra Leone which formed the first colonial settlement in Africa. This settlement would, from that time onwards, have a very important symbolic meaning to the

African struggle for independence (Geiss, 1974, pp. 34-37). One point which we could certainly add to the list by Geiss was the impact of the Haitian Revolution of 1791-1804. This remarkable series of events, resulted in a European imposed Black slavocracy being overthrown by its very victims, the Black masses.

Geiss was not alone in making this kind of proposition. Tony Martin (2012) in the preface to his book, pointed out that although the concept was coined by Henry Sylvester Williams in 1897 when he established the Pan African Association which met in London, what Williams established was the 'popularisation of an expression.' The concept had been established long before 'without the benefit of a name' (Martin, 2012, p. V11). Furthermore, Falola makes a similar point with regard to the fact that discussons about African nationalism actually started in the nineteenth century by writers such as Edward Blyden and James Africanus Beale Horton, amongs others, and extended to twentieth century writers like Kwame Nkrumah and Amilcar Cabral (Falola, 2013, p. 102).

Additionally, Vincent Bakpetu Thompson (1969) in the opening page of his introduction to his work declared that the seeds of Pan Africanism go back to the centuries of slave trading. He, however, like many other writers on this topic, then focused his attention on the twentieth century flowering of the ideology and movement, thereby discarding any significant discussions pertaining to the seeds of the movement prior to 1900. Geiss, also made reference to a proposed organisation in 1859 partly at the request of Thomas Hodgkin who suggested to Thomas Hughes at Cape Coast, Ghana, that there had been a meeting in that year to create an association of Africans, West Indians, and Afro Americans. Interestingly enough, the proposed name of this organisation included the key words 'African Association.' Even though the proposed association never materialised, this clearly demonstrates that there were people who were thinking seriously about such a Pan African organisation (Geiss, 1974).

One of the features of the Pan African movement has been the desire on the part of Africans in the Diaspora to relink with Africa. During the period of slavery and colonialism there was, among some Back people, the overwhelming desire to actually make efforts to physically (if not spiritually and culturally) reconnect with the African Continent. In this sense there was a need to organise initiatives to reconnect and even repatriate to Africa. These kinds of initiatives were often popularly labelled as 'back to Africa' campaigns. Chevannes, quite rightly asserted that the doctrine of repatriation is kindred to a lineage of ideas and forms of actions four hundred years old (Chevannes, 1995, p.1). These ideas were, as a few of the studies in this chapter suggest, closely linked to the onset of European slavery and colonialism and did not wait until Garvey popularised the concept in the twentieth century. Chevannes speaks of an 'idealisation of Africa' which was a feature which could be identified in the nineteenth century if not before, not only in Jamaica, where he focused much of his work, but also in the wider African Diaspora. For him, this attempt to reconnect with Africa took two main forms. The first was on the physical need to return or repatriate to Africa as an 'ideal home,' while the second centred upon attempts or movements pertaining to a symbolic point of reference denoting a sense of identity.

Furthermore, Geiss pointed out that just as America had used the Monroe Doctrine of the 1820s to declare to the world that Americas was for Americans, so, some Black people had, in the same nineteenth century, declared that Africa was for the Africans (Geiss, 1974, p. 41). According to Fryer, it was Martin Delaney, an African-American, who was one of the very first people to use the phrase, 'Africa for the Africans' (Fryer, 1984, p. 273). From as early as 1861 a meeting had taken place in London involving twelve people to discuss plans for the collaboration between British abolitionists, Africans, African Americans and Haitians (Fryer, 1984, p. 273). In 1859 Delany was responsible for setting up an initiative voluntary re-emigration to Africa to help build up a modern nation on African soil and for the halting of European imperialism. According to Delaney, his policy and thinking was that Africa should be for the African race and for Black men to rule them (Geiss, 1969, p. 190). Although this particular expedition failed to materialise, it was important in terms of the formulation of a movement which sought specifically to engage in the physical repatriation of Black people to Africa.

Even though Dr Martin Delaney is often considered as one of the earliest architects of the back to Africa campaigns, there were a number of other notable Black people involved in repatriation initiatives to Africa. One such individual was Paul Cuffee. He attempted to help free Black people in America settle in Sierra Leone and, in 1815 actually succeeded in transporting thirty eight people to Africa. The Barbadian, Dr Albert Thorne was a firm advocate of the idea of Black people repatriating to Africa during the period 1890s-1920s. William Henry Ellis led an expedition to Ethiopia in 1903 and Alfred Charles Sam of Oklahoma sought to link his back to Africa initiative, with his Akim Trading Company in Ghana in 1912 (Thompson, 1969, pp. 6, 7).

Martin (2012) also supports this point by pointing out that from the moment some Africans were separated from their homeland, there was a longing and desire to return. This is why a physical return or a symbolic reconnection to Africa is such a key feature of the Pan African struggle. Black people in the Americas and Britain had been, from as early as the eighteenth and nineteenth centuries, organising campaigns, or actively pursuing or considering the cause for a return to Africa. Cuffee, Equaino, Hall and chief Sam of Ghana are good examples of this. This was a crucial point that Traoré made in is chapters on maronage, in which there was a longing or desire on the part of some Caribbean slaves and ex-slaves to return or relink with Africa.

For many Black people in the Diaspora who were unable to make a physical return to Africa, they at least wanted to be closely identified with the continent and often referred to themselves as

Africans. Geiss informs us that such terms as 'African and Ethiopian' had been proudly used by former slaves such as Cugoano and Equiano and also African Americans in the nineteenth century. Very importantly, the term was not used in reference to single entities, but to the idea of a much wider collective community of Africans. This would become a significant feature of later twentieth century Pan African thought. Marable and Mullings (2000) also considered Edward Wilmot Blyden as the first important theorist of Pan Africanism who argued that the Black struggle and resistance should transcend national boundaries (Marable and Mullings, 2000). From the late nineteenth century Blyden advocated the repatriation of Black people from America to Africa. He declared that the Black people needed to be free in body and mind and bid farewell to the scenes of bondage and discipline and return to the land of their fathers where they could achieve larger opportunities and loftier achievements (Marable and Mullings, 2000, p. 152). Even though most of these early initiatives such as Chief Alfred Charles Sam's campaign to re-settle Black people in Africa were not totally successful, they should be considered as significant milestones in the back to Africa movement which is widely considered as one of the key features of Pan Africanism.

Before concluding this section of the chapter, it is worth making reference to the British Government's controversial attempt in the 1780s to send Black people who were living in Britain to settle in Sierra Leone. This initiative is not considered in this study as a Black-led campaign to reconnect Black people with the African continent, but demonstrates how the British Government was also thinking about repatriation but for entirely different reasons. According to Walvin (1973) this particular back to Africa plan, influenced and encouraged by Granville Sharp, was partly in response to Britain's attempts to offload the cause of some of its social problems which were closely associated with the Black population. This was supposed to be an opportunity to repatriate Black people to Africa in a society free from the social evils which they were experiencing in Britain. In fact, it was even argued that Black people would find life much better in Africa because the mildness of the climate and fertility of the land would help ensure that life would be so much easier there. It was assumed that with very little effort, it would be relatively easy for a person equipped with such basic tools as an axe, a hoe and a pocket knife, to make a very good living (Walvin, 1973, p. 147).

Some seven hundred Black people had signed the agreement to go on this trip to Sierra Leone in 1786. In fact, the government was not pleased that more people had not signed up and serious attempts were made to capture or press gang any Black person found on the streets begging or lurking about the streets under the Vagrant Act (Shyllon, 1977, p. 137). In the end, however, about four hundred of the original number of Black people who had signed up to go on the Sierra Leone expedition, refused to be part of the programme due in part to their doubts over the intentions of the British Government. They also questioned the reasons for the departure as well as expressed fears over their safety and security once in Sierra Leone itself (Shyllon, 1977, p. 137). As Shyllon pointed out, Cugoano had warned that the Sierra Leone expedition failed to really meet the expectations of the Black community in Britain or those in Africa and that it seemed to have been a plan put together in haste and based on racial discrimination (Shyllon, 1977, pp. 138-142).

Notwithstanding the failure of this Sierra Leone campaign, it is evident that many Black people were at least willing to consider the possibility of returning to Africa, but there might have been greater success, if this particular drive had been based on a genuine desire on the part of the Black people to leave Britain, not out of sympathy or to get rid of them, but as a means of turning their backs on an environment which discriminated against so many of them. Had this been the case, they, like the Maroons of the Caribbean, would have escaped from European colonial bondage to establish their own political independence and freedom.

The Black-led back to Africa campaigns of the nineteenth century, were not significantly different from the initiatives of Marcus Garvey's movement in the twentieth, which also failed to meet this central objective of actually bringing about a large-scale physical repatriation to Africa. What these different Pan African campaigns have in common, was their resolution to challenge and resist European control and domination by proclaiming the significance of Black pride and identity through the forging of close links with the African mainland. Significant for this study, is the fact that Black people in the Diaspora had been attempting to relink with Africa in terms of a physical repatriation long before Marcus Garvey popularised this concept in the twentieth century.

Religion, Resistance and Black Identity

A central theme which has been discussed in various chapters of this book, for example, Botchway in chapter three and Beckford and Charles in chapter five, has been the ways in which Black communities in Africa as well as the Diaspora used religion as forms of resistance. Indeed, this is the second feature of Pan Africanism which is examined in this section of the chapter. There was a need within the Black communities in Africa, the Americas and Britain to form organised Black-based religious groups and churches to counteract the racial discrimination which prevailed in the mainstream churches. These organisations specifically focused on the desire to improve the conditions under which many within the Black population lived and worked and worshipped in the Americas or Britain. In this regard, the Black populations in the United States as well as in Britain in the eighteenth and nineteenth centuries, sought to engage in resistance campaigns by organising a variety of Black churches specifically designed to challenge European domination and control in mainstream religious groups and churches, from which many of them were excluded. Such religious or church groups were very active Black-based institutions specifically established to promote, or even preserve aspects of Black identity and culture and as such, would definitely fit the criteria of Pan African organisations, in much the same way as some of the Black churches in America still do today.

That religion and Black resistance were crucial elements in the history of the Pan African struggle can hardly be denied. The Name Ethiopia has had great symbolic significance within the Pan African movement from the eighteenth century. As early as 1784, the name or word Ethiopia became identified with salvation, when an African American Baptist preacher, a former slave, founded the first Baptist Church which he called the 'Ethiopian Baptist Church' (Nelson, 1994, p. 66). By the 1920s and 1930s many followers of Marcus Garvey and later Rastafarians, would come to see Ethiopia as the land of freedom or a symbolic representation of a safe place of refuge from 'Babylon' which was taken, by Rastafarians in particular, to refer to European and colonial systems of political and cultural oppression against Black people.

Campbell goes even further by suggesting that whereas White missionaries were seeking to take part in the civilising aspect of European colonialism and so contribute to the partitioning and subsequent underdevelopment of Africa, Black Christian preachers of the Ethiopianism were doing the opposite. Their central mission was to unite Africans wherever they were, under the umbrella of a religious and political movement which had, as a significant part of its focus, the centrality of Africa (Campbell, 1994, p. 288). Therefore, evangelical Pan Africanism was a key feature of Black resistance in which people used religion as a form of political protest. This can further be seen from the fact that Marcus Garvey established the African Orthodox Church as an integral part of the UNIA (Martin, 1983). In this way, therefore, the Black churches or evangelical Pan Africanism was concerned with promoting Christianity with a Black political emphasis based on freedom from discrimination, oppression and suffering in the here and now.

The presence of such evangelical Pan Africanism was very evident in America in the nineteenth century. Richard Allen was particularly instrumental as one of the founders of the Independent Free African Society in 1787. It is interesting to note that this was also the very year when the Anti-Slavery Society was established in Britain, primarily to put pressure on the government to bring an end to the trans-Atlantic slave trade in Britain. In this same year, a group of Black people in America were establishing campaigns to bring about their own religious or cultural emancipation from White domination. Precisely because of the openly discriminatory practices towards the Black members of the St George's Methodist Church on Fourth Street, Philadelphia, Richard Allen and others would later form the African Methodist Episcopal (AME) Church in 1816 (Marable and Mullings, 2000).

Black people in America were actively involved in organised resistance campaigns for their own liberation. These include people like Nat Turner, Frederick Douglas, Martin Delaney and also Joseph Cinque both on board the Amistad in 1839, and even after he landed in America. Black Christian evangelical preachers such as George Alexander McGuire of Antigua who was also the first Bishop in America of the African Orthodox Church, was associated with the Marcus Garvey Movement and the UNIA (Thompson, 1969, p. 6). Similar to the case of Appiah in chapter three of this study, McGuire was dis-satisfied with Anglican Church and sought to establish, and be involved in a religion which had, as its central mission, the uplifting of Black people. As Thompson importantly points out, the fact that these Christian believers used the name 'African' suggests that there were attempts to establish solidarity with Africa, brought about largely in response to the prevailing European domination and racial discrimination towards the Black community in America (Thompson, 1969, pp. 8, 9).

Those individuals, who were not advocating for the establishment of alternative Black-led churches, used the church or very Biblical-based language as a means of getting their message of Black radicalism across to whole groups or a collectivity of people. In this regard, a Christian minister, Henry Garnet, was also a very active Black anti-slavery campaigner in America and became particularly famous for his controversial speech at the National Negro Convention in 1843 in New York. These meetings had been held to discuss issues of racial equality and the emancipation of the Black slaves in the South of the country. That this convention was actually taking place at all, in the middle of the nineteenth century is testimony in itself of a Pan African spirit of collectively seeking to challenge the discriminatory practises which were prevalent in many of the established or conventional ideologies and policies in America at that time. In this meeting, Garnet virtually called for the Black community to take up arms and fight for their freedom. As far as he was concerned, a person's Christian beliefs did not justify them being obedient to oppressive leaders. It was their duty, therefore, to use every moral, intellectual and physical means available to ensure their prosperity and success, even to the point of death (Marable and Mullings, 2000, p. 60). This very radical, outspoken preacher and activist went on to declare that Black people could plead their own cause and do the work of emancipation themselves. Using a combination of Biblical language contextualised within a political framework, he declared that there would be very little redemption without the shedding of blood (Marable and Mullings, 2000, pp. 61, 62). Though Garnet provided no clear cut method of resistance in this delivery, he nonetheless suggested that people should use whatever means necessary to 'torment the God-cursed slave-holders until they are glad to let you go free' (Marable and Mullings, 2000, p. 63). These churches in America were important tools in providing information pertaining to Black political consciousness.

Of course, Garnet was not alone in attacking the orthodox Christian religion. Another example of a politically and intellectually Black activist in this regard was Edward Wilmot

Blyden (1832-1912) who left St Thomas in what is today the US Virgin Islands in the Caribbean in 1850 for Liberia via the United States. He became one of the most distinguished Pan African intellectuals of his day, who amongst other ideas, suggested that Black people should reject Christianity as it had stifled and thwarted the development of Black people (Blyden, 1992,). In this way, Blyden and some of the other individuals mentioned above, started a movement or Black Theology which has continued to the present day with such studies as Beckford (1998) which posits the view that much of the Christian religion, followed by so many Black people today in Britain, needs to have more of an Afrocentric focus.

In the Caribbean there were similar Pan African religious resistance movements, some of which were discussed in Beckford and Charles' chapter on Jamaica. Wherever the slaves found themselves, many of them resisted the mainstream ideologies and teachings of the Christian religion. Vincent Thompson has correctly pointed out that many slaves resisted the established religious systems and conventions and stuck to their own variations of African worship and religions (Thompson, 1987). Such religious gatherings by Black people were occasions not only to engage in acts of worship, but also to socialise and also attack the exploitative colonial establishment, either through speeches or songs. Thompson, for example, makes mention of the fact that some of the slaves in Africa used satire through songs as a means of engaging in subtle forms of resistance against their slave masters (Thompson, 1987, pp. 262, 263). Patterson also made mention of the same practice among the slave populations in Jamaica (Patterson, 1973).

The development of the Myal religion in Jamaica by the middle of the eighteenth century was a very good example of an attempt to form a religious movement based on the broad association of Pan Africanist ideology. Its prevailing feature was its ability to embrace a wide cross section of the Black population in Jamaica and unite them in their pursuit of freedom of worship not confined to European conventions. The focus centred on the dominance of getting into the spirit as well as the almost total obedience to their charismatic leaders (Chevannes, 1995, pp. 18-21).

John Sayers Orr or the 'Angel Gabriel' was described by Martin as a coloured Guyanese whose ideology included hostility to Roman Catholic 'popery,' insistence on the right of free speech and opposition to slavery (Martin, 2012, p.199). Because of his international travel to places like England, the USA as well as Australia, he had an African world view in which he opposed the exploitation being experienced among the poor Black people in Guyana. His criticisms of the Catholic Church and the Portuguese in Guyana, many of whom were Catholic, meant, from the outset, there were bitter hostilities between Orr's Black and coloured followers and the Portuguese. Furthermore, Orr was able to mobilise people and, at one time, had ten thousand followers in Manhattan and two thousand followers in a procession into Brooklyn (Martin, 2012, p. 200). In 1856 in Guyana there were days of widespread riots between the followers of Orr and the Portuguese. Orr was, even though not personally involved in the riots, arrested and later died in Jail in November 1856. For Martin, Black resistance campaigners Like Orr, were part of a larger group of predominantly middle class Black and coloured professional individuals who were conscious of their 'historical mission of racial uplift' (Martin, 2012, p. 207).

In Britain the pattern of using religion as a vehicle of Black resistance was not dissimilar to those practices in the Americas. The colonial authorities in Britain were often reluctant to allow Black missionaries to travel from the country to engage in missionary work among fellow Black people in Africa. According to Shyllon, the Society for the Propagation of the Gospel in Foreign Parts, had been educating Black young people in Britain from at least the 1750s so that they could go to Africa to help train the Africans in Christian missions (Shyllon, 1977, p. 56). A reading of Equiano's biography demonstrates the extent to which his own life was one filled with examples of struggles not only for his freedom but also for those of his fellow countrymen, and also for the equality of all peoples based on Christian brotherhood. He became a Christian quite early in his life in the Americas and, upon arriving in England, sought to get involved in becoming a missionary to help spread the Christian message in Africa. Although Martin described Equiano, as 'England's foremost Black abolitionist', he was denied his official appointment or ordination as a missionary and so was denied this opportunity (Martin, 1983, p. 39).

A contemporary and associate of Equiano was Quobna Ottobah Cugoano (1757-1791?) whose publication in 1787, 'Thoughts and Sentiments' on the Evils of Slavery was the first book written by a Black British person on the topic. He too had a Christian perspective in his writings and anti-slavery campaigns. He, like Equiano, argued from a moral and Christian perspective about the evil associated with slavery and called upon fellow Bible-believing Christians in Britain to treat all peoples, including Black people, with dignity and equality. Cugoano thus became one of the first outspoken anti-slavery campaigners in the eighteenth century. Having been kidnapped from what is present day Ghana at about the age of thirteen, he was taken to the Caribbean as a slave before eventually coming to England. His book became a powerful and personal attack on the trans-Atlantic slavery system. Cugaono's brand of Christianity was neither meek nor mild. He used the Bible as a tool with which to both appeal to, as well as attack the White authorities. He famously warned, in his book, of dire possible punishments from God which would befall those engaged in treating Black people unjustly (Cugoano, 1999, p. 79).

Far more radical than Cugoano, was the Jamaican born Robert Wedderburn, who was briefly discussed in the first chapter of this book; by the early nineteenth century he had joined the outlawed radical Spencean Movement. It was partly because he, like so many of the people mentioned above, had become so disillusioned with Christianity that he was eventually arrested in 1820 for Blasphemy. He became very critical of the Christian religion which seemed to support slavery and discrimination against Black people on the hand one, while openly declaring a message of peace, love and happiness on the other. Although as we have seen, his central mission was linked to the Spencean Movement which was more politically aligned with the ideals of providing social benefits such as land and property rights to the poor, Wedderburn was also very definitely concerned with the plight of the Black population in Britain and in his homeland of Jamaica. According to Fryer, up to two hundred people a week would gather to attend presentations or lectures on 'theology, morality, natural philosophy, and politics by this self-taught West Indian' (Fryer, 1984, p. 223). Although he was at one time a licensed preacher, he was very clearly not always inclined to follow the Christian doctrine of turning the other cheek, in the face of any form of injustice. For example, following the Peterloo disturbances or massacre in Manchester in 1819 where thousands of people had gathered to demand Parliamentary reform, but were met with police or military brutality in which about a dozen of them were killed and several hundreds wonded by these government forces, he suggested people should learn to 'use the gun, the dagger, the cutlass and the pistol (Fryer, 1984, p. 224). But with regard to Jamaica more specifically in relation to slave reistance, he suggestsd that the slaves in Jamaica should go on an annual one hour strike. Wedderburn's radical views, some of which supported violent actions against the government forces, was the main reason for which he was subsequently arrested and charged with sedition and blasphemy.

As Fryer explained, Wedderburn had two objectives. The first was to campaign for improvements in the living conditions of the poor White people in Britain and secondly, he was an anti-slavery campaigner. Drawing upon examples from his own experience as an eye witness to the evils of slavery, Wedderburn held meetings where he 'preached' and was said to have audiences of up to two hundred people clapping and cheering his speeches. According to one source, Wedderburn was actually planning to 'incite revolution on the streets of the imperial capital' (Rice, 2003, p. 11). His radical speeches soon came to the attention of the government and he was actually charged and sentenced by the Lord Chief Justice in 1820 to two years in Dorchester Prison for preaching 'blasphemous words' against the Bible and Christianity, the official state religion. As Hoyles points out, Weddeburn was very much a radical preacher who had never forgotten how his own parents had been mistreated physically at the hands of their White plantation owners and in this sense was certainly one of Britain's most radical Black anti-slavery campaigner (Hoyles, 2004).

With regard to his campaigns pertaining to the Black population, he was against slavery and colonialism and in this regard, a vocal critic of these systems. He was, for example opposed to the idea of Black Christian missionaries going to the colonies in Africa or the Caribbean to help spread the Christian message (Fryer, 1984, p. 224). Wedderburn, largely through the political group and ideology of Spencean Movement, used this as a vehicle to speak out against the 'horrors of slavery' and general injustices being experienced by Black people in Britain and throughout the Caribbean. His call for African unity amidst a common colonial oppressor was captured in this powerful quote in Fryer's work:

> Oh ye Africans and relatives now in bondage to the Christians because you are innocent and poor; receive this the only tribute the offspring of an African can give... I am a West Indian, a lover of liberty and would dishonour human nature if I did not shew myself a friend to the liberty of others (Fryer, 1984, p. 225).

In these ways, Wedderburn sought to appeal to the Black community to be aware of the political and economic plight they found themselves in and was prepared to use the language of the Bible and religion as tools in his campaigns.

Rather than accepting the teachings or doctrines of the conventional churches, and being submissive or docile with regard to resisting European colonialism, many Black people were using organised religion as a vehicle of resistance based on their own variation of broad-based African traditions. These were clearly seen both in the twentieth century and also in the two centuries before this. These Black initiatives were evident throughout the African Diaspora and were entirely independent of each other. There were two inter-related reasons which stimulated this interest in establishing Black-based or Pan African religious movements. The first was dissatisfaction with mainstream European religions, and the second was the subsequent breakaway and formation of a radical Black alternative. This is what drove so many Black people to become labelled by the colonial White establishment as 'radical preachers' because they used their newly established religious organisations as political instruments through which to attack European slavery, colonialism and discrimination.

Conclusion

From the discussions above, two main points have emerged which are briefly summarised here. The first key point which this chapter has tried to postulate is that many essential features within the Pan African Movement existed in the African Diaspora long before the twentieth century. In fact, the origins of the Pan Africanist Movement has its roots in the very fabric of slave and colonial society and culture which emerged from the sixteenth century when Europeans first attempted to engage in large-scale operations of exploitations of Africa and Africans on the continent and subsequently in the Americas and Britain. From the outset, Africans everywhere engaged in resistance at every level and through a variety of means. Many of these forms of Black resistance were carefully and systematically organised campaigns targeting

European systems of slavery and colonialism. These Black resistance campaigns which ensued, focused on alternative Black ideologies and organisations in direct opposition to established Eurocentric systems and values. Some of these Black campaigns also stressed the need for unity as well as calls for a reconnection with, and repatriation to, Africa through various back to Africa campaigns. The fact is, that such initiatives were evident among slaves and their immediate descendants throughout the African Diaspora long before Henry Sylvester Williams coined the phrase 'pan-African' at the very end of the nineteenth century.

The second issue which this chapter has demonstrated is that throughout the Black Diaspora, there were numerous groups or individuals who questioned aspect of Eurocentric and exploitative religions which seemed to justify racial discrimination, slavery and colonialism. There was very often a rejection of a particular European model or framework in favour of a more African centred approach. This is why, for example, Blyden and Wedderburn eventually turned their backs on the mainstream Christian religion. In keeping with the spirit and central mission of such twentieth century Black resistance religious and political organisations such as Rastafarianism and Nation of Islam, these eighteenth and nineteenth century church organisations were able to pre-empt and articulate similar sentiments of dissatisfaction and Eurocentric dominance in religion. It seems very clear that Black communities were not only establishing their own ideologies and institutions of resistance through religious organisations, but were doing so from the eighteenth and nineteenth centuries. From the foregoing discussion, it becomes evident that Pan-Africanism ought to be examined more within this broader framework incorporating the struggles and campaigns which predate the year 1919 when the first official Pan- African Conference took place.

CHAPTER TEN

Fight For Freedom: A Summary

Moussa Traoré and Tony Talburt

The central objective of this book has been to demonstrate that Black People, wherever they found themselves, and through a variety of different strategies, challenged European systems of dominance and oppression. The focus in this study has centred upon the resistance campaigns that were often characterised by sophisticated levels of planning and organisation. This brief summary outlines a number of key themes that have emerged throughout the book. Specifically, it highlights the three main forms of resistance that were carried out in Ghana, before examining the resistance strategies carried out in the Diaspora, particularly in the Caribbean and Britain.

Two of the unique features and strengths of this book have been its eclectic and interdisciplinary approach, coupled with its examination of case studies of Black people in Africa and throughout the Diaspora, engaging in resistance campaigns in order to fight for their own political, economic and socio-cultural survival and identity. Drawing upon original material from different academic disciplines such as African and Caribbean history, literature, politics and psychology, this central theme of organised Black resistance campaigns has been emphasised. In particular, the study has shown that wherever systems of European slavery and colonialism existed, examples of Black resistance against such European exploitation, were equally present and active. The over-riding motive behind most of these resistance initiatives was a desire among Black people to preserve and assert their own forms of existence and identity.

Some of these forms of resistance that have been examined in this study included: African oral narratives, Black Nationalism and religion in Africa, local African resistance to colonial integration, an examination of Jamaica as a micro-study of radical Black traditions, case studies of Maroons in the French Caribbean, skin bleaching and Black identity, and also the historic roots of Pan Africanist ideology and resistance.

One of the methods used by Africans to resist European slavery and colonialism was the use of songs and oral narratives. Many of these songs and oral accounts by Africans in the Northern Region of Ghana, focused on their reflections of attempts by slave raiders to capture their people, and also of the different strategies they used to resist such attempts to enslave them. One of the main points that emerged from an examination of these African songs was the extent to which they presented African communities, hitherto perceived as victims, as places where they were able to present a completely different perspective of their own, based upon narratives of resistance and common struggle to retain their own freedom and identity.

These songs of resistance not only revealed the very subtle ways and attempts by these cultures to rewrite their collective history, but also demonstrated that many of these slave raids were accompanied by some degree of violence. Therefore, fighting back became a significant cultural response mechanism, and is portrayed in some of the songs through images of war. One of the songs, for example, performed by men in Navrongo, involved a call to arms in which the strong men were called to meet their enemies on the battle field. In another song, reference was made to the shooting of arrows, which in itself does not suggest weakness, docility or victimhood, but rather, demonstrates evidence of a determined desire on the part of these Africans to fight back even in the midst of sophisticated weaponry. These songs, therefore, demonstrate the level of importance that these communities attached to these historical accounts of resistance and Black pride.

The second major form of resistance examined in this study was the issue of religion and Black Nationalism in Ghana. The Eurocentric brand of Christianity only served to strengthen European dominance over African communities. As Europeans attempted to use the Christian religion as a form of control in Africa, many African leaders used their own interpretations of Christianity to challenge such domination. This was precisely what was done by Prophet Jemisimiham Jehu-Appiah. He conceptualised religion as a force of social change that should be regarded as more than just a matter of personal worship and spiritual salvation. Religion, he argued, should be a potent tool for the physical redemption of the African. Appiah viewed his church as Afrocentric, born and controlled by Africans, and instituted to restore the lustre of Afrocentricity to Christianity, which he suggested was a universal religion of freedom and self-determination.

The central point for Black Nationalists like Appiah, was that Black people should be in charge of their religious destinies as well as their affairs in the secular space. Black religious campaigns, therefore, could not be divorced from the secular affairs of the world. For him, the essence of religion was for ensuring of a Black Nationalist perspective, predicated upon the significance of ethnic pride, self-determination, and self-reliance. For example, he disagreed with the notion that indigenous instruments and singing and dancing were heathen and uncivil and should be excluded from church services. The Black Nationalist religious ideas of Appiah served to raise awareness of the significance of safeguarding Black identity by resisting the dominance of Eurocentric systems in Christianity.

The third major example of Black resistance carried out in Ghana was based around the case study of one particular African ethnic community, the Ewe, fighting for their own Black identity and self-determination. The main conflict was between the Black-led Togoland Congress and the British Colonial Office, working in tandem with local political parties and officials, over attempts to integrate the Trust Territory in the Gold Coast. In essence, this struggle was carried out between two groups of African nationals who were caught up in a wider colonial conflict, where the British, were actually using one group of Africans against another, to satisfy its own interests. It was expedient for the British Colonial Office to create a Trust Territory that was based on integrating different peoples into one larger country. This, act of integrating different communities into the Gold Coast, however, would bring an end to any agitation for a separate Togoland unification. Such an action would result in the erosion of the very existence of the Ewe ethnic community in the Gold Coast. This became a source of resentment, disenchantment and agitation among the Ewe, who came under the British-controlled Togoland.

It was this sense of powerlessness and the gradual erosion of their cultural and historic significance, that resulted in the local people engaging in resistance campaigns against this British colonial policy, and was also one of the factors that led to the development of Togoland/Ewe Nationalism. This particular Togoland Nationalist resistance also resulted in the development of their shared colonial experiences and, a common identity. The local people of Ewedome sought to resist by attempting to reclaim and also assert their own political and cultural autonomy. The various resistance strategies such as protests, demonstrations and attempted boycotts were used among the Ewe, as they sought to fight for their own independence and freedom.

Outside of Africa the various forms of Black Resistance continued. In this respect, the country of Jamaica served as a unique example of a society where all the major forms of Black resistance actually took place at one time or another during the course of its history and development. In this regard, it was demonstrated that Jamaica has had a long history of engaging in resistance against European domination and oppression through its various manifestations of a Black radical tradition. These forms of resistance were clearly evident from the era of initial European contact until the present period.

Captive Africans, working on commercial plantations, along with the Maroon wars, created serious problems for the colonial militias because of their continued forms of resistance to European domination and control. The Black radical tradition manifested itself in the 1865 Morant Bay Rebellion and was also observed in the subversive preaching of Reverend Alexander Bedward, as well as in the Black Nationalism of Marcus Garvey. It was also demonstrated in the 1938 labour protests, and also the rise of Leonard Howell and other Rastafari founders who promoted Ethiopianism and Garvey's conception of Black Nationalism. The resistance continued through Reverend Claudius Henry's suspected coup, and the Walter Rodney protests of the 1960s. Black resistance also manifested itself over the brutality of some Chinese merchants, and through the controversial and conscious lyrics of popular songs, especially those belonging to the genre of reggae music. These examples indicated a coherent and constant theme of Black people in Jamaica engaging in radical opposition to systems of White exploitation.

Another area of Black resistance that was emphasised in this study was the significant role played by female Maroons in the Francophone Caribbean. One Maroon woman in particular, was determined to reconnect physically and emotionally with Africa, which she regarded as the ancestral home of Black people. This was clearly demonstrated in *Heremaknhonon,* where, Veronica, the young Black Gadeloupean, sought to find her cultural identity, especially because she felt isolated and also as though she was merely existing in a state of 'unhomliness.' That state of confusion and identity conflict led her to embark upon a physical journey from the Caribbean to Guinea, in Africa, where she hoped to find her roots and her Black identity.

Veronica manages to resist the various forms of Eurocentrism she encounters, and then fights to repatriate to Africa. In this regard, therefore, this novel is an example of a literary work that incorporates one of the themes of Pan African resistance to Eurocentrism through a search for a feminist Black Caribbean identity. One can regard Veronica's trip to Guinea, as a brave, strong and vigorous form of Maronage. Whereas most of the slaves in the Caribbean who fought for their freedom were primarily concerned with establishing Maroon communities in the same country, this woman completely leaves the Americas and journeys all the way across the Atlantic Ocean to Africa where she forcefully looks for freedom.

The second novel, also about Maroons in the Francophone Caribbean, followed a trans-historical 'collective' protagonist, the Nègre Marron or Maroon Negro, who refused to accept enslavement or assimilation, and never stopped resisting exploitation and White hegemony. The Nègre Marron is a symbolic figure whose personality constantly changes in the novel. From the run-away slave who refused the submission of the plantation system and seeks refuge in the forest, he then later became the one who organised the workers and eloquently taught them how to discuss and argue for better salaries and working conditions when slavery ends and Blacks become workers on the fields of the rich land owners. Siméon Louis Jerome, the Negro Maroon and protagonist, first appears in the novel when he leaves his White master's plantation, flees to the hilly forests and begins to think of actual and practical ways in which he can kill the White master and then return to Africa. At a later stage in the novel, we find ourselves at a period which corresponds to the Cold War era of tensions between the West and the Soviet bloc. The Nègre Marron's character switches into a labour activist whose companion in the workers' struggle is Leon, a name that is reminiscent of Leon Trotsky, one of the main ideologists of the Soviet Revolution. The key point to take from this novel, is the fact that throughout the different narratives pertaining to Siméon Louis Jerome, he never stops being an activist, seeking to improve the conditions of the Black people and also ways to empower them.

Unlike the Maroons who engaged in resistance campaigns to gain their freedom from slavery and oppression by physically escaping, many Black people who were unable to leave, arising from their miseducation relating to colourism, challenged their feelings of oppression and exploitation by engaging in skin bleaching in order to improve their social aspirations and positioning in society. Far from assuming that Black people engaged in skin bleach primarily because they have low self-esteem, or because they hate themselves, this study showed that such practises are carried out precisely to challenge the systems of oppression they find themselves in. In fact, it is colourism that actually influences the behaviour of some Blacks because they are miseducated to believe that the standard for beauty, status, intelligence, moral integrity, progress, enlightenment and so on, are determined by Whites and their culture.

This miseducation occurred because these Blacks were indoctrinated in schools about European heroes, culture, history and achievements. As far as they were concerned, light skin is prettier than dark skin, and ultimately derives greater benefits from society, and this desire, on their part, to succeed, drives them to this course of action. In seeking to address this situation, those individuals who felt powerless and oppressed, sought to take back control of their own destiny. Engaging in skin bleaching, therefore, like the Maroons seeking to escape from slavery and exploitation, should be regarded as acts of resistance to achieve greater levels of control of their own destiny and identity.

The final issue dealt with in this study was Pan Africanism and Black resistance. The central objective that has been presented, is that both the seeds and many actual manifestations of the Pan African resistance in America and Europe, have been present for centuries, and should not be exclusively regarded as twentieth century Black initiatives. Discussions about Pan Africanism very often centre upon the twentieth century initiatives, campaigns and ideologies propounded by such leading personalities as: Henry Sylvester Williams, Marcus Garvey, William Dubois or Kwame Nkrumah. As a consequence, many aspects of Pan Africanism, as well as the individuals involved in such initiatives during the eighteenth and nineteenth centuries, throughout the African Diaspora, have been largely ignored.

The concept of Africa for the Africans, or back to Africa campaigns, were actively pursued by a number of people in the nineteenth century such individuals as Martin Delaney, Paul Cuffee, and Alfred Charles Sam of Oklahoma who all sought, independent of each other, to raise awareness of these ideas about African repatriation. In addition, many people, through their Christian beliefs and influences also pursued this Pan African agenda of Black liberation. Whilst European missionaries were seeking to take part in the civilising aspect of European colonialism and so contribute to the partitioning and subsequent underdevelopment of Africa, a number of Black Christian preachers of the Ethiopianism or the Pan African tradition, were doing the opposite. For example, Robert Wedderburn was in no mood to wait for God to exact judgement upon White oppressors for their exploitative behaviour towards Black people, but suggested a much more radical approach where people should learn to 'use the gun, the dagger, the cutlass and the pistol.' In America Henry Garnet in 1843, virtually called for the Black community to take up arms and fight for their freedom. Through these means, it is clear that a number of Black people saw religion as a means to help resist European exploitation through Black collective organisation.

This study has demonstrated, therefore, that Black people used a wide range of resistance strategies and initiatives to confront European exploitation and dominance. Whether on the African continent, or in the Diaspora, Black people were fighting for the own freedom. These forms of resistance were aimed at helping to ensure the continued existence of Black pride, freedom and identity. In Africa, exploited Black people fought for freedom and identity from the moment Europeans arrived to exploit them. In the Diaspora, according to the words of Bob Marley, Black people were fighting on arrival and continue to fight for their survival.

References

American Society of African Culture eds. (1962). *Pan Africanism Reconsidered*, Berkeley and Los Angeles, University of California Press.

Apter, David and Coleman, James. (1962). 'Pan Africanism or Nationalism in Africa' in the American Society of African Culture eds. *Pan Africanism Reconsidered*, Berkeley and California, University of California Press.

Beckford, Robert. (1998). Jesus is Dread: *Black Theology and Black Culture in Britain*, London, Darton, Longman and Todd Ltd.

Blyden, Edward. W. (1992). *Christianity Islam and the African Race*, San Francisco, California, First African Arabian Press.

Campbell, Horace. (1994). 'Pan-Africanism and African Liberation' in Lemelle, Sidney and Kelly, Robin eds. Class, *Imagining Home: Class, Culture and Nationalism in the African Diaspora*, London, New York, Verso Publishers.

Chevannes, Barry. (1995). *Rastafari: Roots and Ideology*, New York, Syracuse University Press.

Cugoano, Quobna Ottobah. (1999). *Thoughts and Sentiments on the Evil of Slavery and Other Writings*, New York, Toronto and London, Penguin Books.

Davis, John. (1962). 'Pan Africanism: Nascent and Mature' in American Society of African Culture (eds.) *Pan Africanism Reconsidered*, Berkeley and Los Angeles, University of California Press.

Directorate of Information and Communication of the African Union Commission, (2013). *The AU Echo*, Issue No. 5, 27 January.

Edwards, Paul eds. (1989). *The Life of Olaudah Equiano*, New York and Ontario, Longman Publishers.

Falola, Toyin. (2013). *The African Diaspora: Slavery, Modernity and Globalisation*, Universty of Rochester Press.

Fryer, Peter. (1984). *Staying Power: The History of Black People in Britain*, London, Pluto Press.

Geiss, Imanuel. (1969). 'Pan-Africanism' in *Journal of Contemporary History*, Vol. 4 No. 1 January, pp. 187-200.

Geiss, Imanuel. (1974). *The Pan-African Movement*, London, Methuen and Company Ltd.

Harris, Joseph in collaboration with Zeghidour, Slimane, (1999). 'Africa and its Diaspora Since 1935' in Mazrui, Ali eds. *General History of Africa Vol. V111: Africa Since 1935*, California, James Currey Publishers.

Hoyles, Martin. (2004). *The Axe Laid to the Root: The Story of Robert Wedderburn*, London, Hansib Publishers.

Marable, Manning and Mullings, Leith eds. (2000). *Let Nobody Turn Us Around: Voices of Resistance, Reform and Renewal, An African American Anthology*, Lanham, Boulder, New York, Oxford, Rowman and Littlefield Publisher Inc..

Martin, Tony. (2012). *Caribbean History: From Pre-Colonial Origins to the Present*, Boston, London, Pearson Publishers.

Martin, Tony. (1983). *The Pan African Connection From Slavery to Garvey and Beyond*, Dover, Massachusetts, The Majority Press.

Mazrui, Ali A. eds. (1999). *General History of Africa Vol. V111; Africa Since 1935*, California, James Curry Publishers.

McKay, Vernon. (1963). *Africa in World Politics*, New York, Harper and Row Publishers.

Nelson, Gersham. (1994). 'Rastafarians and Ethiopianism', in Lemelle, Sidney and Kelly, Robin eds. Class, *Imagining Home: Class, Culture and Nationalism in the African Diaspora*, London, New York, Verso Publishers.

Olisanwuche, P. Esedebe. (1982). *Pan-Africanism: The Idea and Movement 1776-1963*, Washington, Howard University Press..

Patterson, Orlando. (1973). *The Sociology of Slavery: An Analysis of the Origins, Development and Structure of Negro Slave Society in Jamaica*, Jamaica, Sangsters's Book Stores Limited in

Association with Granada Publishing Limited London, New York, Verso Publishers.

Rice, Alan. (2003). *Radical Narratives of the Black Atlantic*, London, Continuum Publishers.

Shyllon, Folarin. (1977). *Black People in Britain 1555-1833*, Oxford University Press.Thompson, Vincent Bakpetu (1987). *The Making of the African Diaspora in the Americas 1441-1900*, New York, Longman Publishers.

Thompson, Vincent Bakpetu. (1969). *Africa and .Unity: The Evolution of Pan Africanism*, London and Harlow, Longman Publishers.

Walvin, James. (1973). *Black and White, The Negro and English Society 1555-1945*, London, Allen Lane the Penguin Press.

Index

A

African Methodist Episcopal *53, 56, 233, 241*
Afrocentric *50, 51, 53, 54, 55, 59, 61, 110, 122, 126, 136, 138, 146, 149, 167, 213, 215, 243, 252*
an Oroonoko *148*

B

Black Gadeloupean *143, 254*
Bulsa *18, 25, 26, 27, 29, 31, 32, 36, 39, 40, 41, 43, 45, 48*

C

captive rebellions *111*
Caribbean Antilleans *154*
Caribbean identities *146, 167*
Christianity *11, 16, 19, 49, 50, 51, 53, 54, 55, 59, 61, 62, 64, 65, 67, 68, 69, 70, 72, 73, 75, 181, 240, 243, 245, 246, 247, 252, 259*
Colonialism *22*
Colonial Office *78, 82, 84, 88, 103, 104, 253*
Colourism *129, 201, 202, 203, 219*
Communal *34, 41*

D

Diaspora *vi, 1, 2, 3, 4, 6, 8, 11, 18, 22, 24, 48, 51, 53, 54, 61, 75, 144, 146, 149, 152, 153, 168, 169, 171, 176, 197, 199, 224, 225, 228, 229, 230, 231, 232, 235, 236, 239, 248, 249, 250, 257, 258, 259, 260, 261*

E

Eurocentric *50, 51, 55, 59, 67, 69, 73, 122, 127, 138, 145, 147, 149, 151,*
157, 158, 160, 167, 174, 178, 184, 187, 193, 197, 202, 203, 212, 213, 224, 249, 252
Ewe *19, 78, 80, 81, 82, 85, 86, 87, 93, 94, 95, 103, 252, 253*
Ewedome *iii, vii, 78, 79, 80, 81, 82, 84, 85, 86, 87, 88, 90, 91, 92, 93, 95, 97, 98, 99, 100, 101, 102, 103, 253*

F

Francophone Caribbean *20, 143, 145, 146, 150, 155, 156, 157, 162, 164, 166, 167, 171, 174, 196, 254, 255*
Freedom *iv, 24, 48, 105, 139, 142, 170, 175, 220, 250*
Futa Djalon mountain *180*

G

Grandy Nanny *160, 161, 167, 176*
gree-gree *149, 150*

I

Identity *iii, 1, 26, 47, 48, 139, 141, 143, 169, 218, 220, 222, 239*
Integration *iii, 78, 87, 98*

J

Jemisimiham Jehu Appiah *iii, 11, 19, 49*

K

Kasena *18, 25, 26, 27, 29, 31, 32, 35, 37, 38, 45, 47*

M

Maronage *110, 255*
Maroon wars *107, 108, 215, 254*

www.ingramcontent.com/pod-product-compliance
Lightning Source LLC
Chambersburg PA
CBHW022305280326
41932CB00010B/993